立信实验实训教材系列

上海市职业教育公共实训基地建设项目
上海市重点课程"国际贸易实务"教材

出口贸易情景模拟实训

主　编　马慧敏
副主编　张　珉

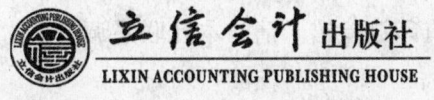

图书在版编目(CIP)数据

出口贸易情景模拟实训/马慧敏主编. —上海:立信会计出版社,2011.6
 立信实验实训教材系列
 ISBN 978-7-5429-2945-7

Ⅰ.①出… Ⅱ.①马… Ⅲ.①出口贸易—教材 Ⅳ.① F746.12

中国版本图书馆 CIP 数据核字(2011)第 121420 号

责任编辑　洪梅春
特约编辑　李沂轲
封面设计　周崇文

出口贸易情景模拟实训

出版发行	立信会计出版社
地　址	上海市中山西路 2230 号　邮政编码　200235
电　话	(021)64411389　传　真　(021)64411325
网　址	www.lixinaph.com　电子邮箱　lxaph@sh163.net
网上书店	www.shlx.net　电　话　(021)64411071
经　销	各地新华书店
印　刷	常熟市梅李印刷有限公司
开　本	787 毫米×1092 毫米　1/16
印　张	17.25
字　数	390 千字
版　次	2011 年 6 月第 1 版
印　次	2011 年 6 月第 1 次
印　数	1—3 100
书　号	ISBN 978-7-5429-2945-7/F
定　价	30.00 元

如有印订差错　请与本社联系调换

前言

现代国际贸易活动对从业人员的知识结构、实践能力和基本素质提出了新要求。围绕培养国际贸易应用型人才的目标,根据国际贸易职业岗位所需的知识、技能及素质要求,特别是操作能力的要求,对学生进行最大化的贴近实际业务的操作训练,全面、系统、规范地掌握主要操作技能,缩小理论与实践、课堂与业务、书本知识与实际操作间的差距,提高职业适应能力是国际经济与贸易及其他相关专业实训课程的主要教学目的。

《出口贸易情景模拟实训》是为国际经济与贸易及其他相关专业的"专业模拟实训环节"提供的专用教材。"专业模拟实训环节"是在学生完成与专业相关的各门课程的理论学习及单项技能训练的基础上,以提高学生对专业所需各项基本技能在具体业务流程中的综合运用能力为目的所设置的重要环节,也是实现理论知识向实践运用过渡的必要环节。

本教材是"上海市职业教育公共实训基地(第六期)——立信国际商务实训中心"项目的建设成果,也是上海市重点课程"国际贸易实务"的建设成果。

本教材遵循"理论与实践相结合"、"知识的转化与能力的内化相结合"以及"教学要素之间相结合"的教育教学基本规律,根据学生学习要求和认知特点,以假想设定的一位国际贸易行业新入职的大学毕业生李新完成出口合同履行基本流程的亲身经历为主线,设置了"交易前准备"、"报价核算与发盘"、"还盘与盈亏测算"、"成交谈判与合同签订"、"落实信用证"、"托运订舱和报检"、"投保与原产地认证"、"报关与装运"、"交单结汇"以及"收汇核销与退税"等十个环节的工作场景。按照"将典型的业务背景、仿真的交易操作场景和对应的知识点有机融合"的原则,在每一个工作环节的学习中都安排以下四部分内容(简称为"LTAD"):

1. LOOK——情景示范:以典型的业务背景模拟每一个环节的工作场景,通过对话形式全面体现该环节所涉及的知识点和规范操作要求,与教材配套的视频以生动活泼全真的方式演示工作实景,提高学生对国际贸易实务工作环境的感性认识和实际操作的真实感受,对学生的模拟操作起到示范作用。

2. THINK——理论思考:用提问的方式帮助学生复习该环节所涉及的基本原理即重要知识点和规范操作要求,引导学生以基本原理为依据,规范实务操作过程,达到"温故知新"的目的。提问内容覆盖该环节操作中所必须掌握的所有基本原理内容,涉及《进出口贸易实务》、《国际商务谈判》、《商务英语》、《外贸函电》、《国际结算》等课程。

3. ACT——模拟训练:按照该工作环节实训要求,提供多份背景资料,方便教师通过情景模拟实训室的配合使用,带领学生以角色分工的形式进行模拟训练。

4. DISCUSS——个案讨论:提供有别于"情景示范"和"模拟训练"部分的工作条件或贸易条件的个案,引导学生根据个案提供的工作条件和贸易条件讨论实务操作方案,锻炼学生对重要知识点和规范操作要求的灵活运用能力,帮助学生掌握不同贸易条件下的实务操作技能,提高综合运用素质。

本教材可以作为各类高等院校国际经济与贸易专业以及相关专业的实训教材,还可以作为从事国际贸易或企业经营管理人员专业培训的参考用书。

本教材由马慧敏担任主编,张珉担任副主编。马慧敏负责编写大纲拟订、体例设计和内容结构确定,并编写了实训一至实训三、各个实训中的"THINK——理论思考"内容以及全书的定稿工作;张珉负责实训四至实训十的其余内容编写,以及全书的校订工作;彭江燕、尚超英参与了部分内容的编写。

在本教材编写过程中,国内外专家及同行的大量文献资料和研究成果给予我们不少启迪和借鉴,上海立信会计学院的领导及同事给予我们鼓励、支持和指导,立信会计出版社给予我们大力协助,在此一并表示感谢。疏漏之处,敬请广大读者批评指正。

编 者
2010年4月

目录

情景模拟实训一　交易前准备 …………………………………………………………… 1
情景模拟实训二　交易磋商一——报价核算与发盘 …………………………………… 25
情景模拟实训三　交易磋商二——还盘与盈亏测算 …………………………………… 52
情景模拟实训四　交易磋商三——成交谈判与合同签订 ……………………………… 64
情景模拟实训五　履行合同一——落实信用证 ………………………………………… 92
情景模拟实训六　履行合同二——托运订舱和报检 …………………………………… 114
情景模拟实训七　履行合同三——投保与原产地认证 ………………………………… 144
情景模拟实训八　履行合同四——报关与装运 ………………………………………… 162
情景模拟实训九　履行合同五——交单结汇 …………………………………………… 187
情景模拟实训十　收汇核销与退税 ……………………………………………………… 205

参考答案 …………………………………………………………………………………… 215

附录　出口贸易英语口语——示范对话 ………………………………………………… 254

参考文献 …………………………………………………………………………………… 269

表目

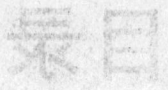

情景模拟实训一

交易前准备

 LOOK——情景示范

王经理：李新！欢迎你加入上海立信国际贸易有限公司(Shanghai Lixin International Trading Co., Ltd.)，很高兴你成为我们轻纺产品部(Textiles and Light Industry Products Department)团队的一员。我们公司是一家专业外贸公司，公司已经经营了13年，尽管时间不长，但公司资产规模已经过亿元。我们主要经营纺织品和轻工业品，包括纺织品面料、服装、鞋类、运动器械和运动装备、化妆品等，经营范围还是比较广的。我们的业务覆盖美国、日本、东南亚等多个国家和地区。我们所经营的产品市场竞争非常激烈，所以要不断地推出新产品以确保稳定的利润。目前公司与国内有关厂家联合开发出了一系列纺织品功能面料，希望借此找到公司新的利润增长点，相信你的加入一定会给我们带来新的活力。你以前有没有接触过进出口贸易啊？都学了哪些课程？

李新：接触过一点，我们学校安排了《国际贸易实务》、《国际商务单证实务》、《国际结算》、《国际商务函电》、《商务谈判》等课程。

王经理：你们学校有没有安排你们参加实习啊？

李新：学校没有统一安排校外实习，但我们在校内有《外贸模拟实习》课，所以我对进出口环节的操作知道一点。

王经理：好，我们公司与绍兴轻纺开发公司合作开发了一系列纺织品功能面料，我们希望通过这些含有一定高新技术的产品经营，寻找公司新的利润增长点，你愿不愿意一起来开发这些新产品的市场啊？

李新：当然愿意！

王经理：好的，我们合作开发的产品中有一种产品是具有抗菌防臭功能的面料，你可以一边熟悉公司的业务，一边试着找找这类产品的市场和买家。具体的产品资料你可以通过货源部的张经理向工厂了解，业务操作方面有什么问题可以随时问我。祝你成功，加油！

李新：谢谢王经理，我会努力的。

（与王经理交谈后，李新找到了货源部的张经理）

李新：张经理好！我是新来的员工李新，要请您多多关照噢！王经理让我找您了解一下抗菌防臭功能面料的货源情况,麻烦您啦!

张经理:没问题的。抗菌防臭功能面料是我们公司和绍兴轻纺开发公司共同新开发的面料,用这种面料做成的产品具有抗菌防臭效果,在医疗、婴儿用品、运动产品、军用装备等方面都有很大的用处。这是产品的详细宣传资料,我另外给你一张名片,具体的产品信息与样品,你可以与绍兴轻纺开发公司的梁厂长联系。

李新:谢谢张经理,有问题我再向您请教好吗?

张经理:没问题的。

(李新回到工位上,仔细阅读了产品宣传资料,然后按照名片上的电话,给绍兴轻纺开发公司的梁厂长打了电话)

李新:请问是梁厂长吗?我是上海立信国贸公司新来的李新,我公司货源部张经理给了我您的联系方式。我想向您了解一下抗菌防臭功能面料的商品信息,具体的等一下我会给您发传真的,麻烦您尽早给我答复好吗?

……

李新:好的,谢谢梁厂长,保持联系,请您多多关照噢!

(李新拟了一份传真发了过去)

询价索样传真文稿:

上海立信国际贸易有限公司
Shanghai Lixin International Trading Co., Ltd.
5/F, No. 2230 West Zhong Shan Road, 200235, Shanghai, P. R. China
Tel: 86-21-64391520   Fax: 86-21-64391530   E-mail: li_xin@lixin.com.cn

致:绍兴轻纺开发公司
梁厂长:

您好!经我公司王经理、张经理介绍,得知贵公司与我公司共同开发的纺织品功能面料含有一定的高新技术,市场潜力较大,希望在贵公司的帮助下能够尽快打开国际市场。

现我司准备向国外客户推销抗菌防臭功能面料,希望贵厂提供一些产品目录及样品,并请附上含税价格单,同时注明包装方式、交货时间、地点、付款方式及最低起订数量等详细的产品信息。

盼复!
顺颂商祺!

李新
2010年7月1日

(半小时后,李新收到了梁厂长的回复)

供货商报价寄样文稿：

绍兴轻纺开发公司

浙江省绍兴市会稽路 367 号

电话：86 – 575 – 85780676　传真：86 – 575 – 85781739

李新先生：

　　您好！很高兴接到您的传真。现将有关情况介绍如下：

1. "银河"牌抗菌防臭功能漂白布

　　货号：KJ1001

　　规格：漂白，100％棉，坯布经纬纱 20×20，每英寸经纬密度 108×58，每匹幅阔 57/58 英寸，每匹长 120 米

　　出厂价：人民币 18 元/米（含税）

　　包装：布包，每包 4 匹（体积：长 1.50 米×宽 0.50 米×高 0.60 米）

　　每包毛净重：毛重 135 千克，净重 130 千克

2. "银河"牌抗菌防臭功能染色布

　　货号：KJ2001

　　规格：染色，100％棉，坯布经纬纱 20×20，每英寸经纬密度 108×58，每匹幅阔 57/58 英寸，每匹长 120 米

　　出厂价：人民币 20 元/米（含税）

　　包装：布包，每包 4 匹（体积：长 1.50 米×宽 0.50 米×高 0.60 米）

　　每包毛净重：毛重 135 千克，净重 130 千克

　　上述样品各 4 米三日内寄到贵司。全棉织物的增值税率：17％；出口退税率：16％；生产周期：月产量 300 万米；最低起订数量：每色 1000 米；交货期：白度样或染色色版确认后 20 天在工厂交货；支付方式：预付 50％货款，交货后 10 日内支付余下货款。

　　如有什么问题，请随时来电，我们将全力配合。

　　此致

敬礼

梁瑞德
2010 年 7 月 1 日

（收到了梁厂长的回复后，李新上网查找了一些相关的信息，找到了王经理，向他汇报了自己的一些想法）

李新：王经理好！

王经理：你好！准备得怎么样啊？

李新：王经理，我刚才已经向张经理和绍兴的梁厂长了解了产品的情况，想向您汇报一下我的一些想法和打算。您现在方便吗？

王经理：好的，你说吧。

李新：我感到，如果将这种产品推销给国外运动鞋制造厂商，也许会有机会。

王经理：为什么呢？

李新： 我前几天看到有报道称，有些客户在投诉某国际知名运动鞋供应商，说他们的鞋容易孳生细菌，一天穿下来就很臭，有的还因此生脚癣。专家回应说这是运动鞋的通病，无法解决的。我看了我们的新产品介绍后，感到如果用我们的面料生产运动鞋，这个问题就可以解决，所以我想试一试。

王经理： 好啊，你真的很用心，可以试试看。那你认为如何收集国外运动鞋制造厂商的联系方式呢？

李新： 这个很简单，我只要去互联网上搜索一下就可以找到的。然后我再给他们发信息就可以了。

王经理： 很好，你试试看吧。

（李新回到自己的工位上，拟写了一封商品信息E-mail——建交函，并根据从互联网上查到的众多国外运动鞋制造厂商的联系方式一一发出）

商品信息——建交函：

发件人：	li_xin@lixin.com.cn
收件人：	f.taldelli@palmavito.com
日　期：	2010-07-02
主　题：	Innovative Textile Made in China

Dear Mr. Taldelli,

We have obtained your name and address from Global Sources online. We know that you are one of the most famous manufactory of sport shoes in Europe. We write the letter to you for the establishment of business relations.

We specialize in the exportation of textiles products and light industrial products which have enjoyed great popularity in world markets such as textiles, garments, shoes, exerciser, cosmetics, etc. Recently, we made an innovative kind of textile with special antibacterial finished material. We think this kind of textile may be useful for you to improve the function of your sport shoes.

We will send you our latest catalogue and relevant samples per 10 M for your reference in a few days and hope that you would contact us if any item is of interest to you.

For our business and financial standing, we may refer you to our bankers:
BANK OF CHINA SHANGHAI BRANCH
NO. 34 EAST ZHONG SHAN ROAD, SHANGHAI, P. R. CHINA

In addition, would you please let us have your bank reference?

We are looking forward to your favorable reply.

Yours truly,
Shanghai Lixin International Trading Co., Ltd.
Li Xin (Mr.)

(一周以后,李新打开电脑,收到一封来自意大利知名运动鞋制造商 Palmavito 公司的 E-mail)

进口商询盘函:

From:	f.taldelli@palmavito.com
To:	li_xin@lixin.com.cn
Date:	2010-07-09
Re:	Inquiry for Antibacterial Finished Textiles

Dear Mr. Li,

We are pleased to receive your E-mail and your samples of textiles as well as the catalogue on July 6, 2010. As you know, we are one of the largest manufactory of sport shoes in southern Europe and wish to improve the function of our products.

We have checked the samples you send to us. We are particularly interested in the antibacterial finished textiles. Please quote us FOB SHANGHAI, CFR GENOVA, CIF GENOVA both bleached and dyed (effected by FCL). For your information, we usually settle the payment with new suppliers by L/C at 30 days after sight. In the meantime, would you please send the inspection report to us as early as possible.

Please advise us the cost of the samples including postal charges so that we could remit to you. Our bank information is as follows:
BANCA INTESA SANPAOLO S.P.A.
VIA MONTE DI PIETA, 8, 20121 MILANO, ITALY

We hope to hear from you soon.

Yours sincerely,
Fabio Taldelli
Palmavito Articoli Sportive S.P.A.

(拿到了客户的询盘函,李新非常兴奋地找到了王经理)

李新:王经理,太好了!已经有客户来询价要货了。

王经理:(边看客户来函边说)先别急,客户的经营实力及信用度如何与我们的报价高低及交易能否顺利进行有着很大的关系。所以,我们在与客户建立业务关系前,先要对客户的资信情况进行调查,这是一份资信调查表,你可以根据客户提供的开户银行信息填写后委托中国银行上海分行向这家开户银行发出资信调查申请。

李新：我知道了，马上就去办！

（李新根据客户提供的信息填写了资信调查申请书，交给公司财务送银行）

资信调查申请书：

<table>
<tr><td colspan="5" align="center">资信调查申请书</td></tr>
<tr><td colspan="3">致：中国银行上海分行</td><td colspan="2">日期：2010-07-10</td></tr>
<tr><td colspan="3">兹委托贵行对下述对象作资信调查：</td><td colspan="2">编号：1009261</td></tr>
<tr><td rowspan="4">调查对象</td><td>国外客户全称（中英文）</td><td colspan="3">Palmavito Articoli Sportive S. P. A.</td></tr>
<tr><td>地址（中英文）</td><td colspan="3">Via G. Mazzini, 46, 20116 Milano, Italy</td></tr>
<tr><td>电传号</td><td>39-02-369052</td><td>电话</td><td>39-02-369010</td></tr>
<tr><td>往来银行名称及账号</td><td>Banca Intesa Sanpaolo S. P. A. Via Monte di Pieta, 8, 20121 Milano, Italy</td><td>电传</td><td>39-02-366241</td></tr>
<tr><td colspan="2">调查内容及目的</td><td colspan="3"></td></tr>
<tr><td colspan="2">调查方式</td><td>你行　电询　函询</td><td colspan="2">代理行　电复　函复</td></tr>
<tr><td colspan="2">委托须知</td><td colspan="3">1. 银行对调查结果的真实性不负任何责任。
2. 你行对调查过程中邮电、通信造成的延误、丢失以及代理行的延误或不回复概不负责。
3. 委托人同意支付银行有关费用（包括你行费用和国外行可能收取的外币费用）。
4. 委托人保证对调查内容保密，并保证对由此引起你行蒙受的一切损失负全部责任。</td></tr>
<tr><td rowspan="4">委托单位</td><td>全称及地址</td><td colspan="3">上海立信国际贸易有限公司
上海市中山西路2230号5楼，200235</td></tr>
<tr><td>开户行及账号</td><td colspan="3">中国银行上海分行
4447071295522031474</td></tr>
<tr><td>联系人</td><td>吴知文</td><td>电话</td><td>021-64391520</td></tr>
<tr><td>银行审核意见</td><td>经办日期</td><td colspan="2">委托单位签章
负责人：　　　日期</td></tr>
</table>

THINK——理论思考

Think 1-1　国际货物买卖主要包括哪些阶段？

国际货物买卖的基本流程如下：

交易前准备	出口商： 　　通过市场调查、广告宣传、参加展览会、交易会、网上发布供货信息、机构推荐、客户介绍、出国推销等多种方式寻找国外买家信息，主动与其联系以建立业务关系 进口商： 　　通过市场调查、接受客户委托等方式明确国内买家 　　通过浏览供货信息、参加展览会、交易会、网上发布求购信息、机构推荐、客户介绍等多种方式寻找国外卖家信息，主动与国外卖家建立联系或在收到国外卖家来函后积极回应
↓	
交易磋商	询盘(Inquiry)：交易的一方向另一方询问进行交易的条件 ↓ 发盘(Offer)：交易的一方向另一方提出达成交易的各项条件 ↓ 还盘(Counter Offer)：交易的一方对另一方的交易条件提出变更或修改 ↓ 接受(Acceptance)：交易的一方对另一方的交易条件表示同意
↓	
合同签订	出口商寄送《销售确认书》(Sales Confirmation, S/C)→进口商会签 　或 进口商寄送《购货订单》(Purchase Order, P/O)→出口商会签 　或 进口商寄送《购货确认书》(Purchase Confirmation, P/C)→出口商会签
↓	
合同履行	出口商：交付货物并收取货款 进口商：支付货款并收取货物

Think 1-2　出口合同履行主要包括哪些环节？

出口合同履行的基本环节(以 CIF 术语成交、集装箱班轮运输、凭信用证付款为例)如下：

催证	出口商提醒进口商按约定时间开出信用证
审证	出口商审核信用证是否符合合同约定和其他规定
备货	安排生产或向供应商采购
订舱	缮制《集装箱货物托运单》(又称"十联单"),向船公司或其代理订舱 ↓ 如委托货代订舱,需提交《出口货物订舱委托书》,随附《商业发票》、《装箱单》 ↓ 船公司接受订舱后,在《集装箱货物托运单》的"装货单"联上加盖船公司签单章后,连同"配舱回单"等其他联一并退还
报检	如货物属于法定检验范围,或进口商要求提交相应检验证书,则需办理出口报检 ↓ 在规定的时间内,向出入境检验检疫机构提交《出境货物报检单》,并随附《商业发票》、《装箱单》,办理货物出境报检手续 ↓ 如委托工厂报检,则需同时提交《报检授权委托书》 ↓ 货物经检验合格后,出入境检验检疫机构签发《出境货物通关单》和/或《商检证书》
投保	填制《出口货物投保单》,随附《商业发票》,向保险公司投保 ↓ 保险公司接受投保申请后,收取保险费并出具《保险单》
认证	根据进口商要求,办理出口认证、出证手续 例如:进口商要求提交《原产地证明》 填制《一般原产地证明书申请书》、《原产地证明》 ↓ 在规定的时间内,持《一般原产地证明书申请书》、《原产地证明》至出入境检验检疫局或中国国际贸易促进委员会(CCPIT,简称中国贸促会)申请出证 ↓ 出入境检验检疫局或中国国际贸易促进委员会审核确认无误后,在《原产地

(续上)

	证明》上签字确认并退还 ↓
	例如：进口商要求提交《普惠制原产地证明》 填制《普惠制原产地证明书申请书》、《普惠制原产地证明》 ↓
	在规定的时间内，持《普惠制原产地证明书申请书》、《普惠制原产地证明》至出入境检验检疫局申请出证 ↓
	出入境检验检疫局审核确认无误后，在《普惠制原产地证明》上签字确认并退还
进 港 ↓	出具《集装箱装箱单》(Container Load Plan, CLP)，并派集装箱卡车至指定地点装运货物 ↓
	货物运抵海关监管区(港区)，场站人员根据CLP核对实际装箱情况并签收
报 关 ↓	在规定的时间内，向海关递交《出口货物报关单》、《集装箱货物托运单》中的"装货单"、"大副联"、"场站收据"三联、《出口收汇核销单》，并随附《商业发票》、《装箱单》，申报货物出口 ↓
	如货物属于法定检验范围，则需同时提交《出境货物通关单》 ↓
	如委托货代报关，则需同时提交《报关授权委托书》 ↓
	海关查验完毕，在《集装箱货物托运单》中的"装货单"联上加盖海关放行章，连同"大副联"、"场站收据"等联一并退还，在《出口收汇核销单》上加盖海关验讫章后退还
装 船 ↓	将《集装箱货物托运单》的"装货单"和"大副联"交给船公司，凭此装货 ↓
	船方装妥货物，在"大副联"上签字后返还 ↓
	凭经船方签署的"大副联"向船公司换取正本已装船《海运提单》
通 知 ↓	向进口商发出装船通知(Shipping Advice)
结 汇 ↓	备妥缮制的各种单据，在信用证规定的交单有效期内交银行办理议付和结汇手续

(续上)

核销 ↓	货款收妥后,收到银行加盖"出口收汇核销专用章"的结汇水单 ↓ 结关后,收到海关加盖验讫章的《出口货物报关单》"收汇核销联"以及"出口退税专用"联 ↓ 在规定的时间内,持银行出具的盖有"出口收汇核销专用章"的结汇水单、盖有验讫章的《出口收汇核销单》及《出口货物报关单》"收汇核销联",向外汇管理部门办理出口收汇核销 ↓ 受理核销后,外汇管理部门在《出口收汇核销单》"出口退税专用联"和银行结汇水单上加盖已核销章后退还
退税 ↓	向税务机关提供购进货物时的《增值税专用发票》"抵扣联"、盖有验讫章的《出口货物报关单》"出口退税专用联"、盖有已核销章的《出口收汇核销单》"出口退税专用联",办理出口退税手续 ↓ 税务机关核准后退税

Think 1-3　出口贸易交易前的准备阶段主要包括哪些工作?

出口贸易交易前的准备是四个阶段中的第一阶段,也是整个交易的基础。其主要包括组织出口货源、市场行情调研、出口方案制定、寻找贸易机会、开展广告宣传和办理商标注册等工作。

Think 1-4　如何了解出口货源情况?

外贸企业在进行出口贸易交易前准备工作时,首先应该注意做好国内货源及需求方面的调查,了解出口货源供应商的资信情况和生产能力,以及货源的具体情况(参见表1-1)。

Think 1-5　市场行情调研主要包括哪些内容?

国际市场行情调研是为了获得与贸易有关的各种信息,通过对信息的分析,得出国际市场行情特点,判定贸易的可行性并进而据此制定贸易计划。从国际贸易商品出口角度看,国际市场行情调研主要包括:国际市场环境调研、国际市场商品情况调研、国际市场营销情况调研、国外客户情况调研等。

(一)国际市场环境调研

企业对国际市场环境调研的主要内容为:

(1)国外市场营销的经济环境分析。国际市场营销的经济环境分析包括世界经济环境分析和目标国家经济环境分析两个方面。对世界经济环境的分析,通常包括世界经济格局及发展趋势、国际贸易构成和国际金融体系等方面的分析。目标国家经济环境分析主要是

表 1-1 供应商信息数据表

供应商名称、地址	
厂长姓名	
电话	
传真	
电子邮件	
开户行及账号	
纳税人识别号	
经营范围	
货物名称	
货号	
规格	
出厂价(税前)	
出口退税率	
包装种类	
内包装数量	
包装箱规格	
毛重	
净重	
月产量	
最低起订量	
交货期	
交货地点	
支付方式	
付款时间	
样品提交时间	
产品优势	
需要改进的地方	
主销地区	
竞争对手	
备注	

为了了解一个国家或地区的自然条件、总体经济状况、生产力发展水平、产业结构特点、国家的宏观经济政策、货币制度、经济法律和条约、价值观念、商业习惯、消费水平和基本特点等。

(2) 国外市场营销的政治和法律环境分析。国际市场营销不可避免地受到有关国家或地区政治法律环境的制约。目标国家的政治和法律环境构成了市场进入的直接障碍，国际营销企业不仅要注意了解和分析目标国家政治和法律环境的特征，遵守当地的法律法规，而且也要采取措施避免或减少可能的政治风险，维护自己的合法权益。国外市场营销的政治和法律环境分析包括政府的重要经济政策、政府对贸易实行的鼓励、限制措施、特别有关外贸方面的法律法规，如关税、配额、国内税收、外汇限制、卫生检疫、安全条例等。

(3) 国外市场营销的文化环境分析。国际营销活动与国内营销的主要区别在于企业在其他国家面临着不同的文化环境。各国文化背景的不同，导致了各国顾客的需求不同。企业要想在国际营销中满足异国顾客的需求，就必须进行文化环境分析，根据各国文化的差异性判断各国顾客需求的差异性。包括使用的语言、教育水平、宗教、风俗习惯、价值观念等。

(4) 其他分析。其他分析包括国外人口、交通、地理等情况。

(二) 国际市场商品情况调研

国际市场商品情况调研是为了了解国际市场消费者的需求和偏好；捕捉国际市场营销机会；为企业国际营销活动提供决策依据以及控制企业国际营销的发展进程，规避风险。企业要把产品打入国际市场或从市场进口产品，除需了解外市场环境外，还需了解国外商品市场情况，主要包括：

(1) 市场适销商品调研，包括品种、规格、用料、颜色、包装、商标使用等。

(2) 市场供给情况调研，包括市场容量、供货主要来源、主要生产者、生产能力、数量及库存情况等。

(3) 市场需求特点调研，包括消费水平、质量要求、消费习惯、销售季节、产品销售周期。

(4) 市场商品价格情况，包括国际市场商品的价格、商品供求价格变动规律等。

(三) 国际市场营销情况调研

国际市场营销情况调研要学会贸易技巧，运用有效的推销手段扩大商品出口。

(1) 产品销售渠道的调研，包括各大类商品的主要销售渠道，各个销售渠道的特点和地位及它们之间的相互关系，哪些销售渠道最合适，推销网点如何合理分布，如何选择经销代理户，销售渠道由谁控制等。

(2) 广告宣传的调研，包括商品在某个国家和地区最好的宣传媒介是什么，国外广告宣传中有哪些好的方式和方法等。应结合商品特点、消费习惯、顾客心理进行比较和分析。

(3) 选择计价货币的调研，包括选择什么货币计价较为有利，怎样制定价格策略，怎样使用佣金和折扣及奖励办法，采用何种支付方式，即期支付还是远期支付等。

(4) 售前售后服务的调研，包括如何设立国外服务中心，怎样进行设备安装、技术培训、维修服务、零配件供应，售前售后服务有哪些形式（委托、派驻、合营），利弊如何等。

(5) 制定产品发展规划的调研,包括哪些市场要开拓,哪些市场要挤进,哪些市场要维持,哪些产品已为市场所淘汰,哪些产品趋向淘汰,哪些产品有发展前途,新产品如何试销等。

(6) 竞争分析,包括竞争者产品质量、价格、政策、广告、分配路线、占有率等。

（四）国外客户情况调研

每个商品都有自己的销售(进货)渠道。销售(进货)渠道是由不同客户所组成的。企业进出口商品必须选择合适的销售(进货)渠道与客户,做好国外客户的调查研究。一般说来,商务企业对国外客户的调查研究主要包括以下内容:

(1) 客户政治情况,主要了解客户的政治背景,与政界的关系,公司、企业负责人参加的党派及对我国的政治态度。

(2) 客户资信情况,包括客户拥有的资本和信誉两个方面。资本指企业的注册资本、实有资本、公积金、其他财产以及资产负债等情况。信誉指企业的经营作风。

(3) 客户经营业务范围,主要指客户的公司、企业经营的商品及其品种。

(4) 客户公司、企业业务,指客户的公司、企业是中间商还是最终用户或专营商或兼营商等。

(5) 客户经营能力,指客户业务活动能力、资金融通能力、贸易关系、经营方式和销售渠道等。

Think 1-6　国外市场行情调研有哪些渠道和方法?

企业进行国外市场环境、商品及营销情况调研一般可通过下列渠道、方法进行:
(1) 派出国推销小组深入国外市场以销售、问卷、谈话等形式进行调查(一手资料)。
(2) 通过各种媒体(报刊、杂志、新闻广播、计算机数据库等)寻找信息资料(二手资料)。
(3) 委托国外驻华或我驻外商务机构进行调查。

通过以上调研,企业基本上可以解决应选择哪个国家或地区为自己的目标市场、企业应该出口哪些产品以及以什么样的价格或方法出口等问题。

Think 1-7　对于国外客户资信情况的调查,主要可以通过哪些途径?

对于国外客户资信情况的调查,主要可以通过下列途径:
(1) 通过国内往来银行,向对方的往来银行调查。
(2) 直接向对方的往来银行调查。
(3) 通过国内的咨询机构调查。
(4) 通过国外的咨询机构调查。
(5) 通过国内外商会调查。
(6) 通过我国驻外商务机构调查。
(7) 通过国外的亲朋好友调查。
(8) 由对方来函自己判断调查。
(9) 要求对方直接提供资信资料。

(10) 通过我国外贸公司驻外分支机构和商务参赞处,在国外进行资料收集。
(11) 利用交易会、各种洽谈会和客户来华做生意的机会了解有关信息。
(12) 派遣专门的出口代表团、推销小组等进行直接的国际市场调研,获得第一手资料。
通过上述各途径的调查,企业可有针对性地选择国外客户进行交易。

Think 1-8 国外客户资信调查主要包括哪些内容?

国外客户资信调查的内容有:

(1) 厂商企业的组织情况。厂商企业的组织情况包括公司、商号企业的组织性质、创建历史、主要领导人员、分支机构、要弄清英文名称及公司是有限责任的还是无限责任的。

(2) 往来对象的性格和道德。贸易往来对象诚实可靠是交易成功的基础。在国际贸易中,如果遇到不可靠的贸易对象,就难免出现货物的品质不良、开来与合同不符的信用证、延交货物等现象。

(3) 贸易经验。选择一个具有国际贸易经验的贸易对象至关重要。

(4) 资信情况。所调查对方的资信情况包括企业的资金和信用两方面,资金指的是企业的注册资金、实收资金、公积金、其他财产及资产债务的情况等。信用是指企业的经营作风,履约守信用等。这些情况对客户要求作经销、代理、独家包销、寄售等业务做出决定时是十分重要的。

(5) 经营范围。调查对方的经营范围也是较重要的,同时还要调查经营的性质,如代理商、零售商、批发商、最终用户等。

(6) 经营能力。该企业每年的经营金额、销售渠道、贸易关系、经营做法等。

(7) 往来银行名称。了解对方往来银行的名称、地址同样重要。

Think 1-9 如何进行国外客户情况(资信)调查?

在选择贸易伙伴,建立国际业务关系之初,首先要对新的贸易对象进行资信调查,以免蒙受经济损失。调查内容主要包括调查对象的资金状况、经营能力、商业信誉等。资信调查的途径主要有:与对方有开户关系的银行(例如本实训 LOOK 环节中向银行提交的"资信调查申请书");与对方有业务关系的公司;国际上专业的资信调查代理机构。对于已获得的资信调查资料,必须严格保密。

向对方往来银行进行资信调查的函电一般包括以下部分:

(1) 开头部分:告知如何获得贵方的名称和地址。
(2) 承接部分:准备咨询的内容。
(3) 结尾部分:保证你方将对所获资料予以严格保密。

Think 1-10 如何制定出口商品经营方案?

出口商品经营方案(参见表 1-2)是企业国内外市场、企业经营决策及目标对其所经营的出口商品所做的一种业务计划安排,是企业同客户洽商交易的依据。它可使企业交易有计划、有目的地顺利进行。出口商品经营方案的内容一般包括:

表1-2 出口商品经营方案

商品情况	品名：		规格：		生产商：	
	包装：		尺码：		产品特色：	
	收购价：		每件毛重：		竞争对手及特点：	
	实际成本：		每件净重：		产品改进：	
进销存情况	项　目		金　额		数　量	
	库　存					
	成交待运					
	预计收购					
	预计出口					
历年情况	年　份		出口数量		利润情况	主销地区
	2006年					
	2007年					
	2008年					
	2009年					
	2010年					
2011年	外销计划	国别地区	数　量	单　价	FOB净价	换汇成本
出口安排	主要客户	性质(佣金率)	市场特点	年(月)销量	销售额	存在问题
	主要措施					
备注	备货资金的来源：自有资金 　　　　　　　　银行贷款 　　　　　　　　打包放款					

(1) 商品和货源情况，包括商品的特点、品质、规格、包装，国内生产数量、可供出口数量、当前库存及国内需要量等。

(2) 国外市场情况，包括国外商品生产、消费、贸易情况，主要销往国家的交易情况，今后发展变化的趋势，国外主要市场经营该商品的基本做法、销售渠道等。

(3) 经营历史情况，包括我国出口商品在国际市场上所占的地位，主要销往国家及销售情况，国内外客户的具体反映，经营该商品的经验、教训等。

(4) 经营计划安排，主要包括出口商品的数量、金额，对某国或某地区出口的数量、进度等。

(5) 营销策略，包括客户利用措施，采取的贸易方式、价格的掌握、收汇方法、出口销售的原则策略等。

出口企业一般只在经营大宗或重点出口商品时才逐个制订商品出口方案，对其他商品可只按商品大类制订，对中小商品可制订内容简单的价格方案，仅对市场和价格提出分析意见，规定对各个地区的出口价格以及掌握出口价格的原则和幅度。

应当说完成出口商品经营方案的制订只是做好出口贸易的第一步，要把它变成现实还要经过许多努力。在执行方案的过程中，我们应注意经常检查方案的执行情况、定期总结经验，及时修订方案中不再适用的内容。

Think 1-11 寻找贸易机会的主要方法有哪些？

国际贸易中，企业寻找客户关系的渠道方法很多，归纳起来大体有以下三种类型：

(1) 他人介绍：即企业通过委托我驻外使领馆的商务参赞、代办处或国外驻华使领馆的商务参赞、代办处，国内外各种商会、银行及与我有业务关系的企业介绍寻找客户。

(2) 媒体寻找：即企业利用各国商会、工商团体、国内外出版的企业名录及国内外报刊、杂志上的广告以及计算机数据库中提供的客户信息、资料查找客户，也利用 Internet，开展网上营销。

(3) 主动出击：由驻外分支机构开发新顾客，也可以通过在国内外参加或举办各种交易会、展览会的方式找到客户，或者利用一些特殊渠道，如联合国采购、跨国采购等平台和方式；国内或驻外机构（如贸易中心）常年开设的展厅，进行商品展览等。

Think 1-12 商业展览在国际贸易中的作用，中国主要的国际贸易展览会有哪些？

展览会有别于其他营销方式。它是唯一充分利用人体所有感官的营销活动，人们通过展览会对产品的认知较全面和深刻。同时，展览会又是一个中立场所，不属于买卖任何一方私有，从心理学角度看，这种环境易使人产生独立感，从而以积极、平等的态度进行谈判。这种高度竞争而充分自由的气氛，正是企业在开拓市场时最需要的。国际性商业展览是代理商接触进口产品最直接的途径，当然也是参展厂商寻求代理商，并与潜在客户商谈的绝佳商机。

中国主要的国际贸易展览会主要有"中国进出口商品交易会"以及"中国华东进出口商品交易会"、"中国昆明进出口商品交易会"和"中国的大连进出口商品交易会"等区域性展览会。

Think 1-13 如何撰写建交函？

国际贸易中，买卖双方业务关系的建立，往往是由交易一方通过主动向对方写信、发传真或 E-mail 形式进行。建立业务关系的函件一般包括下列内容：
　　一笔具体的交易往往始于出口商主动向潜在客户发函建立业务关系。就标准规范的层次而言,建立业务关系的信函一般应包括如下内容:
　　(1) 信息来源,即如何取得对方的资料,像通过他人介绍、网上信息等。
　　(2) 言明去函目的,如扩大交易或地区、建立长期业务关系等。
　　(3) 本公司情况,包括公司性质、业务范围、宗旨、公司经营优势等。
　　(4) 产品介绍,分两种情况:一是明确对方需求,此时宜选取某类特定产品,进行具体的推荐;二是不明确对方需求,此时宜对企业产品整体情况(质量标准、价格、销路等)作笼统介绍(可能的情况下,附上商品目录、报价单或另寄样品供对方参考)。
　　(5) 激励性结尾,即希望对方给予回应或采取行动。

Think 1-14　如何撰写询盘函?

　　询盘(Inquiry)是交易的一方打算购买或出售某种商品,向对方询问买卖该项商品的有关条件。询盘主要是试探对方的诚意和了解对方的交易条件,内容涉及价格、规格、品质、数量、包装、交货期及索取样品、商品目录等,而多数是询问价格,也称询价。询盘不是交易磋商的必经步骤,对于询盘人和被询盘人均无法律约束力,发出询盘的目的通常是要求对方作出发盘。

　　询盘函一般包含以下内容:
　　(1) 怎样得知对方公司名称和地址的。
　　(2) 表明建立业务关系的愿望。
　　(3) 本公司简介(公司性质、业务范围、优势、拟与对方合作的方式)。
　　(4) 销售的商品及有关条件(需求明确的,作具体介绍;否则,作笼统介绍)。
　　(5) 介绍一下市场状况(供需情况、客户购买意向、购买力等)。
　　(6) 告知对方向何处了解其信用情况。
　　(7) 激励对方回应的结尾。

 ACT——模拟训练

　　上海海纳进出口有限公司(Shanghai Haina Import & Export Company Limited)主要经营不锈钢真空器皿,产品远销美洲、欧洲、澳洲、东南亚、中东等地区,现公司计划向国际市场推销不锈钢真空杯。

Act 1-1　出口商向供货商询价索样

　　2010 年 9 月 15 日,业务员钱晓俊就准备参加下个月在上海举办的国际日用品展销会事宜,向浙江省永康市的采薇杯业有限公司发出传真,询问商品信息(真空保温杯、含税价格单、包装方式、交货时间、交货地点、付款方式、最低起订数量等)和索要产品目录及样品。
　　请以钱晓俊的身份向采薇杯业公司的刘松泉总经理发去传真。

询价索样传真文稿：

上海海纳进出口有限公司
Shanghai Haina Import & Export Company Limited
Rm. 905 Yong An Mansion, No. 12 Huashan Rd., Shanghai, P. R. China
Tel: 0086-21-54105623   Fax: 0086-21-54742511   E-mail: sales@hainaco.com

---

接到出口商钱晓俊的询价索样传真后，采薇杯业有限公司的刘松泉总经理于2010年9月18日回复传真如下：

供货商报价寄样文稿：

永康采薇杯业有限公司
浙江省永康市长英工业园区东湖路 126 号
电话：0579 - 87442170　传真：0579 - 87442180　E-mail：sales@caiweicup.com

钱晓俊先生：

　　您好！

　　很高兴收到您的传真，我对与贵司的合作前景很有信心。经过我司负责设计、供应、生产的人员研究，并对原材料的供应情况和成品真空保温杯的销售情况作了进一步了解，下列产品近来销路很好，国外不少客户询问、订货，市场看好，希望能有较好的结果。现将有关情况介绍如下：

1. 真空运动水壶
　　　货号：CWS3 - 50
　　　容量：500 毫升
　　　材质：不锈钢、单胆
　　　出厂价：12.6 元/个（含税）
　　　包装：纸箱，每箱 40 个装
　　　每箱毛净重：29.4 千克/21.8 千克
　　　纸箱尺寸：61 厘米×39 厘米×26 厘米＝0.0619 立方米
2. 真空旅游水壶
　　　货号：CWT2 - 100
　　　容量：1000 毫升
　　　材质：不锈钢、双胆
　　　出厂价：19.2 元/个（含税）
　　　包装：纸箱，每箱 20 个装
　　　每箱毛净重：27.3 千克/20.7 千克
　　　纸箱尺寸：65 厘米×41 厘米×29 厘米＝0.0773 立方米

　　上述真空保温杯样品各 1 个将于 3 日内交到贵司。不锈钢真空保温杯的增值税率：17%；出口退税率：11%；生产周期：日产 8000 个；最低起订数量：3000 个；交货期：收到订单后 10 天在工厂交货；支付方式：预付 70% 货款，交货后 5 日内支付余下货款。

　　如有什么问题，请随时来电，我们将全力配合。

　　此致

刘松泉
2010 年 9 月 18 日

Act 1-2 出口商与进口商建立业务关系

业务员钱晓俊在上海参加国际日用品博览会期间,从美国驻华商务参赞处获知一家美国大型日用品采购商欲更换中国供应商的信息。2010年10月12日,钱晓俊向该美国采购商发出了一封E-mail,表示欲与其建立业务关系的愿望。

请以钱晓俊的身份向美国采购商 Gulfland Dainecess Inc. 的采购经理 Raymond Sinclair 先生发去一封建交E-mail。

出口商建交函:

发件人:	damonchan@hainaco.com.cn
收件人:	ray.sinclair@gulfday.com
日 期:	2010-10-12
主 题:	Establishment of Business Relations

Act 1-3　进口商向出口商询盘

　　Sinclair 先生收到钱晓俊的 E-mail 及快递来的商品目录,感到海纳的不锈钢真空器皿质量上乘,价格有竞争力,遂于 2010 年 10 月 22 日通过 E-mail 向钱晓俊询盘,在询盘中感谢钱晓俊去电,介绍 Gulfland Dainecess Inc. 是美国西南部最大的日用品进口商之一并对质优价廉的商品需求很大,现对海纳公司的真空运动水壶(货号 CWS3-50)和真空旅游水壶(货号 CWT2-100)很感兴趣,要求报价(集装箱整箱)及寄送样品,最后给出了其公司的往来银行信息。

　　请以 Sinclair 先生的身份,撰写该询盘 E-mail。

进口商询盘函：

From：	ray.sinclair@gulfday.com
To：	damonchan@hainaco.com.cn
Date：	2010-10-22
Re：	Inquiry

 **DISCUSS**——个案讨论

Discuss 1-1

2011年3月1日,上海立信国际贸易有限公司作为参展出口商参加了"中国华东进出口商品交易会",当时李新与一家澳大利亚进口商的业务代表 Kurt Sheldon 先生进行过面谈,现此公司直接向立信公司发来了建交函 E-mail,李新将怎样回复?

进口商建交函:

From:	k. sheldon@claco. com
To:	li_xin@lixin. com. cn
Date:	2011-03-10
Re:	Having a Start

Dear Mr. Li,

One week ago we had the opportunity to see a display of your products at the East China Imports and Exports Trade Fair, and we were most impressed by the quality and low prices of your product of textiles.

We should like to offer you our service as a trading firm, and would mention that we are experienced importers of our country, and are enjoying a good reputation all over the world.

We foresee a bright prospect for your products in our market. We shall be able to send you considerable orders if the price is suitable. We should be obliged if you send us some samples with the best terms as soon as you can.

Our financial standing information is as follows:
AUSTRALIA AND NEW ZEALAND BANKING GROUP LIMITED
ANZ MEDIA RELATIONS, LEVEL 9
833 COLLINS STREET, MELBOURNE, AUSTRALIA

Yours early reply will be highly appreciated.

Yours sincerely,
Kurt Sheldon
Glamour International Company Limited
16 Pentagon Square, P. O. Box 463, Melbourne, Australia

延续以上讨论,若王经理要求李新在回复澳大利亚公司的建交函前,先向其提供的账户银行去函对其进行资信调查,李新将如何撰写这封E-mail?

资信调查函:

发件人:	li_xin@lixin.com.cn
收件人:	enterprise@anzbank.com
日　期:	2011-03-10
主　题:	Credit Inquiry

出口商询盘函：

发件人：	li_xin@lixin.com.cn
收件人：	k.sheldon@claco.com
日　　期：	2011 - 03 - 15
主　　题：	Inquiry for Innovative Textile

Discuss 1 - 2

李新在中国华东进出口商品交易会(华交会)上接洽过的一家阿拉伯客户将派员亲至上海立信国际贸易有限公司进行交易磋商，请将相关情境进行角色扮演，并请体现适用于阿拉伯客商的商务礼仪。

情景模拟实训二

交易磋商一——报价核算与发盘

 LOOK ——情景示范

(两天后,财务结算部吴经理拿着银行来函找到了李新)

吴经理: 小李,你提出的客户银行资信调查,银行已经接受办理并给了回复,Palmavito 公司是意大利一家知名企业,银行信用评级是 3A 级,资信方面应该是没有什么问题的。

李新: 谢谢您啦!

(李新随即找到王经理,将上述情况进行汇报)

李新: 王经理好!刚才吴经理已经得到了银行的回复,告知 Palmavito 公司银行资信评级是 3A 级。

王经理: 噢,非常不错啊,这应该是一个大客户。

李新: 是的,我前两天也在网上查询了一下,这家公司的运动鞋销量一直很好,拥有很多品牌,而且还是不少著名运动队的指定用鞋,知名度很高的。

王经理: 这很好啊,如果这个公司能够下单的话,数量也不会少的啊。

李新: 我还了解到现在市场对抗菌防臭用品的关注度在不断提高,我们应该抓紧推销我们的产品,尽快打开销路。

王经理: 是呀,市场竞争向来很激烈,好不容易开发出的新产品一定要抓紧上市,否则就会痛失良机的,呵呵!

李新: 那我现在就去拟写给客户的报价函吧。

王经理: 噢,在写报价函之前我们先要将价格计算出来,你先去将工厂提供的供货资料整理一下,然后我们来一起讨论如何报价好吗?

(李新回到了工位上,将工厂的传真拿了出来,整理了一份资料,然后拿着资料去找王经理)

李新: 王经理,工厂供货资料已经整理出来了。

王经理: 先讲讲,出口商品的价格条款应该由哪几项内容构成啊?

李新: 这个问题,我们老师在课上讲过的,一共由四元素构成:计价货币、单价金额、计量单位和贸易术语。

工厂供货资料：

绍兴轻纺开发公司
供货资料

1. "银河"牌抗菌防臭功能漂白布
   货号：KJ1001
   规格：漂白，100%棉，坯布经纬纱 20×20，每英寸经纬密度 108×58，每匹幅阔 57/58 英寸，每匹长 120 米
   出厂价：人民币 18 元/米（含税）
   包装：布包，每包 4 匹（体积：长 1.50 米×宽 0.50 米×高 0.60 米）
   每包毛净重：毛重 135 千克，净重 130 千克

2. "银河"牌抗菌防臭功能染色布
   货号：KJ2001
   规格：染色，100%棉，坯布经纬纱 20×20，每英寸经纬密度 108×58，每匹幅阔 57/58 英寸，每匹长 120 米
   出厂价：人民币 20 元/米（含税）
   包装：布包，每包 4 匹（体积：长 1.50 米×宽 0.50 米×高 0.60 米）
   每包毛净重：毛重 135 千克，净重 130 千克

   其他：
   增值税率：17%
   出口退税率：16%
   生产周期：月产量 300 万米
   最低起订数量：每色 1000 米
   交货期：白度样或染色色版确认后 20 天在工厂交货
   支付方式：预付 50% 货款，交货后 10 日内支付余下货款

王经理： 外贸业务中最常用的贸易术语是哪三个啊？
李新： FOB、CFR 和 CIF。
王经理： 我们公司通常用的计价货币是美元，纺织品面料的计量单位是每米或者每码，所以我们现在需要计算的就是商品在不同贸易术语条件下的单价金额了，是吗？
李新： 是的。
王经理： 商品的报价主要由哪几部分组成啊？
李新： 成本、费用和利润。
王经理： 成本应该如何计算啊？能否直接用从工厂进货的采购成本计算啊？
李新： 不行的。
王经理： 为什么？
李新： 因为从工厂进货的采购成本是含增值税或者消费税的，我们外贸公司待产品出

口后可以获得出口退税,出口退税可以看作是我们出口的收入,所以在计算成本时我们应该将这部分出口退税从采购成本里扣除得到实际成本,用实际成本计算才是正确的。

王经理: 很好,那费用主要有哪些呢?

李新: 费用主要分国内费用和国外费用,国内费用按照实际情况计算,国外费用按照不同的贸易术语分别计算国外运费、保险费等。

王经理: 如果是 CIF 贸易术语的话,运费如何计算呀?

李新: 我想先问您一个问题,客户在询盘函中要求的集装箱流转形态是 FCL,但没有写清是 20 英尺还是 40 英尺集装箱,我们公司一般是算 20 英尺还是 40 英尺啊?

王经理: 根据公司的惯例,一般是先以 20 英尺算运费。

李新: 我还有个问题,客户没有明确提出要多少个 20 英尺集装箱的货,我们怎么处理呢?

王经理: 记住,我们现在是报价,是以 20 尺箱能装货物的数量作为核算的基础。比如你手头上这票货有两个货号,相当于一个货号装入一个 20 尺箱,共两个集装箱的数量,算出报价,当客户收到报价后,就有了进口核算的依据,就能最终决定到底要多少数量货物。

李新: 哦,我明白了。这样的话,单个 20 英尺集装箱的运费就能直接从集装箱运价表中查出,然后再乘以集装箱的数量,就能得到这票货物的总运费。

王经理: 不错,思路清楚!那么保险费怎么算呢?

李新: 根据投保险种在保险公司提供的保险费率表中查出保险费率,再把商品的 CIF 价值乘以保险加成算出保险金额,最后把保险金额乘以保险费率得到保险费。

王经理: 好的。那你再考虑一下我们的利润率应该如何设定?

李新: 我认为,我们的商品是新品种,产品在市场上应该处于成长期,所以价格不宜太低,利润在销售价格的 10% 左右差不多的,您看呢?

王经理: 好的,那你就按照 10% 的销售利润率来核定一下价格吧。运费、保险费率表你可以到报关运输部查,资金周转周期你可以到财务结算部查,其他费用可以请教货源部张经理。还有什么问题吗?

李新: 我先试试看吧。

王经理: 好的。

(李新回到工位上埋头算了起来,其间他找到了报关运输部的陈老师)

李新: 陈老师好!我是公司新来的员工李新,现在有个意大利客户要求报价,我想找您了解一下有关集装箱运价。

陈老师: 好的,没问题。你这票是什么货物啊,作整箱还是拼箱啊?

李新: 是纺织品面料,作整箱。

陈老师: 目的港是哪里啊?

李新: 是意大利热那亚港。

陈老师: 这是一份船公司提供的最新的中国—地中海航线的集装箱运价表(见表 2-1),你可以查到相应的运价。

表2-1 中国—地中海航线的集装箱运价表(节选)　　　　　　单位：USD

航　　线	FCL 整箱货			LCL（W/M）拼箱货(重量/尺码)
	20′	40′	40′HQ	
上海—热那亚 SHANGHAI-GENOVA	1800.00	3500.00	3600.00	80.00

李新：谢谢您！

陈老师：我再考考你，你觉得这是哪一种集装箱运价表啊？

李新：您给我的是 FAK 运价表，就是 Freight for All Kinds，是不分货物级别统一收取运费的，是集装箱包箱费率 Box Rate 中最常用的形式。我这票货先按照 20 英尺整箱算运费，所以从这张运价表中查到运价是 1800 美元。

陈老师：回答得很好。你还有什么问题要问吗？

表2-2 价格构成表

价格构成	项　　目
成　本	生产成本：制造商的投入
	加工成本：加工商的投入
	采购成本：贸易商向供货商购货的价格
费　用	包装费(Packing Charges)：通常包括在进货成本中，如果客户有特殊要求，则需另加
	仓储费(Warehousing Charges)：购货后存仓的费用
	国内运输费(Inland Transport Charges)：装货前发生的内陆运输费用,如卡车、内河运输费、路桥费、过境费及装卸费等
	认证费(Certification Charges)：出口商办理出口许可、配额、产地证以及其他证明所支付的费用
	港区港杂费(Port Charges)：货物装运前在港区码头支付的各种费用
	商检费(Inspection Charges)：出口检验检疫机构检验货物所发生的费用
	报关费(Customs Clearance Charges)：向海关申报出口所发生的费用
	捐税(Duties and Taxes)：国家对出口商品征收、代收或退还的有关税费,通常有出口关税、增值税等
	垫款利息(Interest)：出口商结汇前因垫付资金发生的利息
	业务费用(Operating Charges)：出口经营过程中发生的费用,如：通讯费、交通费、交际费等
	银行费用(Banking Charges)：出口商委托银行向国外客户收取货款、作资信调查等产生的费用
	出口运费(Freight Charges)：出口支付的海、陆、空运及多式联运费用
	保险费(Insurance Premium)：出口商购买货运或信用保险的费用
	佣金(Commission)：出口商向中间商支付的报酬
利润	预期利润(Estimated Profit)：出口商所得

李新：陈老师，除了海运费外，货物在出口前还会发生哪些费用呢？

陈老师：这得按照不同货物的特点和客户所需货物的数量来核算，一般的一个 20 英尺集装箱国内运杂费需 2000 元，出口商检费 350 元，出口报关费 150 元，港区港杂费 600 元。这里有份价格构成表（见表 2-2），你可以先了解一下，以备核算价格时用。

李新：陈老师，保险费怎样处理呢？

陈老师：这是海运保险费率表（见表 2-3），你可以根据客户要求的投保险种和投保加成查得相应的费率，然后计算出保险费。

表 2-3 海运保险费率表

洲别	目的地	平安险	水渍险	一切险
亚洲	中国港澳台地区、日本、韩国	0.08	0.12	0.25
	约旦、黎巴嫩、巴林、阿拉伯联合酋长国、菲律宾	0.15	0.20	1.00
	尼泊尔、阿富汗、也门			1.50
	泰国、新加坡等其他国家			0.60
欧洲、美国、加拿大、大洋洲		0.15	0.20	0.50
中、南美洲		0.15	0.25	1.50
阿尔巴尼亚、罗马尼亚、南斯拉夫、波兰、保加利亚、匈牙利、捷克、斯洛伐克、独联体国家		0.15	0.25	1.50
非洲	埃塞俄比亚、坦桑尼亚、赞比亚、毛里求斯、布隆迪、科特迪瓦、贝宁、刚果、安哥拉、佛得角群岛、卢旺达	0.20	0.30	2.50
	加纳利群岛、毛里塔尼亚、冈比亚、塞内加尔、尼日利亚、利比里亚、几内亚、乌干达			3.50
	其他地区			1.00

李新：谢谢陈老师，有问题我再向您请教好吗？

陈老师：好的，有问题尽管问。

（李新又找到了财务结算部的钱老师）

李新：钱老师好！我是公司新来的员工李新，现在有个意大利客户要求报价，我想了解一下我们公司出口业务的资金周转周期。

钱老师：这和出口成交合同约定的支付方式以及工厂要求的付款方式有关系。如果国外客户预付款，就基本不占用资金，只有部分退税资金占用。如果我们和国外客户之间采用信用证方式或者是货到付款，工厂又要求我们预付款或者带款提货的话，除了退税资金外还要占用一部分资金。我们公司按照 3 个月来结算，银行年利率为 4.98%，现在你手上的这个意大利客户要求 30 天远期信用证支付，那就要按照 4 个月的周期来计算利息了。这样你会计算吗？

李新：我知道的，采购成本×4.98%×4/12，谢谢您啦！还有个问题，我们公司的业务费用一般是按照多少比例来算的啊？

钱老师：噢，我们公司的业务费用一般是按照报价的 2% 的比例计算的。

李新：好的,谢谢钱老师!

(李新回到工位上埋头算了起来,半小时后,李新找到了王经理)

李新：王经理,我算好了,按照10%的销售利润率,2%的业务费用率计算,报价是……

王经理：(打断李新的话)对不起,我打断一下。你先别给我看最后结果,说说你的计算过程吧。

李新：根据我刚才向您请教过的,分为成本、费用和利润三块进行核算。首先我根据"供货资料"中的数据做成本核算,最基本的关系式是"实际成本＝采购成本－退税收入"。您看我算得对吗?

李新的计算过程——成本核算：

(1) KJ1001 的实际成本：

$$退税收入 = \frac{采购成本}{1+增值税率} \times 退税率 = \frac{18}{1+17\%} \times 16\% = 2.46 \text{ 元/米}$$

实际成本＝采购成本－退税收入＝18－2.46＝15.54 元/米

(2) KJ2001 的实际成本：

$$退税收入 = \frac{20}{1+17\%} \times 16\% = 2.74 \text{ 元/米}$$

实际成本＝20－2.74＝17.26 元/米

王经理：很好!

李新：然后我核算了费用,包括国内费用和国外费用,不过在核算费用前我先确定了报价基础数量。

王经理：为什么?

李新：因为有些费用是按照一批货物报价收取的,比如说运费,当然集装箱运价还分整箱运价和拼箱运价。还有报关费,往往也是按照一批货物来收的。而我们向客户报价往往采用单位价格,比如说纺织品面料就是一米或者一码。所以我就要先算出一个集装箱能装下多少货物,就是基础数量,然后再将相关费用分摊到每一个基础数量上。

王经理：很好,很仔细的。

李新的计算过程——报价基础数量确定：

核算 20 英尺集装箱整箱所能装货物数量：

该货物的积载因数＝外包装体积÷毛重＝0.450÷0.135＝3.33 立方米/吨

20 英尺集装箱内容积约为 25 立方米,因为积载因数大于1,属于轻货,故按体积法计算

外包装数量＝集装箱内容积÷单位外包装体积＝25÷0.45＝55.56 包,即 55 包

基础数量＝55×4×120＝26400 米

李新：在确定了报价基础数量后,我再计算相关的费用。这是我列出的费用核算表(见表 2-4),您先看一下是否正确,然后我就可以根据这个表上的内容来计算费用了。

表 2-4 费用核算表

	项 目	总 价	单价(每米)
费用	包装费		
	仓储费		
	国内运输费	2000 元/20′	2000÷26400=0.076 元
	认证费		
	港区港杂费	600 元/20′	600÷26400=0.023 元
	商检费	350 元/20′	350÷26400=0.013 元
	报关费	150 元/20′	150÷26400=0.006 元
	出口海关税费		
	垫款利息		KJ1001：18×4.98％×4/12=0.30 元 KJ2001：20×4.98％×4/12=0.33 元
	业务费用		美元报价×2％
	银行费用		
	出口运费	1800 美元/20′	1800÷26400=0.068 美元
	保险费		美元报价×(1+10％)×0.15％
	佣 金		

王经理：很好,很详细的。我问个问题,在你的计算中,保险加成率为什么是 10％啊?

李新：因为如果客户没有提到保险加成率的话,我们一般就按照 10％加一成。

王经理：那为什么保险险种按照平安险来计算呢?

李新：同样的,如果客户没有提到保险险种的话,我们一般就按照平安险投保。

王经理：好的,下一步如何计算?

李新：最后我将成本加上费用,再加上利润就完成了价格的核算。

王经理：好的,你最后的报价分别是多少啊?要注意统一成美元哦。

李新：这是我美元报价的具体核算过程,请您过目。**(见第 32 页)**

王经理：很好!你现在就按照这个价格给客户写发盘函吧,注意发盘函的格式和内容噢。

李新：好的,我写好后拿给您看。

(李新回到工位上很快拟写了一份发盘 E-mail 交给王经理审核)**(见第 33 页)**

李新的计算过程——报价核算：

(1) KJ1001 的报价核算（美元的汇率为 6.8 人民币元/1 美元）：

实际成本：15.54 元/米，换算成美元＝15.54/6.8＝2.29 美元

人民币费用：国内运输费 0.076＋港区港杂费 0.023＋商检费 0.013＋报关费 0.006＋垫款利息 0.3＝0.418 元/米，换算成美元＝0.418/6.8＝0.061 美元

美元费用：业务费用报价×2%＋出口运费 0.068＋保险费报价×(1＋10%)×0.15%

利润：报价×10%

报价＝实际成本＋人民币费用＋美元费用＋利润

FOB 报价＝2.29＋0.061＋报价×2%＋报价×10%

FOB 报价＝2.67 美元/米

CFR 报价＝2.29＋0.061＋报价×2%＋0.068＋报价×10%

CFR 报价＝2.75 美元/米

CIF 报价＝2.29＋0.061＋报价×2%＋0.068＋报价×(1＋10%)×0.15%＋报价×10%

CIF 报价＝2.76 美元/米

(2) KJ2001 的报价核算：

实际成本：17.26 元/米，换算成美元＝17.26/6.8＝2.54 美元

人民币费用：国内运输费 0.076＋港区港杂费 0.023＋商检费 0.013＋报关费 0.006＋垫款利息 0.33＝0.448 元/米，换算成美元＝0.448/6.8＝0.066 美元

美元费用：业务费用报价×2%＋出口运费 0.068＋保险费报价×(1＋10%)×0.15%

利润：报价×10%

报价＝实际成本＋人民币费用＋美元费用＋利润

FOB 报价＝2.54＋0.066＋报价×2%＋报价×10%

FOB 报价＝2.96 美元/米

CFR 报价＝2.54＋0.066＋报价×2%＋0.068＋报价×10%

CFR 报价＝3.04 美元/米

CIF 报价＝2.54＋0.066＋报价×2%＋0.068＋报价×(1＋10%)×0.15%＋报价×10%

CIF 报价＝3.06 美元/米

报 价 汇 总

	KJ1001（美元/米）	KJ2001（美元/米）
FOB Shanghai	2.67	2.96
CFR Genova	2.75	3.04
CIF Genova	2.76	3.06

发盘函(初稿):

发件人:	li_xin@lixin.com.cn
收件人:	f.taldelli@palmavito.com
日　　期:	2010-07-12
主　　题:	Offer for Innovative Textile

Dear Mr. Taldelli,

We are in receipt of your inquiry dated Jul. 9, 2010. We are glad to know that you are interested in our antibacterial finished textiles. As requested, we have sent the inspection report to you. Moreover, the samples of the textiles are free of charge. We hope they will reach your demand and help to improve the function of your products.

In order to start a concrete transaction between us, we take pleasure in making you a special offer as follows:

1. "Milky Way" antibacterial finished bleached twill
   Art No. KJ1001
   Specification: 100% cotton twill, 20×20, 108×58, 57/58'×120 M
   USD2.67/M FOB Shanghai
   USD2.75/M CFR Genova
   USD2.76/M CIF Genova
2. "Milky Way" antibacterial finished dyed twill
   Art No. KJ2001
   Specification: 100% cotton twill, 20×20, 108×58, 57/58'×120 M
   USD2.96/M FOB Shanghai
   USD3.04/M CFR Genova
   USD3.06/M CIF Genova

Packing: In bales of 4 pieces each, 135 kgs in gross and 130 kgs in net, 1.5×0.5×0.6 m in measurement, 26400 meters/20'(FCL)
Shipment: to be effected within 30 days after receipt of the relevant L/C
Payment: by L/C 30 days after sight
Insurance: for 110% invoice value covering FPA
Please note the above quotation is subject to the quantity of full container load (FCL).

Looking forward to your favorable reply.

Yours truly,
Shanghai Lixin International Trading Co., Ltd.
Li Xin

发盘函(定稿):

发件人:	li_xin@lixin.com.cn
收件人:	f.taldelli@palmavito.com
日　期:	2010-07-12
主　题:	Offer for Innovative Textile

Dear Mr. Taldelli,

We are in receipt of your inquiry dated July 9, 2010. We are glad to know that you are interested in our antibacterial finished textiles. As requested, we have sent the inspection report to you. Moreover, the samples of the textiles are free of charge. We hope they will reach your demand and help to improve the function of your products.

In order to start a concrete transaction between us, we take pleasure in making you a special offer as follows:

1. "Milky Way" antibacterial finished bleached twill
   Art No. KJ1001
   Specification: 100% cotton twill, 20×20, 108×58, 57/58'×120 M
   USD2.67/M FOB Shanghai
   USD2.75/M CFR Genova
   USD2.76/M CIF Genova
2. "Milky Way" antibacterial finished dyed twill
   Art No. KJ2001
   Specification: 100% cotton twill, 20×20, 108×58, 57/58'×120 M
   USD2.96/M FOB Shanghai
   USD3.04/M CFR Genova
   USD3.06/M CIF Genova

Packing: In bales of 4 pieces each, 135 kgs in gross and 130 kgs in net, 1.5×0.5×0.6 m in measurement, 26400 meters/20' (FCL)
Shipment: to be effected within 30 days after receipt of the relevant L/C
Payment: by L/C 30 days after sight
Insurance: for 110% invoice value covering FPA
Please note the above quotation is subject to the quantity of full container load (FCL). This offer is firm subject to your immediate reply which should reach us not later than 10 days.

Looking forward to your favorable reply.

Yours truly,
Shanghai Lixin International Trading Co., Ltd.
Li Xin

李新： 王经理，我写好了，您看看。

王经理： 好的，我来看看。商品规格有了，数量有了，包装有了，价格有了，交货时间和交货地点有了，支付方式也有了。对了，有效的发盘有一项很重要的内容是什么啊？

李新： 噢，是发盘有效期。

王经理： 为什么说发盘有效期很重要啊？

李新： 因为如果不规定发盘有效期，就表明对方接受发盘的时间不受限制，而市场行情在不断变化，特别是生产原料价格会不断变化。如果对方等到对自己有利的时候接受发盘，而此时恰好生产成本涨价，生产工厂不愿意按照原价提供产品时，我们就会很被动。如果发盘规定有效期，那么这个发盘只在有效期内受到约束，也就是对方只要在有效期内表示接受，我们就必须和他按此发盘签约成交，但如果有效期内对方没有表示接受，过后我们就不用负责了。这样的话，我在发盘函结尾处加上 "This offer is firm subject to your immediate reply which should reach us not later than 10 days."就可以了吧？

王经理： 很好，你把发盘有效期加上去，然后就直接发给客户吧。

（李新将发盘函修改完并请王经理签字后发送给了客户）（见第 34 页）

THINK —— 理论思考

Think 2-1 出口商品的价格条款主要有哪些内容构成？

出口合同中的价格条款，一般包括商品的单价（unit price）和总值或总金额（total amount）两项基本内容。商品单价在表述上由计价货币、单价金额、计量单位和贸易术语四个部分组成。总值或总金额是单位和数量的乘积，也就是一笔交易的货款总金额。总值所使用的货币必须与单价所使用的货币一样。总值除使用阿拉伯数字填写外，一般还用文字表示。

Think 2-2 出口商品的价格由哪些要素构成？

出口商品价格主要由三大要素构成。

（一）成本

成本（cost）指出口货物的实际成本。如果是专业的外贸公司，为得到一批货物需要付出一定的收购成本；如果是工贸公司，则需付出生产成本或加工成本。收购成本、生产成本或加工成本减去出口退税部分即为实际成本。

（二）费用

费用（expenses, charges）主要包括国内费用和国际费用，其中：

（1）国内费用：主要包括国内运输费、国内保险费、包装费、仓储费、认证费、商检费、报关费、港口费、相关捐税、购货垫款利息、经营管理费、银行手续费和其他种种为进行贸易活动而付出的费用。

(2) 国际费用：主要包括国际运费、国际保险费和佣金。

(三) 预期利润

在对外报价中还应该包括预期利润(expected profit)部分。

Think 2-3　如何核算出口商品的成本？

一般情况下，出口方的成本为含税成本。但很多国家为鼓励出口，往往对出口商品采取退还全部或部分增值税的做法。因此，出口方的实际成本应为含税成本减去出口退税部分。具体计算方法如下：

(1) 实际成本＝含税成本－出口退税

(2) 出口退税＝[含税成本/(1＋增值税率)]×出口退税率

(3) 实际成本＝含税成本－[含税成本/(1＋增值税率)]×出口退税率

或：实际成本＝含税成本×[1－出口退税率/(1＋增值税率)]

或：实际成本＝含税成本/(1＋增值税率)×(1＋增值税率－出口退税率)

(4) 含税成本＝实际成本×(1＋增值税率)/(1＋增值税率－出口退税率)

Think 2-4　出口商品的国际费用如何计算？

出口商品的国际费用主要包括国际运费、国际保险费和佣金。

(一) 国际运费的计算

国际贸易运输方式有多种，海洋运输因其具有通过能力大、运载量大、单位运费低、对货物的适应性强等优点而成为国际贸易中使用最为广泛的运输方式。

海洋运输分为班轮运输和租船运输两种方式，在国际贸易中，除大宗初级产品的交易外，一般采用班轮运输的方式。

班轮运费分为件杂货物运费和集装箱货物运费两种。

1. 件杂货物运费

1) 计算方法：

件杂货物运费＝基本运费＋附加费＝基本运费费率×运费吨＋附加费

2) 计算步骤：① 查询商品列名等级和运费计收标准；② 查明本次运输航线的基本运费率；③ 查明各种附加费用；④ 计算单位运价；⑤ 计算总运费。

3) 计收标准有以下几种：

(1) 重量吨(Weight Ton, W/T)，即以货物的毛重作为运费的计收标准。

(2) 尺码吨(Measurement Ton, M/T)，即以货物的体积作为运费的计收标准，1立方米相当于1吨。

(3) 从价运费(Ad Val., A.V.)，即按货物总价值的一定百分比收取运费。

(4) 选择运费，即由轮船公司在多种运费计收标准中选择一种方式收取运费。常见的有以下四种选择方法：① W/M，即在重量吨和尺码吨中选择，轮船公司一般选择运费较高者作为计收标准。② W or A.V.，在重量吨和从价运费中选择。③ M or A.V.，在尺码吨和从价运费中选择。④ W/M or A.V.,在重量吨、尺码吨和从价运费中三选一。

(5) 综合运费,W/M plus A.V.,即先在重量吨和尺码吨中选择,再加收一定的从价运费。

(6) 按货物的件数计收。

(7) 船货双方临时议定。

2. 集装箱货物运费

集装箱运输可分为整箱货(Full Container Load,FCL)和拼箱货(Less than Container Load,LCL)两种流转形态。若为整箱货,直接按运价表中所列之单箱运费计算;若为拼箱货,应先计算出所装箱的货物数量,再按件杂货物的计算方法计算;若为部分整箱货、部分拼箱货,应混合两种计算方法进行计算。

集装箱运费=包箱费率×集装箱的数量

集装箱数量按货物的总重量或总体积除以集装箱的有效载货重量或有效容积取整得出。通常 20 英尺集装箱的有效载重量为 17.5 吨,有效容积为 25 立方米;40 英尺集装箱的有效载重量为 24.5 吨,有效容积为 55 立方米。

(二) 国际保险费的计算

保险金额=CIF 报价×(1+投保加成率)

保险费=保险金额×保险费率

(三) 佣金计算

佣金=含佣价×佣金率

净价=含佣价-佣金=含佣价×(1-佣金率)

Think 2-5 出口商品的国内费用如何计算?

出口商品的国内费用主要包括国内运输费、国内保险费、包装费、仓储费、认证费、商检费、报关费、港口费、相关捐税、购货垫款利息费、银行手续费、经营管理费和其他种种为进行贸易活动而付出的费用。其中:

(一) 购货垫款利息费

购货垫款利息费=采购成本(含税)×贷款利率×垫款期限

由于贷款利率通常为年利,则在计算时要注意,垫款期限如为 60 天,则需要计算为:垫款利息费=采购成本(含税)×贷款利率×(60/360);如垫款期限为 2 个月,则需要计算为:垫款利息费=采购成本(含税)×贷款利率×(2/12)。

(二) 银行手续费

通常银行手续费是出口议付结汇等费用。在计算时,出口报价为基数,费用率可估算。

银行手续费＝出口报价×银行手续费率

（三）经营管理费

有些外贸公司为了计算方便，将出口的经营管理费以一个定额费用率（国内费用占出口商品采购成本的比率）来核定。

经营管理费＝采购成本（含税）×定额费用率

Think 2-6　贸易术语在国际贸易中有哪些作用？

贸易术语（trade terms）又称价格术语（price terms），是在长期的国际贸易实践中产生的，用简明的语言或缩写字母概括说明交货地点、买卖双方责任、费用和风险划分的固定化的买卖条件。

贸易术语在国际贸易中有以下几个方面的作用。

（一）有利于买卖双方洽商交易和订立合同

由于每种贸易术语都有其特定的含义，因此，买卖双方只要商定按何种贸易术语成交，即可明确彼此在交接货物方面所应承担的责任、费用和风险。这就简化了交易手续，缩短了洽商交易的时间，从而有利于买卖双方迅速达成交易和订立合同。

（二）有利于买卖双方核算价格和成本

由于贸易术语表示价格构成因素，所以，买卖双方确定成交价格时，必然要考虑采用的贸易术语中包含哪些从属费用，这就有利于买卖双方进行比价和加强成本核算。

（三）有利于解决履约当中的争议

买卖双方商订合同时，如对合同条款考虑欠周，使某些事项规定不明确或不完备，致使履约当中产生的争议不能依据合同的规定解决，在此情况下，可以援引有关贸易术语的一般解释来处理。因为，贸易术语的一般解释已成为国际惯例，它是大家所遵循的一种类似行为规范的准则。

（四）有利于其他有关机构开展业务活动

买卖双方离不开船公司、保险公司和银行等机构，而贸易术语及有关解释贸易术语的国际惯例的相继出现，便为这些机构开展业务活动和处理业务实践中的问题提供了客观依据和有利条件。

Think 2-7　常用的贸易术语有哪些？

最常用的适用于海运的贸易术语主要有 FOB、CFR 和 CIF。

FOB：直译为装运港船上交货，是一种常见的国际贸易术语，指卖方在约定的装运港将货物交到买方指定的船上。按国际商会对 FOB 的解释，买卖双方各自承担的基本义务可作如下划分：

（1）卖方的基本义务包括：办理出口清关手续，并承担货物在指定装运港交到船上之前的一切费用与风险,在约定的装船期与装运港内,按通常或约定的方法将货物装到买方指定的船上,并向买方发出已装船的通知,随后向买方提交双方所约定的各项单证或具有效力的电子信息数据。

(2) 买方的基本义务包括:按双方约定好的时间订好船舶开往约定的装运港接运货物并支付相应的运费,同时告知卖方船舶的到达装货日期以及船名,承担货物在指定装运港交到船上之后的各种费用以及一切风险,最后凭卖方所提交的提货凭证提取货物并支付相应的货款。

由于双方要采取的货运方式不同可能会导致装货费用的承担问题,比如班轮运输由船方负担装卸费,而不定期船运则不一定,因此买卖双方通常在FOB术语下加列装货费用由谁负担的附加条件以明确责任。

CFR:直译为成本加运费。此术语是指卖方必须负担货物运至约定目的港所需的成本和运费,这里所指的成本相当于FOB价,故CFR术语的基本含义是在FOB价的基础上加上装运港至目的港的通常运费。

按CFR术语成交,在货价构成因素中,包括自装运至目的港的通常运费,也就是说,主要运费已付,故卖方要负责签订运输合同和安排运送货物,但由于它同FOB术语一样也属于装运港交货,货物风险的划分,也以货物在装运港装上船为界,故货物中途灭失或损坏的风险以及货物装船后中途发生事件产生的任何额外费用,概由买方承担。

CIF:直译为成本加运费加保险费,指卖方需支付从装运港到目的港的全部成本及货运费用并承担相应的保险费用,它与CFR术语下买卖双方的基本义务大致相同,只不过卖方的义务相应增加了一条,即为买方办理货运保险并支付保险费,按照一般的国际惯例,投保金额应按CIF价格加成10%,合同中若无特殊约定,卖方只需购买最低级别的保险,若买方要求加买附加险,险费应由买方承担。需要指出的是:CIF术语下,虽然由卖方支付保险费用,但风险的划分仍以货物在装运港装上船为界,卖方只是代办保险,如果发生承保范围内的损失,应由买方向保险公司进行索赔,卖方概不负责。

Think 2-8 如何核算FOB、CFR、CIF价格(含佣价)?

(1) FOBC=(实际成本+国内费用)/(1-佣金率-预期利润率)

(2) CFRC=(实际成本+国内费用+国际运费)/(1-佣金率-预期利润率)

(3) CIFC=(实际成本+国内费用+国际运费)/[1-(1+投保加成率)×保险费率-佣金率-预期利润率]

Think 2-9 交易磋商的内容主要有哪些?一般情况下,出口交易磋商的程序由哪些环节组成?达成一项交易,哪些环节是必不可少的?

国际贸易合同中的交易条件是交易磋商的主要内容。

交易条件可以分为五类:

(1) 货物条件,包括货物的名称、质量规定、数量、包装、商品检验等。

(2) 价格条件，包括货物的单价、总价、价格术语、佣金或折扣等。
(3) 交货条件，包括交货的时间、地点、运输方式、运输保险等。
(4) 支付条件，包括支付工具、支付时间、地点及支付方式等。
(5) 争议处理条件，包括索赔、不可抗力、仲裁等。

在外贸业务中，出口交易磋商的一般程序可概括为"询盘"、"发盘"、"还盘"和"接受"四个环节。其中"发盘"和"接受"是必不可少的环节。

Think 2-10　发盘环节在交易磋商中有何重要性？

发盘是买方或卖方向对方提出交易条件并愿意按此条件达成交易的表示。发盘是交易磋商中必需的一个环节，在法律上对发盘人具有约束力。发盘在有效期内，发盘人不得任意撤销或修改其内容；一旦受盘人在有效期内表示无条件接受发盘内容，发盘人将承担按发盘条件与对方订立合同的责任。

Think 2-11　发盘应具备哪些条件？

构成一项有效的发盘，必须具备下列条件：

(1) 发盘应向一个或一个以上特定的人提出，即指向有名有姓的公司或个人提出。例如，广告就不能算是发盘，这是因为他没有向一个或一个以上的特定的人提出。

(2) 发盘的内容必须十分确定。所谓十分确定，指在提出的订约建议中，至少应包括三个基本要素：① 标明货物的名称；② 明示或默示地规定货物的数量或确定数量的方法；③ 明示或默示地规定货物的价格或确定价格的方法。

(3) 表明经受盘人接受，发盘人即受约束的意思。

发盘人必须表明其发盘一旦被受盘人接受即受约束的意思。发盘是订立合同的建议，这个意思应当体现在发盘之中，如发盘人只是就某些交易条件建议同对方进行磋商，而根本没有受其建议约束的意思，则此项建议不能视为一项发盘。例如，发盘人在其提出的订约建议中加注诸如"仅供参考"、"须以发盘人的最后确认为准"或其他保留条件，这样的订约建议就不是发盘，而只是邀请对方发盘。

Think 2-12　发盘需要注意哪些问题？

(1) 发盘约束力。发盘具有法律约束力。发盘人发出发盘后不能随意反悔，一旦受盘人接受发盘，发盘人就必须按发盘条件与对方达成交易并履行合同（发盘）义务。

(2) 发盘生效时间。《联合国国际货物销售合同公约》（以下简称《公约》）规定，发盘在"到达受盘人时生效"。公约的这一规定，对发盘人来讲具有非常重要的意义。

(3) 发盘有效期。发盘有效期是发盘人受其发盘约束的期限。在国际贸易中，发盘有效期有两种表现形式：明确规定有效期限、采用合理期限。前者不但很少发生争议而且还可促进成交，使用较多，但不能撤销；后者容易产生争议，但在对方没有接受前可以撤销。采用何者，应视情况，不能一概而论。

(4) 发盘的终止。发盘终止指发盘失去效力。发盘终止有四种情况：① 因受盘人拒绝而失效；② 因发盘人撤销自己的发盘而失效；③ 因规定的接受期限已满而失效；④ 因"合理期限"已过而失效。

交易中，不论哪种原因导致发盘终止，此后发盘人均不再受其发盘的约束。

Think 2-13　发盘在什么情况下是失效的？

发盘的失效是指发盘失去了法律效力，发盘人不再受发盘的约束，受盘人也失去了接受该发盘的权利。发盘的失效有以下几种情况：

(1) 在发盘规定的有效期内未被接受，或虽未规定有效期，但在合理时间内未被接受，则发盘的效力即告中止。

(2) 发盘被发盘人依法撤销。

(3) 被受盘人拒绝或提出还盘后，即拒绝或还盘通知送达发盘人时，发盘的效力即告终止。

(4) 发盘人发盘后，发生了不可抗力事件。在这种情况下，按出现不可抗力可免除责任的一般原则，发盘的效力即告中止。

(5) 发盘人或受盘人在发盘被接受前丧失行为能力，则该发盘的效力也可终止。

Think 2-14　发盘撤回与发盘的撤销有什么不同？

根据《公约》规定，一项发盘（包括注明不可撤销的发盘）在未送达受盘人之前，发盘人可以撤回。而发盘的撤销是发盘已生效但未作出接受之前，发盘人由于某些特殊原因将发盘撤销。《公约》规定，发盘送达受盘人后，在受盘人尚未表示接受前，发盘人将撤销通知送达受盘人，发盘可予撤销。但下列两种情况下的发盘不得撤销：

(1) 在发盘中规定了有效期或以其他方式表示该发盘是不可撤销的。

(2) 受盘人有理由相信该发盘是不可撤销的，并本着对该发盘的信赖采取了行动。

Think 2-15　如何规定发盘的有效期？

从发盘角度来看，在有效期内，发盘人受其发盘内容的约束，即一旦被接受，就要承担订立与发盘内容相符的合同的责任；在有效期之外，发盘人则不受其发盘内容的约束。因此，发盘的有效期既是对发盘人的一种限制，也是对发盘人的一种保障。

凡是发盘，都有有效期。发盘人对发盘有效可以做出明确规定，也可做不明确规定。如果发盘规定有效期，则该有效期从发盘传达到受盘人开始，到规定的有效期届满为止；如果发盘没有规定有效期，则有效期在按法律规定的合理时间内有效。

在实务中，规定有效期的方法有两种。

（一）规定最迟的接受期限

例如，"发盘限15日复"。但是，这种方法有一个问题，即截止期15日是指发出的15日，还是送达发盘人的15日在使用信件或电报表示时，这两个15日之间有一段时间间隔，那么，对于接受应于何时生效，各国法律对此的解释不同。

英美法的国家采用"投邮生效"原则。信件投邮或电报交发，接受即告生效，即使接受的函电在邮递途中延误或遗失,发盘人未能在有效期内收到,甚至根本没有收到,也不影响合同的成立。也就是说,传递延误或遗失的风险由发盘人承担。但是,如果发盘人在发盘中规定,接受必须于有效期内传达到发盘人,则接受的函电传达到发盘人时,接受才能生效。

大陆法的国家则采用"到达生效"原则。接受的函电只有在发盘有效期内到达发盘人时才生效。如果接受的函电在邮递过程中延误或遗失,则合同不能成立。也就是说,传递延误或遗失的风险由受盘人承担。

《公约》采用了"到达生效"原则,接受在到达发盘人时生效。如果接受在发盘的有效期内,或发盘没有规定有效期,在合理时间内未到达发盘人,接受即为无效。

为了明确发盘的截止期,在规定最迟接受期时,可以同时明确以哪方的时间为准。例如:"发盘限15日复,我方时间为准";"发盘有效至我方时间星期五"。

(二)规定一段时间

例如:"发盘3天有效","发盘5天内复"。但是,这种方法也有一个如何计算"一段时间"的起讫时间问题。《公约》第20条规定,发盘人在电报或信件中订定的一段接受期间,从电报交发时刻或信上载明的发信日期起算。如果信上未载明发信日期,则从信封上所载日期起算。发盘人以电话、电传或其他可立即传达到对方的通信方法订定的一段接受期间,从发盘到达受盘人时起算。在计算一段接受期间时,这段期间内的正式假日或非营业日应当计算在内。但是,如果因为那天在发盘人的营业所在地是正式假日或非营业日,接受通知在接受期间的最后一天未能送达发盘人的地址,则这段期间应顺延至下一个营业日。《公约》对合理时间也没有一个确切的解释,但提出要考虑到交易的情况,包括发盘人所使用的通讯方法的迅速程度。但是,对口头发盘,一般要立即接受。

Think 2-16 如何撰写发盘函?

发盘因撰写情况或背景不同,在内容、要求上也有所不同。但从总的情况看,其结构一般包括:

(1)感谢对方来函,明确答复对方来函询问事项。
(2)阐明交易的条件(品名、规格、数量、包装、价格、装运、支付、保险等)。
(3)声明发盘有效期或约束条件。
(4)鼓励对方订货。

  ACT——模拟训练

Act 2-1 出口实际成本核算

接到 Sinclair 先生10月22日的询盘 E-mail 后,钱晓俊着手进行出口报价核算。为了方便核算,钱晓俊先将采薇杯业公司提供的进货资料进行了整理。

工厂供货资料：

采薇杯业公司
供 货 资 料

1. 真空运动水壶
   货号：CWS3－50
   容量：500 毫升　材质：不锈钢、单胆
   出厂价：12.6 元/个（含税）
   包装：纸箱，每箱 40 个装，纸箱尺寸：61 厘米×39 厘米×26 厘米＝0.0619 立方米
   每箱毛净重：29.4 千克/21.8 千克

2. 真空旅游水壶
   货号：CWT2－100
   容量：1000 毫升　材质：不锈钢、双胆
   出厂价：19.2 元/个（含税）
   包装：纸箱，每箱 20 个装，纸箱尺寸：65 厘米×41 厘米×29 厘米＝0.0773 立方米
   每箱毛净重：27.3 千克/20.7 千克

其他：
增值税率：17%
出口退税率：11%
生产周期：月产量 8000 个
最低起订数量：3000 个
交货期：收到订单后 10 天在工厂交货
支付方式：预付 70% 货款，交货后 5 日内支付余下货款

根据以上供货资料，请以钱晓俊的身份核算出口实际成本。

出口实际成本核算：

出口实际成本核算

Act 2-2　报价基础数量确定

钱晓俊在核算出口费用前先确定报价基础数量,以便计算每单位货物发生的费用。
请以钱晓俊的身份计算报价基础数量。

出口报价基础数量计算:

报价基础数量计算

Act 2-3　出口费用核算

钱晓俊从公司有关部门获取了"中国—美国墨西哥湾航线"集装箱运价表(见表2-5)、海运保险费率表(见表2-3)及各项费用数据,整理出费用构成表(见表2-6)。

表2-5　中国—美国墨西哥湾航线的集装箱运价表(节选)　　单位:USD

航　线	FCL 整箱货			LCL (W/M)拼箱货 (重量/尺码)
	20′	40′	40′HQ	
上海—休斯敦 SHANGHAI - HOUSTON	2300.00	4500.00	4600.00	135.00

表2-6　费用构成表

	项　目	已知费用或费率
费用	20′集装箱包干费	1250元
	业务费用	美元报价×5%
	垫款周期	3个月
	银行贷款年利率	6%
	保险费	保险加成率10% 平安险保费率0.15%
	银行手续费	美元报价×0.35%
	出口运费	2300美元/20′FCL

请以钱晓俊的身份填制下列费用核算表(见表2-7)。

表2-7 费用核算表

费用	项　　目	CWS3-50	CWT2-100
	包干费		
	业务费用		
	垫款利息		
	保险费		
	银行手续费		
	出口运费		

Act 2-4　出口报价核算

钱晓俊请示了经理,本笔贸易的期望销售利润率是10%,接下来进行出口报价核算(美元的汇率为6.8人民币元/1美元)。

请以钱晓俊的身份进行出口报价核算。

出口报价核算:

出口报价核算

Act 2-5　出口商向进口商发盘

完成出口报价核算后,钱晓俊着手撰写发盘E-mail。

请以钱晓俊的身份,撰写该发盘E-mail。

出口商发盘函：

发件人：	damonchan@hainaco.com.cn
收件人：	ray.sinclair@gulfday.com
日　　期：	2010 - 10 - 25
主　　题：	Offer

DISCUSS——个案讨论

Discuss 2-1

在本实训 LOOK 环节中,假设意大利进口商 Palmavito 订货的数量是两种纺织品面料每色 6000 米,共 12000 米,并明确要求集装箱流转形态为拼箱货(LCL),货物的实际成本和销售利润率不变,根据报关运输部陈老师提供的费用构成表(见表2-8)、常用货物等级表(见表2-9)、集装箱运价表(见表2-10),李新将如何进行出口报价核算?

表2-8 费用构成表

项 目		单位费用或费率
费用	包装费	包干费 0.5元/米
	仓储费	
	国内运输费	
	港区港杂费	
	商检费	
	报关费	
	认证费	
	出口海关税费	
	垫款利息	KJ1001: 0.30元/米 KJ2001: 0.33元/米
	业务费用	美元报价×2%
	银行费用	美元报价×0.35%
	出口运费	待计算
	保险费	美元报价×(1+10%)×0.15%
	佣金	美元报价×3%

表2-9 常用货物等级表

货 名	Commodity	W/M
干、蓄电池	Batteries, dry & storage	8
矿泉水	Mineral Water	7
啤 酒	Beer	7
餐 具	Table Ware	10
香 皂	Soap, Toilet	11

(续表)

货 名	Commodity	W/M
药 品	Medicines & Drugs	12
纸	Paper, on Bales, Reels, Pallets & Wooden Clamps	5
文 具	Stationery	9
玩 具	Toys	8
陶瓷器	Porcelain Ware	8
汽车及零件	Motor Cars & Trucks, Parts & Accessories	9
电冰箱	Refrigerator	10
纺织品面料	Textiles	10
自行车及零件	Bicycles & Parts	9
体育用品	Sport Goods	10
木筷子	Wooden Chopsticks	5
皮 箱	Suitcases, Leather	12
未列名鞋	Footwear N.O.E.	9
手 套	Gloves	9
糖 果	Confectionery	9
蜡 烛	Candle	6
毛 毯	Blankets, Woolen	12

表2-10 集装箱运价表(节选)　　　　单位：USD

CLASS 等级	BASIS 计算标准	LCL 拼箱货	FCL 整箱货	
			20'	40'
1—7	M	78	1750	3500
8—10	M	84	1900	3800
11—15	M	91	2050	4100
16—20	M	97	2200	4400
1—7	W	108	1850	3600
8—10	W	117	2000	3900
11—15	W	126	2150	4200
16—20	W	135	2300	4500

提示：

（1）在表2-8中，包装费、仓储费、国内运输费、港区港杂费、商检费和报关费整合为包干费，收取标准为0.5元/米。

（2）在表2-8中，增加了银行手续费用，收取标准为美元报价的0.35%；增加了支付给中间商的佣金，收取标准为美元报价的3%，即该报价为含佣价，佣金率为3%。

（3）表2-10是FCB包箱费率表，但也可用于拼箱货。关于拼箱货的运费计算，采用传统的件杂货运费计算方法，即先在表2-9中查出货物等级并判断货物计算标准（W还是M），然后根据不同等级和计算标准在表2-10中查出运价，最后乘以运费吨得到运费。

出口报价核算：

出口报价核算

Discuss 2-2

2011年3月16日,李新收到国外E-mail如下:

进口商询盘函:

发件人:	k.eisenbach@ulschelke.com.de
收件人:	li_xin@lixin.com.cn
日 期:	2011-03-16
主 题:	Inquiry

Dear Sir or Madam,

Karulos & Therman Handel GmbH inform us that you are exporters of all cotton bed-sheets. We would like you to send us details of your various ranges and some samples. Please indicate terms of payment and discounts you would allow on purchases of not less that 8000 of individual items.

We believe there is a promising market in our area for moderately priced and good quality goods of the kind mentioned.

Looking forward to your favorable reply.

Yours sincerely,
Ulsch & Elke Handel A. G.
Kirsten Eisenbach (Mrs.)

李新将如何回复,他准备在回信中告知对方:
(1) 商品的详细资料,诸如规格、价格和包装等,可参见随附的目录和价目表。
(2) 样品另寄。
(3) 通常采用即期信用证付款。
(4) 所提数量可给予5%的优惠。
(5) 订货若早于本月底,可保证在到证日后30天内交货。

出口商发盘函：

发件人：	li_xin@lixin.com.cn
收件人：	k.eisenbach@ulschelke.com.de
日　期：	2011 - 03 - 18
主　题：	Offer for All Cotton Bed-sheets

情景模拟实训三

交易磋商二——还盘与盈亏测算

 LOOK——情景示范

（李新向客户发盘后的第二天,收到客户的回复E-mail,要求对货号KJ2001的CIF报价每米降低0.50美元,另外再加5%的佣金）

还盘函：

发件人：	f. taldelli@palmavito. com
收件人：	li_xin@lixin. com. cn
日　期：	2010 - 07 - 15
主　题：	Reply for Offer

Dear Mr. Li,

Thank you for your offer of July 12, 2010 and the relevant inspection report.

Based on our evaluation, we request you to revise your price 0.50/M for Art No. KJ2001 and also include 5% commission on the basis of CIF Genova. Once the price declines, we will place the order for you as early as possible.

Expecting your revisionary price.

Yours sincerely,
Fabio Taldelli
Palmavito Articoli Sportive S. P. A.

李新：王经理，客户回 E-mail 了。

王经理：客户怎么说？

李新：客户要求货号 KJ2001 的 CIF 报价每米降低 0.50 美元，然后还要再加进去 5％的佣金，但客户没有提到货号 KJ1001。

王经理：你是怎么考虑的呢？

李新：这是一个大客户，如果这笔交易成功的话以后很可能一直会有比较多的机会。另外我也了解到同类商品会不断地出现，如果这次机会没有抓住的话，以后就更难了，所以我想还是要尽力成交。

王经理：好，我支持你。但因为是新客户，价格也不能轻易降低，这样吧，对于 KJ2001，先不要考虑降价，佣金考虑给，你和工厂商量一下，工厂的出厂价是否可以再低一点，同时我们也作些让利，将销售利润率由 10％调整到 8％吧。至于 KJ1001，看来客户目前不感兴趣。

李新：我明白了，我先测算一下。

（李新回到工位测算利润率，然后直接给绍兴轻纺开发公司的梁厂长打电话）

李新：梁厂长好！我按照您的出厂价给客户报价了，现在客户对货号 KJ2001 还价，我们公司考虑到这是个新客户，而且是个大客户，希望能够成交，所以在利润上作了让步，不知您那里能不能也做些让步争取成交啊？

梁厂长：考虑到与你们公司的长期合作和新产品联合开发，我们先前报给你们的就已经是最优惠价格了，现在再要让步的话，空间就比较小了啊，更何况数量也不大。

李新：梁厂长，看现在的数量，估计客户也是试单，如果质量好的话，一定会有大批量的需求的。因为客户是意大利一家非常知名的运动鞋制造商，而且现在国际市场对抗菌防臭面料的需求旺盛，潜力很大，请您考虑支持一下好吗？

梁厂长：好吧。考虑今后的合作机会，我们就将 KJ2001 的供货价格降低 0.50 元/米，也就是 19.50 元/米吧。

李新：谢谢梁厂长的支持！

（李新找到了财务结算部的钱老师）

李新：钱老师好！客户回函要求降低价格，王经理要求我按照 8％的销售利润率测算，但我算下来还是差一点，无法达到 8％的利润率，我想请教您还有什么办法能将银行相关的费用降低一点吗？

钱老师：你手上这笔业务中银行相关的费用主要就是指垫款利息，如果要降低垫款利息的话，有两条途径：一条途径是要求客户做即期信用证，这样就能把垫款周期从 4 个月降低到 3 个月；另一条途径是要求工厂把给我们的账期从 10 天延长到 45 天，这样也能把垫款周期从 4 个月降低到 3 个月。如果上面两条能同时办到，我们就能以 2 个月来计算垫款利息，那么银行这块的费用降低还是比较可观的。

李新：我明白了，谢谢钱老师！

（李新回到工位上又给梁厂长打电话）

李新：梁厂长好！刚才我和我们财务商量了一下，您能不能再给我们一些优惠啊，能把账期延长到45天吗?

梁厂长:工厂资金很紧张,真的很困难啊。

李新:梁厂长,这笔业务数量不大,占用资金不会很多,您能考虑一下吗?

梁厂长:好吧。刚好最近银行对我们民营企业的资金支持有所倾斜,我就答应你了,不过到了账期日一定要按时付款啊。

李新:请梁厂长尽管放心,我一定保证。

(李新向王经理汇报最新情况)

李新:王经理,我刚才和梁厂长进行了反复沟通,还请教了钱老师,现在有了些进展,我向您汇报一下。意大利客户对KJ2001的还价是USD3.06/M CIFC5% Genova,我是这样想的,报价由成本、费用、利润三部分组成,为了迎合客户的还价,我们对这三块都有可能要适当降低。您已经把销售利润率调低为8%,我刚才想办法通过工厂把成本和费用也降低了些,梁厂长现在把供货价降低到19.50元/米并且把账期延长到了45天,如果我再争取让意大利客户接受即期信用证付款,我们就能把垫款周期从4个月降低为2个月,银行的垫款利息就能降低不少,费用这块也就能降低一些。

王经理:好,思路清楚!接下来你准备再怎么操作下去啊?

李新:接下来我准备测算一下现在的利润率是多少,能不能达到8%。

王经理:具体怎么算利润呢?

李新:用收入减去支出,具体就是"销售收入-实际成本-各项费用",都采用单价,得出的也是单位利润。

王经理:慢着,有点问题,你刚才用的是"单价法",这是新业务员的常见问题,因为在报价核算中用的都是单价,所以自然而然在还价核算中也用单价了。记住,业务中在计算经过还价后的利润时,一般采用"总价法",因为比较直观,也能够减少计算中许多小数点产生的误差,比较精确,你明白其中的道理了吧?

李新:哦,我明白了,在还价核算中,应该算这笔业务的利润总额,就是"总销售收入-总实际成本-总费用",然后再把利润总额除以总销售收入,就得到利润率了。您看这样对了吗?

王经理:对,现在你去算吧。

李新:谢谢王经理的点拨!

(李新回到工位上再次测算利润率,20分钟后,李新向王经理汇报)

李新:王经理,这是按照客户的还价重新核算利润率的计算过程,新的利润率是8.38%,请您过目。

王经理:好的,我看看。(见第55页)

王经理:不错,计算过程没有问题。既然超过我们8%的期望销售利润率了,我看就先这样定了,你尽快答复客户吧。

李新:好,谢谢王经理。

(李新回到工位上,写E-mail回复客户的还盘)(见第56页)

李新的计算过程——利润率核算：

(1) 还价后 KJ2001 的总销售收入：

总销售收入 = 3.06×26400×6.8 = 549331.20 元

(2) 还价后 KJ2001 的总实际成本：

单位退税收入 = $\dfrac{19.50}{1+17\%}\times 16\%$ = 2.67 元/米

总实际成本 = (19.50−2.67)×26400 = 444312 元

(3) 还价后 KJ2001 的各项费用：

费用项目	总 价
国内运输费	2000 元
港区港杂费	600 元
商检费	350 元
报关费	150 元
垫款利息	19.50×26400×4.98%×2/12 = 4272.84 元
业务费用	3.06×26400×2%×6.8 = 10986.62 元
出口运费	1800×6.8 = 12240 元
保险费	3.06×26400×(1+10%)×0.15%×6.8 = 906.40 元
佣金	3.06×26400×5%×6.8 = 27466.56 元

总费用 = 2000+600+350+150+4272.84+10986.62+12240+906.40
　　　　+27466.56 = 58972.42 元

(4) 还价后 KJ2001 的利润总额：

利润总额 = 总销售收入 − 总实际成本 − 总费用
　　　　 = 549331.20 − 444312 − 58972.42
　　　　 = 46046.78 元

(5) 还价后 KJ2001 的利润率 = 利润总额 ÷ 总销售收入 × 100%
　　　　　　　　　　　　 = 46046.78 ÷ 549331.20 × 100% = 8.38%

出口商还盘函：

发件人：	li_xin@lixin.com.cn
收件人：	f.taldelli@palmavito.com
日　　期：	2010-07-15
主　　题：	Price with Commission

Dear Mr. Taldelli,

Thank you for your E-mail of this morning. From it, we know that you are interested in Art. No. KJ2001.

Although we are desirous of meeting your requirements, we regret being unable to comply with your all requests for price reduction. As this is the first time we cooperate with each other, so we accept 5% commission to the price we quoted in our offer dated Jul. 12, 2010. That means — Art. No. KJ2001 USD3.06/M CIFC5% Genova. But in the meantime, payment should be L/C at sight. This price we quoted is accurately calculated. We have cut our profit to the minimum.

Looking forward to your early reply.

Yours truly,
Shanghai Lixin International Trading Co., Ltd.
Li Xin

THINK——理论思考

Think 3-1　什么是"还盘"？还盘环节有什么法律意义？

　　还盘（Counter Offer）也称"反向要约"，是指受盘人收到发盘后，对发盘的内容不同意或不完全同意，为了进一步洽商交易，向发盘人提出修改建议或新的限制性条件的行为。一经还盘，原发盘即失去效力，发盘人不再受其约束；一项还盘相当于是受盘人向原发盘人提出的一项新的发盘。

　　还盘的法律意义：
还盘是对发盘的一种拒绝，还盘一经作出，原发盘即失去效力，发盘人不再受其约束。
辨别还盘还需注意以下几点：
(1) 实质性变更发盘的条件属于还盘性质。
(2) 对发盘表示有条件的接受，也是还盘的一种形式。
(3) 在接受的同时，表示某种希望或愿望，则该接受可视为一项有效的接受。

Think 3-2　在处理还盘时应该注意哪些事项？

　　(1) 还盘可以明确使用"还盘"字样，也可不使用，只是在内容中表示对发盘的修改。

（2）还盘可以针对价格，也可以针对交易商品的品质、数量、装运、支付或者保险。

（3）还盘时，一般只针对原发盘提出不同意见或需要修改的部分，已同意的内容在还盘中可以省略。

（4）接到还盘后要与原发盘进行核对，找出还盘中提出的新内容，结合市场变化情况和我方销售意图认真对待和考虑。

Think 3-3　应该如何考虑是否接受客户的还盘？

当出口商对外报出价格后，最理想的情况是进口商能够接受该报价。但在实际业务中，大多数的情况却是进口商希望降价。在进口商提出降价要求时，出口商在比较有成交把握时，最好能够据理力争，说服进口商接受原报价。但这样做，出口商应该对市场有比较充分的了解，并且所涉货物处于卖方市场时才不会有失去客户的风险。如果出口商没有这样的把握，就要考虑接受进口商的还价或适当降价了。

Think 3-4　如果不考虑接受客户还盘的价格条件，应该如何答复？

在国际贸易中，最常见的还盘是买方对卖方发盘价格的还盘。遇到此种还盘时，卖方一般可按以下方法予以处理和答复：

（1）感谢来函但不能接受其还价。

（2）强调原价格的合理性并陈述理由，进而说服对方接受原报价。

Think 3-5　在考虑接受进口商的还价或适当降价前，应该如何做好价格测算？

在考虑接受进口商的还价或适当降价的策略中，我们要对成本、费用、利润等因素的影响进行充分的计算。在出口报价中，我们的基本要求是在已知出口商品的采购成本、国内费用、国外费用以及公司预期利润的条件下，计算出口报价。这是一个将报价作为计算结果的"正算"过程。而在出口还价核算时，我们是将外商的还价作为一个"已知数"，以此来倒推采购成本、国内费用（国外费用变化的可能性不大）以及公司的预期利润。所以，出口还价的基本要求是：

（1）如果接受外商的还价，在其他条件（采购成本、国内费用等）不变的情况下，计算公司的利润率。因为利润率的多少是能否接受对方还价的基础。

（2）如果接受外商的还价，在其他条件可以改变的情况下，计算公司的利润。这里的其他条件可以改变是指出口公司有可能降低采购成本或国内费用等。

上述两种情况的计算方法是：

销售利润＝销售收入（外商的还价）－实际采购成本－出口费用

（3）如果接受外商的还价，又保持公司的预期利润率不变，计算出能够接受的国内采购成本或费用。

此种情况的计算方法是：

实际采购成本＝销售收入（外商的还价）－出口费用－销售利润

某项费用＝销售收入（外商的还价）－实际采购成本－销售利润－其他费用

Think 3-6 如何答复客户的还盘(如何撰写还盘函)?

(1) 确认对方来函(感谢对方来函,简洁表明我方态度)。

(2) 强调原发盘(原价)的合理性,并列明理由、原因,如符合市价(请客户调查目前市价)、品质超群(请客户检测我方样品)、利润已降低至最低、原料价格上涨、工人成本提升、订单已满,等。

(3) 提出我方意见并催促对方行动,还盘要有说服力,具有促销性质,如给予数量折扣,或以库存紧张为由激励对方早日下订单,或推荐其他代用品,以求新的商机。

 ACT——模拟训练

Act 3-1 出口还价利润率核算

2010年10月30日,钱晓俊收到客户的E-mail。

还盘函:

From:	ray.sinclair@gulfday.com
To:	damonchan@hainaco.com.cn
Date:	2010-10-30
Re:	Counter Offer

Dear Mr. Chan,

We are glad to receive your offer of Oct. 25, 2010 and relative samples.

In reply, we accept your offer for Art. No. CWS3-50 on CIF basis but regret to say that your price of Art No. CWT2-100 is not competitive enough. We really appreciate the good workmanship of your products, but are also aware that the price level counts much, especially in the initial sales stage.

To set up the trade, may we suggest you give a special discount of 6% for Art No. CWT2-100 on CIF basis.

As is known to all, competitive price for a trial order can often lead to a big market share with great profit in the future. We hope you will take this factor into account and wait for your early reply.

Yours sincerely,
Raymond Sinclair
Gulfland Dainecess Inc.

针对以上还盘，钱晓俊与经理商议后，接受客户对 CWT2-100 降价 6% 的要求，并将期望利润率降至 6%，如核算出的还价利润率低于 6%，则将商品数量增加到一个 40 英尺集装箱再行核算（40 英尺集装箱包干费为 2200 元，美元的汇率为 6.8 人民币元/1 美元）。

请以钱晓俊的身份分别以 20 英尺和 40 英尺集装箱核算 CWT2-100 的出口还价利润率，参见表 2-8、表 2-3、表 2-9，完成表 3-1 和表 3-2。

表 3-1　CWT2-100 还价利润率核算表（20′集装箱）

核算项目（总价）	20′集装箱
销售收入	
实际成本	
包干费	
业务费用	
垫款利息	
保险费	
银行手续费	
出口运费	
利润额	
利润率	

表 3-2　CWT2-100 还价利润率核算表（40′集装箱）

核算项目（总价）	40′集装箱
销售收入	
实际成本	
包干费	
业务费用	
垫款利息	
保险费	
银行手续费	
出口运费	
利润额	
利润率	

Act 3-2　出口商回复进口商的还盘

完成出口还价利润率核算后，钱晓俊着手撰写 E-mail 对客户的还盘进行回复。

请以钱晓俊的身份，撰写该回复 E-mail。

出口商还盘函：

发件人：	damonchan@hainaco.com.cn
收件人：	ray.sinclair@gulfday.com
日　期：	2010 - 10 - 31
主　题：	Reply for Counter Offer

DISCUSS——个案讨论

Discuss 3-1

在本实训 LOOK 环节中,假设立信国贸公司接受意大利进口商 Palmavito 的还价,即降低货号 KJ2001 的 CIF 报价 0.50 美元/米并加入 5%的佣金,同时立信又必须保持 10%的销售利润率,在其他费用和订购数量保持不变的情况下,李新将如何进行还价成本核算?

提示:

(1) 所谓"还价成本核算",即计算经还价后的采购成本。在本实训 LOOK 环节中,接受客户还价后,应计算 KJ2001 的原出厂价 20 元/米需降低至多少。

(2) 由于"商品报价=成本+费用+利润",则"采购成本=销售收入-各项费用-利润"。

(3) 根据业务惯例,计算经还价后的采购成本宜采用"单价法",即计算单位商品的采购成本。

还价成本核算:

还价成本核算

Discuss 3-2

2011年3月18日,李新收到国外E-mail如下:

还盘函:

发件人:	fcy@aumedical.com
收件人:	li_xin@lixin.com.cn
日　　期:	2011-03-18
主　　题:	Reply for Your Offer

Dear Mr. Li,

We have carefully studied your offer.

We rather appreciate your non-woven fabrics, bur as you know, nowadays the market is of keen competition. We have to do a lot of sales promotion at the initial stage, which will surely raise our cost.

Therefore we suggest you making a 5% reduction of your price and changing the L/C payment to D/A at 30 days after sight. If then, we will order Art. No. TKM213 as a trial deal with the quantity of 2000 rolls. We have confidence that if our end-users find it satisfactory, they will place repeat orders with you.

We hope you will agree to our above proposal and look forward to receiving your favorable reply.

Yours truly,
A & U Medical Supplies Corp.
Fung Chow Youn (Mr.)

经与王经理商议,同意给予3%的价格折扣,但付款方式必须坚持即期信用证。李新将如何回复E-mail?

出口商还盘函：

发件人：	li_xin@lixin.com.cn
收件人：	fcy@aumedical.com
日　期：	2011-03-19
主　题：	Counter Offer for Non-Woven Fabrics

情景模拟实训四

交易磋商三——成交谈判与合同签订

 LOOK——情景示范

（李新回复客户的还盘后，第二天，接到了来自 Fabio Taldelli 先生的电话）

李新：立信国贸轻纺部，您好！

Mr. Taldelli: Good afternoon. This is Fabio Taldelli from Palmavito company. Could I speak to Mr. Li Xin, please?

李新: Mr. Taldelli, nice to hear from you! This is Li Xin. So what can I do for you?

Mr. Taldelli: Mr. Li, thank you for your E-mail of yesterday. I'm just calling to see if you'd like to set up a meeting between us for further business discussion. I'm going to Shanghai soon.

李新: No problem! You can visit our company at any time you like.

Mr. Taldelli: Is tomorrow afternoon ok for you? Around 4 PM.

李新: Ok!

Mr. Taldelli: Well, see you tomorrow.

李新: See you tomorrow. It's been a pleasure talking to you. Have a good trip!

（结束与客户的通话后，李新向王经理请教）

王经理：的确，国外客户常会在签约前飞过来，与我们进行面谈。一来对各交易条件进行进一步的磋商，二来实地考察一下我们公司的实力。这家意大利客户挺慎重的，明天就过来面谈说明最终签约的可能性是比较大的。小李，你要把握好这次会谈的机会，在"双赢"的基础上力争签下第一份合同，为今后更多的合作机会开个好头！

李新：明白！我一定尽力而为！

（经过了一天充分的准备，Taldelli 先生如约来到了立信国贸公司）

李新: Buon pomeriggio! Benvenuti a Shanghai, benvenuto alla nostra azienda! Piacere di conoscerti, Signore Taldelli.（意大利语：下午好！欢迎您到上海来，欢迎您到我们公司来！很高兴认识您，Taldelli 先生。）

Mr. Taldelli: Buon pomeriggio! Piacere di conoscerti, Signore Li.

李新: How was your journey?

Mr. Taldelli: Well, it was fine.

李新: Is this your first visit to Shanghai?

Mr. Taldelli: To tell you the truth, many times before this.

李新: Then you must be very familiar to Shanghai. Anyway, please allow me to introduce our company and main products to you.

Mr. Taldelli: Yes. All ears.

李新: We are one of the leading exporters of textiles and light industrial products in Shanghai. The products we export include textile fabrics, apparels, shoes, sports equipments, cosmetics and so on. Now, let's move on to the next point — "Milky Way" antibacterial finished dyed twill. Would you please follow me to the sample showroom?

Mr. Taldelli: Yes. I'd love to.

（李新引领 Taldelli 先生来到了样品陈列室）

李新: I think you must be familiar with our products.

Mr. Taldelli: Yes. The quality and the prospect of your new textile fabrics do impress us. However, in your last E-mail, the only concession you could make was to include 5% commission, that is to say, USD 3.06/M CIFC5% Genova. The price is still beyond my consideration.

李新: In fact, the price will be lower as long as you order more than your present quantity.

Mr. Taldelli: In respect that this is the first business transaction between us, the maximum quantity we can purchase, generally, is no more than one 20 feet container.

李新: Just because this is our very first transaction, the price is the lowest we can offer you in the quantity of one 20 feet container.

Mr. Taldelli: I understand. Then how about the trade terms? As a matter of fact, we usually adopt FOB in business of importing textile fabrics. We really hope you will take this into account if we cooperate for a second time.

李新: The VIP clients of our company have the most preferential trade terms, we sincerely hope you will be a member of them.

Mr. Taldelli: I see. Now let's discuss the packing.

李新: Is there anything wrong with the packing?

Mr. Taldelli: Could you pack the bales into cartons in order to reinforce the packages?

李新: So could you pay for the extra cost of cartons?

Mr. Taldelli: I suppose the cost is included into the quotation.

李新: I regret to say it won't be for our account. Actually, bales are more flexible than cartons in loading and unloading the containers. What's more, cartons are easier to be damaged by the forklift than bales.

Mr. Taldelli: Well, forget the cartons. In regard to the time of shipment, I would appreciate the shipment within September for the sake of catch the sales season in our market. Of course, the early, the better. Shipment in early September is the best.

李新: We will do our best to effect early shipment.

Mr. Taldelli: Thank you. Let's move on to the terms of payment. In your last E-mail, you proposed to change the terms of payment from L/C at 30 days after sight to L/C at sight. I'm afraid that won't do. Because of your toughness on the price, we will be burdened with high financial pressure. So you should leave us some time to raise money.

李新: It should have been all right. But we have made a concession on price to a great extent, as your request. Moreover, because the goods are innovative, high in cost and hard to get, we had to bear great cost in sourcing and procuring them in the condition of your no big order. So we really have to stick to sight L/C in the first deal between us.

Mr. Taldelli: Ok, I understand your position. But I do hope that we can use easier terms of payment, like time L/C, when we get more acquainted in the near future.

李新: No problem.

Mr. Taldelli: As to the insurance, you will cover FPA for 110% of the invoice value. What if I want All Risks and 130% of the invoice value?

李新: We can certainly do these, but they are subject to an additional premium.

Mr. Taldelli: Well, in this case, we need to reconsider. Thank you for your information.

李新: You're welcome, it's up to you.

Mr. Taldelli: So, now we have covered all the important points?

李新: Yes. I think so.

Mr. Taldelli: Will you please check up the particulars and see if everything is in order?

李新: Ok. Under this contract, we will supply you with 26400 meters of "Milky Way" antibacterial finished dyed twill, Art. No. KJ2001, at USD 3.06 per meter CIF Genova, including 5% commission, packed in bales of 4 pieces each, 120 meters per piece, all the bales are loaded into one 20 feet container. Shipment is to be made in September, and as early as possible. Payment by irrevocable sight L/C. Insurance is to be effected by us but the types of risks and the percentage of addition to the invoice value are remained to be determined by you. Is that right?

Mr. Taldelli: Yes. I think that's it. Anyway, I'm glad we have put through this deal smoothly.

李新: I certainly owe it to your cooperation. I hope this initial deal will mark the beginning of long-standing and stable business relations between us.

Mr. Taldelli: Definitely!

(李新送别Taldelli先生后,经过了忙碌的三天,收到Taldelli先生的接受E-mail和订

单,希望尽快收到销售合同或销售确认书)

接受函:

发件人:	f. taldelli@palmavito.com
收件人:	li_xin@lixin.com.cn
日 期:	2010-07-20
主 题:	Acceptance

Dear Mr. Li,

Thank you so much for your generous hospitality. Please find attached our order No. PAS-PO-CNSHA10043.

We have decided to accept all of your trade conditions including the terms of insurance, i.e. covering FPA for 110% of CIF value.

We would appreciate shipment within September, the earlier the better.

We look forward to receiving your Sales Contract or Confirmation soonest.

Yours sincerely,
Fabio Taldelli
Palmavito Articoli Sportive S.P.A.

Attachment: Purchase Order No. PAS-PO-CNSHA10043

进口商订单：

PALMAVITO ARTICOLI SPORTIVE S.P.A.
VIA G. MAZZINI, 46, 20116 MILANO, ITALY
TEL: 39-02-369010　FAX: 39-02-369052

PURCHASE ORDER

NO.: PAS-PO-CNSHA10043
DATE: JUL. 19, 2010

TO: SHANGHAI LIXIN INTERNATIONAL TRADING CO., LTD.
　　5/F, NO. 2230 WEST ZHONG SHAN ROAD, 200235, SHANGHAI, P. R. CHINA
　　TEL：86-21-64391520　FAX：86-21-64391530

ITEM DESCRIPTION	QUANTITY	PRICE
"MILKY WAY" ANTIBACTERIAL FINISHED DYED TWILL ART NO. KJ2001 DETAILS AS PER THE SAMPLES DISPATCHED BY THE SELLER ON JULY 12, 2010	26400 METERS	CIF C 5% GENOVA USD 3.06 / METER

TOTAL AMOUNT:　　USD 80784.00
TRADE TERMS:　　CIF C5% GENOVA
PACKING:　　120 METERS IN ONE PIECE
　　　　　　　　4 PIECES IN ONE BALE
　　　　　　　　TOTAL 55 BALES IN ONE 20 FEET CONTAINER
SHIPMENT PERIOD:　NOT LATER THAN SEPTEMBER 2010
　　　　　　　　WITHOUT PARTIAL SHIPMENTS
INSURANCE:　　COVERING FOR 110% CIF VALUE AGAINST F.P.A.
PAYMENT TERMS:　L/C AT SIGHT

FOR AND ON BEHALF OF
PALMAVITO ARTICOLI SPORTIVE S.P.A.
Giuseppe Del Cassano
Giuseppe Del Cassano

General Manager

（李新把客户订单打印后，呈送给王经理）

李新：王经理，意大利客户接受我们所有的交易条件了，把订单也发过来啦。

王经理：（边看客户订单边说）很好！小李，这笔交易能够达成，在很大程度上得归功于你进公司以来的活学活用，加上不错的商务英语口语和商务谈判技巧啊！

李新：班门弄斧啦！接下来我们就要制作合同了吧，好让这笔交易正式达成。

王经理：你的说法有问题。我问你，现在我们和这家意大利客户存在合同关系吗？

李新：还没签合同，两家公司之间不算有合同关系吧。

王经理：问题就在这里。记住，在进出口交易磋商中，一旦买卖双方中的任一方表示接受,那么在法律上,两方之间的合同就告成立,所以现在我们两家公司间已经有合同关系了。

李新:哦,我明白了。那么合同书有什么作用呢?

王经理:的确,绝大多数的进出口贸易要签订纸质的合同书,主要作用是方便进出口双方履行各自在合同关系中的义务及享有各自的权利。如有任一方有违约行为,这份合同书也是另一方维护自身权益的有效依据。

李新:我懂了。现在我的任务就是去起草这份纸质合同书吧。

王经理:根据我们公司的业务流程,在起草合同书前,你得先做另一件事,就是制作"合同核算表"。简单说来,合同核算就是在买卖双方达成交易后,卖方对交易磋商的结果作一份总结。合同核算和还价核算中的总利润额及利润率核算基本相同,只是在性质上有所不同。

李新:好的,我现在就去作"合同核算表"。

王经理:仍旧用总价法哦。

李新:明白!用总价法计算人民币利润总额,得到销售利润率。合同利润额=出口收入总额-出口支出总额。

(李新回到工位上开始制作"合同核算表")(见第70页)

(李新将制作完成的"合同核算表"给王经理过目)

王经理:格式符合公司规范,核算细目明晰,利润核算过程和结果精确,你的"合同核算表"做得不错啊。

李新:谢谢王经理的鼓励!

王经理:做外贸这行,认真仔细的工作态度很重要啊,有时候的确是"细节决定成败"啊。小李,我挺欣赏你严谨细致又不失灵活应变的工作表现的,继续努力哦。

李新:我一定再接再厉!现在我可以开始起草合同了吧。

王经理:接下来起草"签约函"和"销售合同"又是对你的一大考验。

李新:您能和我讲一下签约函吗?

王经理:在出口方向进口方递送销售合同书时,往往会附上一封短函,我们可以称之为"签约函"或是"成交函"。注意,这封函的主要目的是告知客户销售合同已经发出,希望客户签署后自留一份并回发给我们一份。哦,还有,我们这票业务做的是信用证,别忘了在签约函里提一下,让客户把信用证尽早开过来。

李新:知道了,谢谢王经理的点拨!

王经理:你在做销售合同时,记住要多问一下公司各部门的师傅们。

李新:明白,我一定会多向各位老师请教的!

(李新回到工位上开始起草签约函 E-mail 和销售合同……)

(第二天,李新将两份文本呈送王经理)(见第71~73页)

王经理:(边看签约函和销售合同边问)你在合同中订了金额和数量增减幅度条款,后者也就是溢短装条款,为什么要采用这一条款啊?

李新:纺织品面料在加工过程中会出现损耗,成品率很难确定,如合同规定确定的交货数量,工厂就会面临库存或数量短缺的问题,不利合同顺利履行,所以我希望为我们和绍兴轻纺公司争取在一定范围内灵活掌握交货数量的权利。至于金额,要与数量相匹配。

合同核算表：

上海立信国际贸易有限公司
Shanghai Lixin International Trading Co., Ltd.
合同核算表

填表日期：<u>2010</u>年<u>7</u>月<u>20</u>日　　　　填表人：<u>李新</u>　　　　编号：<u>10LXHTE075</u>

核算时，成本、费用及利润项目一律保留2位小数。

进口商		成交术语	装运港	目的港
PALMAVITO ARTICOLI SPORTIVE S.P.A.		CIF	SHANGHAI	GENOVA
国内运输费(CNY)	港区港杂费(CNY)	商检费(CNY)	报关费(CNY)	出口海运费(USD)
2000/20′FCL	600/20′FCL	350/20′FCL	150/20′FCL	1800/20′FCL
增值税率	出口退税率	业务费用	银行年利率	资金周转周期(月)
17%	16%	成交价格2%	4.98%	2
保险加成率	保险费率	佣金率	其他费用	汇率(USD1=CNY)
10%	0.15%	5%	/	6.80

成交信息				
货号	计价单位	采购成本 CNY	成交价格 USD	成交数量
KJ2001	METER	19.50	3.06	26400M IN 1×20′FCL
包装方式	毛重 KGS	净重 KGS	长 CM	宽 CM	高 CM
120M/PC 4PCS/BALE	135	130	150	50	60

(包装)

成交利润核算		
核算项目	计算过程	计算结果
收入(CNY)		
销售收入总额	3.06×26400×6.8	549331.20
支出(CNY)		
实际成本总额	[19.50−19.50/(1+17%)×16%]×26400	444312.00
国内运输费		2000.00
港区港杂费		600.00
商检费		350.00
报关费		150.00
垫款利息	19.50×26400×4.98%×2/12	4272.84
业务费用	3.06×26400×2%×6.8	10986.62
出口海运费	1800×6.8	12240.00
保险费	3.06×26400×(1+10%)×0.15%×6.8	906.40
佣金	3.06×26400×5%×6.8	27466.56
支出总额	444312+2000+600+350+150+4272.84+10986.62+12240+906.40+27466.56	503284.42
利润(CNY)		
利润总额	549331.20 −503284.42	46046.78
销售利润率	46046.78÷549331.20	8.38%

出口商签约函：

发件人：	li_xin@lixin.com.cn
收件人：	f.taldelli@palmavito.com
日　期：	2010-07-21
主　题：	Sales Contract

Dear Mr. Taldelli,

Thank you for your E-mail of Jul. 20, 2010 and your order No. PAS-PO-CNSHA 10043.

Attached is our Sales Contract No. 10LX-PAS075 made out against your order mentioned above. We will forward you the above Sales Contract in duplicate by DHL express courier. If there is no objection, please countersign them and return one copy for our file and establish the relevant Letter of Credit accordingly.

You may rest assured that we shall make up your order upon receipt of credit and effect the shipment during September.

If there is any further information you require, please feel free to contact us. We appreciate your cooperation and look forward to receiving your L/C soon.

Yours truly,
Shanghai Lixin International Trading Co., Ltd.
Li Xin

Attachment: Sales Contract No. 10LX-PAS075

销售合同：

销售合同
SALES CONTRACT

卖方 Seller: SHANGHAI LIXIN INTERNATIONAL TRADING CO., LTD. 上海立信国际贸易有限公司 中国上海市中山西路 2230 号 5 楼（200235） 5/F, NO. 2230 WEST ZHONG SHAN ROAD, 200235, SHANGHAI, P. R. CHINA TEL：86-21-64391520　FAX：86-21-64391530	编号： NO.: 10LX-PAS075 日期： DATE: JUL. 21, 2010 签署地点 SIGNED IN: SHANGHAI, P. R. CHINA
买方 Buyer: PALMAVITO ARTICOLI SPORTIVE S.P.A. VIA G. MAZZINI, 46, 20116 MILANO, ITALY TEL: 39-02-369010　FAX: 39-02-369052	

经买卖双方同意成交下列商品，订立条款如下：
This contract is made by and agreed between the BUYER and SELLER, in accordance with the terms and conditions stipulated below.

货号 Article No.	商品名称及规格 Name of Commodity and Specification	数量 Quantity	单价 Unit Price	金额 Amount
KJ2001	"MILKY WAY" ANTIBACTERIAL FINISHED DYED TWILL SPECIFICATION: 100% COTTON TWILL, 20×20, 108×58, 57/58′×120M DETAILS AS PER THE SAMPLES DISPATCHED BY THE SELLER ON JUL. 12, 2010	26 400 METERS	CIF C5% GENOVA USD 3.06 / METER	USD 80784.00
			TOTAL:	USD 80784.00

金额和数量允许：__%上下幅度
Percentage of allowance for amount and quantity: <u>5</u> % More or Less

总值（大写）：
Total Amount in Words: SAY U. S. DOLLARS EIGHTY THOUSAND SEVEN HUNDRED AND EIGHTY FOUR ONLY

包装：
Packing: 120 METERS IN ONE PIECE, 4 PIECES IN ONE BALE, TOTAL 55 BALES IN ONE 20′ FCL.

运输标志：
Shipping Marks: WILL BE INDICATED IN THE LETTER OF CREDIT.

装运：
Shipment: TO BE EFFECTED DURING SEPTEMBER 2010 FROM SHANGHAI, CHINA TO GENOVA, ITALY BY SEA WITH PARTIAL SHIPMENTS PROHIBITED AND TRANSSHIPMENT PERMITTED.

保险：
Insurance:
由 ____ 方负责，按商业发票金额的 ____ %投保 ____ 险。
To be effected by the <u>SELLER</u> for <u>110</u> % of the invoice value covering <u>F.P.A. AS PER THE OCEAN MARINE CARGO CLAUSES OF P.I.C.C. DATED JAN. 1, 1981.</u>

付款：
Payment:
☐ 买方不迟于 ____ 年 ____ 月 ____ 日前将100%的货款用即期汇票/电汇送抵卖方。
　　The buyers shall pay 100% of the sales proceeds through sight(demand) draft/by T/T remittance to the sellers not later than ____.
☑ 买方应通过 ____ 银行按合同全额开立以卖方为受益人的不可撤销 ____ 天期信用证，并于 ____ 年 ____ 月 ____ 日前开抵卖方，有效至装运日后第 ____ 天在中国议付。
　　The buyers should open through <u>A BANK ACCEPTABLE TO THE SELLER</u> an irrevocable L/C in favor of the sellers payable at <u>*****</u> sight for 100% of the contract value to reach the sellers before <u>AUGUST 15, 2010</u> and valid for negotiation in China until the <u>15TH</u> day after the date of shipment.

（续上）

☐ 付款交单：买方应对卖方开具的以买方为付款人的见票后 ____ 天付款跟单汇票，付款时交单。
Documents against payment(D/P):
The buyers shall duly make the payment against documentary draft made out to the buyers at ___ sight by the sellers.

☐ 承兑交单：买方应对卖方开具的以买方为付款人的见票后 ____ 天承兑跟单汇票，承兑时交单。
Documents against acceptance(D/A):
The buyers shall duly accept the documentary draft made out to the buyers at ___ days by the sellers.

检验：
Inspection:
卖方在发货前由 _____ 对货物的品质、规格和数量进行检验，并出具检验证明书。
The sellers shall have the qualities, specifications, quantities of the goods carefully inspected by ENTRY-EXIT INSPECTION AND QUARANTINE BUREAU OF CHINA , which shall issue Inspection Certificate before shipment.

索赔：
Claims:
如买方提出索赔，凡属品质异议须于货到目的口岸之日起____天内提出；凡属数量异议须于货到目的口岸之日起____天内提出，并均需提供卖方认可的公证机构出具的检验证明。如责任属于卖方，则卖方应于收到异议____天内答复买方并提出处理意见。
The claims, if any regarding to the quality of the goods, shall be lodged within 30 days after arrival of the goods at the destination, if any regarding to the quantities of the goods, shall be lodged within 15 days after arrival of the goods at the destination. In all cases, claims must be accompanied by Survey Reports of Recognized Public Surveyors agreed to by the Sellers. Should the responsibility of the subject under claim be found to rest on the part of the Sellers, the Sellers shall, within 20 days after receipt of the claim, send their reply to the Buyers together with suggestion for settlement.

不可抗力：
Force Majeure:
如因人力不可抗拒的原因造成本合同全部或部分不能履约，卖方概不负责，但卖方应将上述发生的情况及时通知买方。
The sellers shall not hold any responsibility for partial or total non-performance of this contract due to Force Majeure. But the sellers should advise the buyers on time of such occurrence.

仲裁：
Arbitration:
凡因执行本合同或有关本合同所发生的一切争议，双方应协商解决。如果协商不能得到解决，应提交仲裁。仲裁地点在被告方所在国内，或者在双方同意的第三国。仲裁裁决是终局的，对双方都有约束力，仲裁费用由败诉方承担。
All disputes in connection with this contract of the execution thereof shall be amicably settled through negotiation. In case no amicable settlement can be reached between the two parties, the case under dispute shall be submitted to arbitration, which shall be held in the country where the defendant resides, or in third country agreed by both parties. The decision of the arbitration shall be accepted as final and binding upon both parties. The Arbitration Fees shall be borne by the losing party.

法律适用：
Law Application:
本合同之签订地，或发生争议时货物所在地在中华人民共和国境内或被诉人为中国法人的，适用中华人民共和国法律，除此规定外，适用《联合国国际货物销售合同公约》。
It will be governed by the law of the People's Republic of China under the circumstances that the contract is signed or the goods while the disputes arising are in the People's Republic of China or the defendant is Chinese legal person, otherwise it is governed by Untied Nations Convention on Contract for the International Sale of Goods.
本合同使用的价格术语系根据国际商会《INCOTERMS 2000》。
The terms in the contract based on INCOTERMS 2000 of the International Chamber of Commerce.

文字：
Versions:
本合同中、英两种文字具有同等法律效力，在文字解释上，若有异议，以中文解释为准。
This contract is made out in both Chinese and English of which version is equally effective. Conflicts between these two languages arising therefrom, if any, shall be subject to Chinese version.
本合同一式 ____ 份，买卖双方各执一份为证，自双方代表签字（盖章）之日起生效。
This contract is made out in TWO original copies, one copy to be held by each party. Both contracts are effective since being singed/sealed by both parties.

Confirmed by:

卖方   买方
The Seller   **The Buyer**
SHANGHAI LIXIN INTERNATIONAL TRADING CO., LTD.

(signature)   (signature)

王经理：考虑得周全。我再问你，你在合同中为什么用的都是大写字母啊？

李新：我在学校时，专业课老师就强调过，填制外贸业务中的单证，最好用大写字母，这样可以在最大程度上防止篡改。

王经理：对！这也是我们公司的业务习惯。小李，你这两份文本都做得很好，花了不少工夫吧。

李新：各部门的老师们给了我很多指导和帮助啊。王经理，我也想请教您个问题：我们公司一般用"销售合同"而不用"销售确认书"吗？

王经理：问得好。我先问你，这两者的最大区别是什么？

李新：我觉得是条款的繁简。合同一般包括所有交易条件，比如这份合同就包含品名、品质、数量、包装、价格、装运、支付、保险、检验、索赔、不可抗力和仲裁；确认书一般只有八大要件，就是品名、品质、数量、包装、价格、装运、支付和保险。

王经理：对，所以我们公司对新客户一般采用 Sales Contract，成为老客户后才会用 Sales Confirmation，原因就在于此。

李新：哦，我明白了。

王经理：善于提问，并在解决问题中学习提高是你的一大优点。还有什么问题吗？

李新：没有了。谢谢王经理！

王经理：现在你抓紧去把签约函 E-mail 和销售合同发送给客户吧。

李新：好，我这就去办。

THINK——理论思考

Think 4-1 国际贸易谈判有哪些特点？

国际贸易谈判除了具有一般商务谈判的特点之外还有自己的特点，具体有以下几点：① 以取得经济利益为目的；② 价格谈判是核心；③ 政治性强；④ 要坚持平等互利的原则；⑤ 要以国际经济法、国际商法为准则；⑥ 谈判较国内谈判而言要更为复杂和困难；⑦ 谈判的难度大；⑧ 要考虑合同的严密性和准确性。

Think 4-2 商务谈判在资料的收集和准备方面应从哪几点做起？

商务谈判在资料的搜集和准备方面要从以下几点做起：① 国际目标市场信息资料；② 国外交易客户的信息资料；③ 国际技术方面的信息资料；④ 谈判对方政治法律信息资料。

Think 4-3 什么是"接受"？构成有效接受必须具备哪些条件？

接受是买方或卖方同意对方在发盘中提出的各项交易条件，并愿意按这些条件与对方达成交易、订立合同的一种肯定的表示。

构成一项有效接受必须具备的条件是：

（1）接受必须由合法的受盘人作出。由第三者作出的接受，不能视为有效的接受，只能作为一项新的发盘。

（2）接受必须是无条件地接受发盘所提出的交易条件，若只接受部分条件，或对发盘条件提出实质性修改，或提出有条件地接受，均不能构成有效接受，而只能视作还盘。

（3）接受必须在发盘有效期内作出。如发盘中未规定有效期，则受盘人必须在合理的时间内作出。

（4）接受的传递方式应符合发盘的要求。如发盘中未规定传递方式，则受盘人可按发盘所采用的，或采用比其更快的传递方式将接受通知送达发盘人。

Think 4-4 接受的方式有哪些？

接受的表示有两种方式：

（1）用"声明"来表示。即受盘人用口头或书面形式向发盘人表示同意发盘的内容，这是国际贸易中最常用的表示方法。一般来说，如果发盘人以口头形式发盘，则受盘人以口头形式表示接受；如果发盘人以书面形式发盘，则受盘人以书面形式表示接受。

（2）用行为来表示。用行为来表示接受通常是指由卖方发运货物或由买方支付价款（包括汇付货款和开立信用证）来表示，也可以做出其他行为来表示，如开始生产所买卖的货物、为发盘采购有关货物等。在用行为表示接受时，这种行为接受方式是根据该发盘的要求或依照当事人之间确立的习惯做法而行事的，而且该行为必须在发盘明确规定的有效期之内，或在合理时间之内（如果发盘未规定有效期）才有效。

Think 4-5 英美法、大陆法以及公约对接受生效的时间分别采用什么样的原则？什么情况下接受可以撤回？

在接受生效的时间上，英美法采用投邮生效的原则，即接受通知书一经投邮或发出，立即生效；而大陆法采用到达生效的原则，即接受通知书必须到达发盘人时才生效。《公约》采用到达生效原则，因为英美法系的"投邮生效"对发盘人相当不利，接受的函电在邮电途中的风险全部由受盘人承担，这是不合理的。

在接受送达发盘人之前，受盘人将撤回或修改接受的通知送达发盘人，或两者同时送达，则接受可以撤回或修改。接受一旦送达，即告生效，合同成立，受盘人无权单方面撤销或修改其内容。

Think 4-6 有条件接受应该如何处理？

接受应该是无条件的，任何对发盘表示接受但对交易条件有所变更或添加的行为，应视为还盘，接受无效。但是《公约》对发盘的交易条件的变更或添改，分为实质性变更和非实质性变更。

受盘人对货物的价格、品质、数量、支付方式、交货时间和地点、一方当事人对另一方当事人的赔偿责任范围或解决争端的办法等条件提出的添加或变更，均为实质性的变更。此种接受，只能视作还盘。

如果所作的变更属于非实质性的交易条件，如"接受，但需附一张原产地证书"，该项修改并未对实质性利益有影响,则除非当事人及时对这些变更或添加提出异议,否则该接受有效,合同成立。非实质性变更一般是要求提供重量单、装箱单、商检证等单据,或要求增加提供装船样品或某些单据的份数,要求分两批装运等。

Think 4-7 逾期接受应该如何处理?

超过发盘的有效期才到达的接受,为逾期接受。一般情况下逾期接受无效,视为一项发盘。但《公约》规定,如果发盘人毫不迟延地用口头或书面形式通知受盘人,确认该接受有效,则该逾期接受仍有接受的效力,合同于该接受到达时成立。实际上逾期的接受对原发盘人来说是一项新发盘,原发盘人如果愿意接受,则可以毫不迟延地用口头或书面方式通知原受盘人,愿意承受逾期接受的约束,但合同是于接受通知送达原发盘人时成立。如果原发盘人对逾期的接受表示拒绝或不立即发出通知,则该项逾期的接受无效,合同不能成立。

Think 4-8 如何撰写接受函?

1) 感谢对方所作的让步并表示按对方条件成交。例如:
Thank you for your email of today. After due consideration, we decide to accept your price.

2) 重复交易条件并请对方确认。例如:
Now please kindly confirm the following terms and conditions.
(1) Commodity: working boots Art. No. HF865L37
(2) Packing: to be packed in a box, 12 pairs to a carton, size run: 40-45, size assorted:

$$\frac{1}{40} \quad \frac{3}{41} \quad \frac{3}{42} \quad \frac{2}{43} \quad \frac{2}{44} \quad \frac{1}{45}$$

(3) Quantity: 60000 dozens
(4) Price: USD 21.00 per pair CIF C 5% Antwerp
(5) Payment: by irrevocable sight L/C
(6) Shipment: from Shanghai to Antwerp in July, 2011

3) 进一步强调合同履行中的一些需要注意的问题。例如:
The packing material should reach us within 30 days before the time of shipment. Please open the relevant L/C as soon as possible.

4) 表达合同达成的喜悦心情并对未来交易作进一步展望。例如:
We are glad to advise you the shipment will be effected before the end of August.

Think 4-9 如何进行出口合同核算?

出口合同盈亏的核算主要通过两个指标,即换汇成本和出口盈亏额。

(一) 换汇成本

换汇成本是出口商品获得每单位外币的成本,换句话说就是取得出口净收入1单位外币所花费的人民币数额。如果计算出的换汇成本高于当时的银行外汇牌价,则为亏损;反之则为盈利。换汇成本反映出口商品换取外汇的能力。

$$换汇成本=\frac{出口总成本(人民币)}{出口销售外汇净收入(外币)}$$

其中,出口总成本是实际采购成本与出口前的国内费用之和。

出口销售外汇净收入是指出口商品的FOB外汇净收入(即扣除佣金、运保费以后的外汇净收入)。

(二)出口盈亏额

出口盈亏额是出口销售人民币净收入与出口总成本的差额。差额结果为正,为盈利;结果为负,则为亏损。通过盈亏额还可以计算出盈亏率。

出口盈亏额=出口销售外汇净收入(外币折算为人民币)-出口总成本(人民币)

$$出口盈亏率=\frac{出口盈亏额}{出口总成本(人民币)}\times 100\%$$

注意:将出口销售外汇收入折算为人民币时要用银行的外汇买入价来计算。

Think 4-10　为什么要签订书面合同?

签订书面合同的意义在于:① 签订书面合同可作为合同成立的依据,因为我国只承认书面合同有效;② 签订书面合同可作为合同生效的条件;③ 签订书面合同可作为合同履行的依据,特别是通过口头或函电磋商达成交易者,双方当事人有必要以书面合同作为履约的依据。

Think 4-11　合同有效成立的条件有哪些?

合同有效成立的条件包括:① 当事人必须具有签订合同的行为能力;② 合同必须有对价或约因;③ 合同的内容必须合法;④ 合同必须符合法律规定的形式;⑤ 合同当事人的意思表示必须真实。

Think 4-12　规定品名条款时应注意哪些问题?

国际货物买卖合同中的品名条款,是合同中的主要条件。因此,在规定此项条款时,应注意下列事项:

(1) 必须明确、具体。鉴于命名商品的方法多种多样,如有些以其主要用途命名,有些以其使用的主要原材料或主要成分命名,有些以其外观造型或制造工艺命名,有些结合人名或地名命名,也有些冠以褒义词命名,等等。因此,在规定品名条款时,必须订明交易标的物的具体名称,避免空泛、笼统或含糊的规定,以确切地反映商品的用途、性能和特点,并便于合同的履行。

(2) 针对商品实际做出实事求是的规定。条款中规定的品名,必须是卖方能够供应而买方所需要的商品,凡做不到或不必要的描述性词句,都不应列入,以免给履行合同带来困难。

（3）尽可能使用国际上通用的名称。有些商品的名称，各地叫法不一，为了避免误解，应尽可能使用国际上通行的称呼。若使用地方性的名称，交易双方应事先就其含义达成共识。对于某些新商品的定名及其译名，应力求准确、易懂，并符合国际上的习惯称呼。

（4）注意选用合适的品名。有些商品具有不同的名称，因而存在着同一商品因名称不同而交付关税和班轮运费不一的现象，且其所受的进出口限制也不同。为了减低关税、方便进出口和节省运费开支，在确定合同的品名时，应当选用对我方有利的名称。

Think 4-13　为什么商品品质条款是国际货物买卖合同中的重要条款？

因为合同中的品质条款，是构成商品说明的重要组成部分，是买卖双方交接货物的主要依据。《联合国国际货物销售合同公约》规定，卖方交货必须符合约定的质量，如卖方交货不符合约定的品质条件，买方有权要求损害赔偿，也可要求修理或交付替代物，甚至拒收货物或撤销合同。

Think 4-14　国际货物买卖合同中规定货物品质的方法有哪几种？使用时应注意哪些问题？

表示商品品质的方法有许多种，归纳起来，可以分为两大类，即以实物表示和以文字说明表示。

以实物表示品质，有凭成交商品的实际品质和凭样品两种表示方法。前者称为"看货买卖"，是指卖方应按买方验看过的商品交货的方式，适合于鲜活商品、古董、工艺品以及字画等物品的交易；后者称为"凭样品买卖"，是指以样品表示商品品质并以此作为交货依据的方式，适合于难以用文字表示商品品质的商品。凭样品买卖又可分为凭卖方样品买卖、凭买方样品买卖和凭对等样品买卖。凭样品买卖时要注意样品要具有代表性，并做好样品的留样、封样工作。

凭文字说明表示商品品质，可细分为凭规格买卖、凭等级买卖、凭标准买卖、凭说明书和图样买卖、凭商标或牌名买卖、凭地理标志或产地名称买卖。

一种商品并非只用一种方法来表示品质，而是可以用若干种方式来表示它的品质。

Think 4-15　品质机动幅度条款有何作用？

品质机动幅度是指商品的一些特定指标在一定幅度内可以机动。订立品质机动幅度的方法有规定一定的范围、规定一定的极限、规定上下差异三种方法。品质机动幅度比较适合于品质不稳定的初级产品。品质公差是指国际上公认的产品品质的误差。

在国际贸易中，有时候由于商品特性、生产加工条件、自然气候或运输条件的限制，卖方很难做到所交付的货物与合同规定完全相符。在合同中加入品质机动幅度和品质公差这些变通的规定，可以避免因交货品质与买卖合同稍有不符而造成违约，从而保证合同的顺利履行。

Think 4-16　国际货物买卖合同中数量条款包括哪些内容?

国际货物买卖合同中数量条款通常由四部分组成,包括商品名称、计量单位、总重量和单位重量。

Think 4-17　溢短装条款通常在什么情况下使用?应注意哪些问题?

数量机动幅度也称"溢短装条款",是指在规定交货的标准数量的同时,允许多交或少交货物的数量或百分比的条款。在某些大宗商品(如粮食、矿砂、化肥等)的交易中,由于这些商品一般不需要包装,再加上这些商品的特性、船舱容量、装载技术和货源等因素影响,如果要求卖方非常准确地按约定数量交货,会给卖方带来很大的困难。因此在实际贸易活动中,通常买卖双方在合同中规定合理数量的机动幅度,只要卖方交货数量在约定的增减幅度范围内,就算按合同规定数量交货,买方就不得以交货数量与合同不符为由拒收货物或提出索赔。

在订立溢短装条款时应注意:

(1) 数量机动幅度的大小要适当。数量机动幅度的大小通常都以百分比表示。究竟百分比多大合适,应视商品特性、行业或贸易习惯和运输方式等因素而定。数量机动幅度可酌情做出各种不同的规定,其中一种是只对合同数量规定一个百分比的机动幅度,而对每批装运的具体幅度不作规定。在此情况下,只要卖方交货总量在规定的机动幅度范围内,就算按合同数量交了货;另一种是,除规定合同数量总的机动幅度外,还规定每批装运数量的机动幅度。在此情况下,卖方总的交货量,就得受上述总机动幅度的约束,而不能只按每批装运数量的机动幅度交货,这就要求卖方根据过去累计的交货量,计算出最后一批应交的数量。此外,有的买卖合同,除规定一个具体的机动幅度(如3%)外,还规定一个追加的机动幅度(如2%),在此情况下,总的机动幅度,应理解为5%。

(2) 机动幅度选择权的规定要合理。在合同规定有机动幅度的条件下,由谁行使这种机动幅度的选择权呢?一般来说,是履行交货的一方,也就是由卖方选择。但是,如果涉及海洋运输,交货量的多少与承载货物的船只的舱容关系非常密切,在租用船只时,就得跟船方商定。所以,在这种情况下,交货机动幅度一般是由负责安排船只的一方(如FOB的买方)选择,或是干脆由船长根据舱容和装载情况做出选择。总之,机动幅度的选择权可以根据不同情况,由买方行使,也可由卖方行使或由船方行使。因此,为了明确起见,最好是在合同中作出明确合理的规定。

此外,当成交某些价格波动剧烈的大宗商品时,为了防止卖方或买方利用数量机动幅度条款,根据自身的利益故意增加或减少装船数量,也可在机动幅度条款中加订:"此项机动幅度只是为了适应船舶实际装载量的需要时,才能适用。"

(3) 溢短装数量的计价方法要公平合理。目前,对机动幅度范围内超出或低于合同数量的多装或少装部分,一般是按合同价格结算,这是比较常见的做法。但是,数量上的溢短装在一定条件下关系到买卖双方的利益。在按合同价格计价的条件下,交货时市价下跌,多装对卖方有利,但如市价上升,多装却对买方有利。因此,为了防止有权选择多装或少装的一方当事人利用行市的变化,有意多装或少装以获取额外的好处,也可在合同中规定,多装或少装的部分,不按合同价格计价,而按装船时或货到时的市价计算,以体现公平合理的原则。如双方对装船时或货到时的市价不能达成协议,则可交由仲裁解决。

Think 4-18　国际货物买卖合同中包装条款一般包括哪些内容？订立包装条款时应注意哪些问题？

合同中的包装条款一般包括包装材料、包装方式、包装规格、包装标志等。在订立包装条款时,应注意以下事项：

(1) 要考虑商品的特点和不同运输方式的要求。对不同的商品和不同的运输方式,在约定包装材料、包装方式、包装规格和包装标志时,必须从商品在储运和销售过程中的实际需要出发,使约定的包装科学、合理,并达到安全、适用和适销的要求。

(2) 买卖双方对包装的各项事宜在合同中要有具体明确的表述。一般不宜用含义笼统的术语,如"适合海运包装"、"习惯包装"等,以免引起争议。

(3) 按照国际贸易习惯,运输标志一般由卖方决定,并无必要在合同中作出具体规定,但如果买方要求指定,就需要在合同中作出具体规定。

(4) 包装费用一般已包含在商品货价之内,不另在合同中列出;但如果买方要求特殊包装,则超出的包装费用由买方负担,并应在买卖合同中作出具体规定。

Think 4-19　国际货物买卖合同中价格条款包括哪些内容？订立价格条款时应注意哪些问题？

合同中的价格条款,一般包括商品的单价和总值两项基本内容,此外还包括单价的作价办法和与单价有关的佣金与折扣的运用等内容。

订立价格条款时要注意以下问题：

(1) 在充分市场调查、信息分析的基础上合理确定商品的单价,防止作价偏高或偏低。

(2) 根据经营意图和实际情况,在权衡利弊的基础上选用适当的贸易术语,并争取选择有利的计价货币。

(3) 灵活运用各种不同的作价办法,以规避价格变动的风险。

(4) 单价中涉及的计量单位、计价货币、装卸地名称,必须书写正确、清楚,以利合同的履行。对佣金和折扣的规定要符合贸易习惯。

Think 4-20　国际贸易实务中最常用的海洋运输有哪几种经营方式？

海洋运输是国际贸易中最主要的运输方式,其经营方式主要有两大类,即班轮运输和租船运输。其中,班轮运输,又称定期船运输,指按固定的航线和预先规定的时间表航行,沿途停靠若干固定的港口,从事这些港口间的货运业务,并按事先公布的费率收取运费的船舶运输方式。租船运输是指租船人向船主租赁整条船舶进行货物运输。租船运输适用于成交数量大、交货期集中,或对方港口无直达船的情况。按照租船方式的不同,租船运输主要可分为定程租船和定期租船两种。

Think 4-21 国际货物买卖合同中装运条款包括哪些内容？装运时间如何规定？应注意哪些问题？

装运条款包括装运时间，装运港和目的港，分批装运和转运，装船通知，滞期、速遣条款和其他装运条款。

（一）运输条款中装运时间规定的方式

（1）规定明确、具体的装运时间，分为规定一段时间和规定最迟期限两种。此种规定方法明确、具体，使用较为广泛。

（2）规定收到信用证后若干天装运。如规定："收到信用证后 30 天内装运"。为防止买方不按时开证，一般还规定："买方必须不迟于某月某日将信用证开到卖方"的限制性条款。对某些进口管制较严的国家或地区，或专为买方制造的特定商品，或对买方资信不够了解，为防止买方不履行合同而造成损失，可采用此种规定方法。

（3）规定近期装运术语。如规定"立即装运"、"即期装运"、"尽快装运"等。由于这些术语在各国、各行业中解释不一，不宜使用。国际商会制订的《跟单信用证统一惯例》也明确规定不宜使用此类词，如果使用，银行将不予置理。

（二）规定装运时间应注意的问题

（1）买卖合同中的装运时间的规定，要明确具体，装运期限应当适度。海运装运期限的长短，应视不同商品和租船订舱的实际情况而定，装运期限过短，势必给船货安排带来困难；装运期过长也不合适，特别是采用在收到信用证后多少天内装运的条件下，装运期过长，会造成买方积压资金，影响资金周转，从而反过来影响卖方的售价。

（2）应注意货源情况、商品的性质和特点以及交货的季节性等。例如，雨季一般不宜装运烟叶，夏季一般不宜装运沥青、易腐性肉类及橡胶等。

（3）应结合考虑交货港、目的港的特殊季节因素。如北欧、加拿大东海沿岸港口冬季易封冻结冰，故装运时间不宜订在冰冻时期。反之，热带某些地区，则不宜订在雨季装运等。

（4）在规定装运期的同时，应考虑开证日期的规定是否明确合理。装运期与开证日期是互相关联的，为保证按期装运，装运期和开证日期，应该互相衔接起来。

Think 4-22 为什么在国际货物买卖合同中要规定装运通知条款？具体如何规定？

在国际货物买卖合同中要规定装运通知条款的目的是为了买卖双方互相配合，共同搞好车、船、货的衔接和办理货运保险，不论采用何种贸易术语成交，交易双方都要承担互相通知的义务。因此，装运通知也是装运条款的一项重要内容。

按照国际贸易的一般做法，在按 FOB 条件成交时，卖方应在约定的装运期开始以前，一般是 30 天或 45 天，向买方发出货物备妥通知，以便买方及时派船接货。买方接到卖方发出的备货通知后，应按约定的时间，将船名、船舶到港受载日期等通知卖方，以便卖方及时安排货物出运和准备装船。

如按 FOB、CFR 和 CIF 术语签订的合同，卖方应在货物装船后，按约定时间，将合同、货物的品名、件数、重量、发票金额、船名及装船日期等项内容电告买方；如按 FCA、CPT 和

CIP 术语签订的合同,卖方应在把货物交付承运人接管后,将交付货物的具体情况及交付日期电告买方,以便买方办理保险并做好接卸货物的准备,及时办理进口报关手续。

Think 4-23　国际货物买卖合同中支付条款包括哪些内容?

国际货物买卖合同中有关货款收付的规定通常以"支付条款"出现。由于支付条款之间关系到贸易双方的切身利益,因此在制定该条款时应在确保安全收汇、利于扩大贸易和资金周转的前提下,根据不同的客户、商品、市场、结合价格和汇率风险等因素,进行综合考虑,选择适宜的结算方式。具体的支付条款,视不同的交易,特别是所选用的结算方式不同而有所不同,主要有付款时间、地点、金额及条件等。

(1) 使用汇付方式结算货款的交易,在买卖合同中应明确规定汇付的时间、具体的汇付方法和金额等。

(2) 以托收方式结算货款的交易,在买卖合同的支付条款中,必须明确规定交单条件和付款、承兑责任以及付款期限等内容。

(3) 以信用证结算货款的交易,在买卖合同的支付条款中,应明确规定开证时间、开证银行、信用证的受益人、种类、金额、装运期、到期日等。

Think 4-24　汇付方式有什么特点?

汇付方式是由买卖双方根据贸易合同相互提供信用,银行只以委托人代理人的身份参与结算,属于商业信用。由于此方法对交易和收款的安全性完全依赖于交易双方的信誉,因此具有一定的风险性。在国际贸易中,汇付方式通常用于预付货款、随订单付款、交货付现、赊销等业务。

Think 4-25　托收方式有什么特点?

托收方式属于商业信用。在托收业务中,银行只是按委托人的指示办事,并不承担付款人必然付款的义务。因此出口商在托收中的风险较大。不同的托收种类其风险和损失的程度是不同的,其中承兑交单方式下出口人承担的风险最大。从进口人的角度看,托收对其有利,不但可免去进口人申请开立信用证的手续,不必预付银行押金,减少费用支出;而且承兑交单的托收方式有利于其资金融通和周转。由于托收对进口商有利,所以有利于调动进口商采购货物的积极性,从而扩大出口。许多出口商把托收作为推销库存和加强对外竞销的手段。

Think 4-26　信用证业务有哪些特点?

信用证业务的特点是:① 信用证是一种银行信用,开证行负第一性付款责任;② 信用证是一种自足文件,它不依附于贸易合同而存在;③ 信用证业务是一种纯粹的单据业务,它处理的对象是单据。

Think 4-27　国际货物买卖合同中保险条款包括哪些内容?

国际货物买卖合同中保险条款应订明由何方负责投保、明确规定投保险别、保险金额的确定方法以及按什么保险条款保险,并注明该条款的生效日期。

Think 4-28　国际货物买卖合同中商检条款包括哪些内容?

国际货物买卖合同中检验条款内容一般包括:有关检验权的规定、检验或复验的时间和地点、检验机构、检验标准和方法、检验项目和检验证书等。

Think 4-29　国际货物买卖业务中,检验地点规定的方法有哪些?

国际货物买卖业务中,关于检验地点的规定方法有:

(1) 在出口国检验。具体做法可分为:① 工厂(仓库)检验;② 装运港(地)检验。

(2) 在进口国检验。具体做法可分为:① 目的港(地)检验;② 买方营业处所或用户所在地检验。

(3) 出口国检验、进口国复验。具体做法可分为:① 装运港检验,目的港复验;② 装运港检验重量、目的港检验品质。

(4) 装运港(地)检验重量和目的港(地)检验品质。

Think 4-30　国际货物买卖合同履行时解决争议的方式有哪些?

解决争议的方式一般有四种,即协调解决、第三者调解、提交仲裁机构和进行司法诉讼。

Think 4-31　国际货物买卖合同中的索赔条款有哪几种规定方法? 包括哪些内容?

国际货物买卖合同中的索赔条款,大致有两种:一种是异议和索赔条款,一种是罚金条款。

(1) 异议和索赔条款。在一般商品的买卖合同中,多数只订异议和索赔条款,同检验条款合并订在一起。条款的内容包括:① 明确一方如违反合同,另一方有权提出索赔。② 索赔依据,规定索赔时需提供的证件以及检验出证的机构。③ 索赔期限,包括索赔有效期和品质保证期(或称质量保证期)。④ 赔偿损失的估损办法和金额等。例如,规定所有退货或索赔所引起的一切费用(包括检验费)及损失均由卖方负担等。

(2) 罚金条款。在买卖大宗商品或机械设备的合同中,一般还订有罚金条款。内容主要规定:一方如未履行合同所规定的义务时,应向对方支付一定数额的约定罚金,以补偿对方的损失。这种条款一般适用于卖方延期交货等,双方还根据延误时间长短预先约定赔偿的金额,同时规定最高罚款金额。

Think 4-32　合同中的不可抗力条款包括哪些主要内容?

不可抗力条款是买卖双方在合同中对于不可抗力有关内容的规定。不可抗力条款通常包括下列主要内容:

1) 不可抗力的性质与范围。不可抗力事件的范围较广,通常分为两种情况:一种是由于自然力量引起的事件;另一种是由于政治或社会原因引起的。关于不可抗力事件的性质与范围,通常有下面三种规定方法:

(1) 概括式规定。即在合同中不具体订明哪些现象是不可抗力事故,而是笼统地规定"由于公认的不可抗力的原因,致使卖方不能交货或延期交货,卖方不负责任"等等。这种规定办法含义模糊,不宜采用。

(2) 列举式规定。即在不可抗力条款中明确规定出哪些是不可抗力事故。凡合同中没有规定的均不能作为不可抗力事故援引。这种列举的办法虽然明确具体,但文字繁琐,且可能出现遗漏情况。

(3) 综合式规定。列明经常可能发生的不可抗力的同时,再加上"以及双方同意的其他不可抗力事件"的文句。这种规定办法既明确具体,又有一定的灵活性,是一种可取的办法。

2) 不可抗力事件的处理。发生不可抗力事件后,应按约定的处理原则和办法及时进行处理。该部分除规定清楚在哪些情况下可以解除合同、在哪些情况下只能中止合同外,还规定买卖双方都可援引的不可抗力免责。

3) 不可抗力事件的通知和证明。不可抗力事件发生后如影响合同履行时,发生事件的一方当事人,应按约定的通知期限和通知方式,将事件情况如实通知对方。对方在接到通知后,应及时答复,如有异议也应及时提出。此外,发生事件的一方当事人还应按约定办法出具证明文件,作为发生不可抗力事件的证据。在国外这种证明文件一般由当地的商会或法定公证机构出具。在我国一般由中国国际贸易促进委员会出具。

Think 4-33　构成不可抗力事件的条件有哪些?不可抗力事件的法律后果有几种?

构成不可抗力事故需要具备以下三个条件:① 该事故必须发生在合同签订以后;② 该事故不是合同当事人的过失、疏忽或故意行为造成的;③ 该事故是当事人无法预见、无法预防和控制的。

不可抗力事故发生后所引起的法律后果,主要有两种:一种是解除合同;一种是延迟履行合同。至于什么情况下可以解除合同,什么情况下只能延迟履行合同,则要根据该项事故的性质及对履行合同的影响程度来确定。也可以由双方当事人通过协商在买卖合同中加以具体规定。如果合同中未作出明确规定,一般遵循的原则是:如果不可抗力事故的发生使合同的履行成为不可能,如地震使工厂厂房全部倒塌、机器损坏,则可解除合同;如果不可抗力事故只是暂时阻碍合同的履行,如暴风雨使交通中断,那就只能延迟履行合同,而不能解除合同。

Think 4-34　援引不可抗力条款应注意哪些问题?

当一方援引合同中不可抗力条款要求免责时:第一,必须要及时通知对方;第二,必须向对方提交一定机构出具的证明文件;第三,所发生的事件必须是双方约定的不可抗力事件。

Think 4-35　合同中的仲裁条款主要包括哪些内容?

合同中的仲裁条款主要包括:

(1) 仲裁地点,有三种规定方法:① 多数合同规定在中国仲裁;② 有时规定在被申请人所在国仲裁;③ 规定在双方同意的第三国仲裁。

(2) 仲裁机构。我国常设的仲裁机构是中国国际经济贸易仲裁委员会和海事仲裁委员会。

(3) 仲裁规则。

(4) 仲裁裁决的效力。

(5) 仲裁费用的负担。

Think 4-36　仲裁协议的形式和作用分别是什么？

仲裁协议是双方当事人自愿将争议提交仲裁机构进行裁决的书面协议。仲裁协议有两种形式：一种是由双方当事人在争议发生之前订立的，表示同意把将来可能发生的争议提交仲裁裁决的协议。这种协议一般作为买卖合同的一项条款，称为"仲裁条款"。另一种是由双方当事人在争议发生之后订立的，表示同意把已经发生的争议提交仲裁解决的协议，称为"提交仲裁的协议"。

两种仲裁协议的作用是相同的：一是约束双方当事人只能以仲裁方式解决争议，而不得向法院起诉；二是排除法院对有关争议案件的管辖权；三是使仲裁机构和仲裁员取得对有关争议案件的管辖权。

Think 4-37　如何撰写签约函（成交函）？

签约函也称出口成交函，是出口商向进口商寄送出口合同或销货确认书时随附的一封信函，其主要目的是通知进口商有关合同事宜。

在拟写签约函时，通常要表达谢意，感谢对方的合作，能够达成此次交易；此外，还要告知对方合同已寄出，望予以会签(countersign)。在采用信用证结算方式时，通常还在信函中希望买方能够如期或尽快开证。

会签合同是指卖方先在正本一式二份的合同"卖方"处签章后寄给买方，买方签字后自己留一份，再寄回一份给卖方。

进出口业务中，买卖合同一般由我方制作。合同拟好后，我方应及时将其寄给对方让其签署。寄合同时，我方一般要在合同外附上一封简短的书信——签约函。签约函的内容一般包括：

(1) 对成交表示高兴，希望合同顺利进行。常用的表达方式如：

We are pleased to have concluded business with you in the captioned goods.

(2) 告知对方合同已寄出，希望其予以会签。如：

We are sending you our Sales Confirmation No. 765401 in duplicate. Please sign and return one copy for our file.

(3) 催促对方尽早开立信用证。如：

It is understood that a letter of credit in our favour covering the above-mentioned goods will be established promptly.

Think 4-38　在出口贸易业务开展过程中，如何与外商进行英语口语交流？

参见"附录　出口贸易英语口语——示范对话"

ACT——模拟训练

Act 4-1　出口商制作合同核算表

2010年11月5日，钱晓俊收到客户的订单E-mail。

进口商接受和订单函：

From:	ray.sinclair@gulfday.com
To:	damonchan@hainaco.com.cn
Date:	2010-11-05
Re:	Order No. GD-PO-CNSHA129

Dear Mr. Chan,

Thank you for your Email of Oct. 31, 2010. We have decided to accept your price.

Following is our order:

GULFLAND DAINECESS INC.			ORDER NO. GD-PO-CNSHA129	
ART. NO.	COMMODITY	QUANTITY	UNIT PRICE	AMOUNT
			CIF HOUSTON	
CWS3-50	SPORT TYPE VACUUM FLASK	16120 PCS	USD 2.21 / PC	USD 35625.20
CWT2-100	TRAVEL TYPE VACUUM FLASK	14220 PCS	USD 3.33 / PC	USD 47352.60
AS PER SAMPLES DISPATCHED BY THE SELLER ON OCT. 25, 2010				
			TOTAL:	USD 82977.80

PACKING:	CWS 3-50: 40 PCS / CARTON, 403 CARTONS, 1×20′ FCL CWT 2-100: 20 PCS / CARTON, 711 CARTONS, 1×40′ FCL
DELIVERY TIME:	BY THE END OF DECEMBER 2010 WITHOUT PARTIAL SHIPMENTS AND WITHOUT TRANSSHIPMENT
INSURANCE:	FOR 110% OF INVOICE VALUE COVERING F.P.A. RISK AS PER OMCC PICC DATED 1/1/1981
PAYMENT TERMS:	L/C AT SIGHT

If any of the items mentioned above can not satisfy this request, please inform us immediately.

Please try to execute this order soonest.

Yours sincerely,
Raymond Sinclair
Gulfland Dainecess Inc.

在起草销售确认书前，钱晓俊须制作合同核算表以对本笔交易磋商的结果作一总结。请以钱晓俊的身份制作合同核算表。

提示：

在合同核算表的"成交信息"中，应体现两个货号的不同信息，即"分货号成交信息"。在"成交利润核算"中，应将两个货号的相关核算项目相加求得总额。

Act 4-2 出口商制作销售确认书

完成合同核算表后，钱晓俊着手缮制销售确认书。

请以钱晓俊的身份，根据订单 GD-PO-CNSHA129，缮制销售确认书（编号：SCHN-GD10174，日期：2010 年 11 月 6 日）。

提示：自行设计唛头。

销售确认书：

销售确认书				
SALES CONFIRMATION				
卖方： SELLER:			编号： NO.: 日期： DATE:	
买方： BUYER:			地点： PLACE:	
买卖双方同意就以下条款达成交易： This confirmation is made by and agreed between the BUYER and SELLER, in accordance with the terms and conditions stipulated below:				
1. 商品号 Art No.	2. 品名及规格 Commodity & Specification	3. 数量 Quantity	4. 单价及价格条款 Unit Price & Trade Terms	5. 金额 Amount
			Total:	
6. 总值（大写） Total Amount in Words				
允许　　　溢短装，由卖方决定 With　　　More or less of shipment allowed at the sellers' option				
7. 包装 Packing				
8. 唛头 Shipping Marks				
9. 装运期及运输方式 Time of Shipment & means of Transportation				
10. 装运港及目的地 Port of Loading & Destination				
11. 保险 Insurance				
12. 付款方式 Terms of Payment				
13. 备注 Remarks				
The Seller 　　　　　　　　(signature)			The Buyer (signature)	

Act 4-3　出口商撰写签约函

钱晓俊将制作完成的销售确认书交经理审核并签署后,通过 TNT 快递,将销售确认书一式二份发给客户会签,同时准备给客户写一封签约函 E-mail。

请以钱晓俊的身份,撰写签约函。

出口商签约函:

发件人:	damonchan@hainaco.com.cn
收件人:	ray.sinclair@gulfday.com
日　期:	2010-11-06
主　题:	Sales Confirmation

DISCUSS——个案讨论

Discuss 4-1

2011年3月25日,上海立信国际贸易有限公司与越南一家供应商就进口合成纤维面料进行了商务谈判。根据以下谈判纪要,李新该如何缮制购货订单(编号为11TK-LX012,日期为2011年3月26日)?

谈判纪要:

上海立信国际贸易有限公司
Shanghai Lixin International Trading Co., Ltd.

谈 判 纪 要

时间:	2011年3月25日 下午1:30
地点:	上海立信国际贸易有限公司507会议室
客户名称地址:	Thanh Kuang Company Limited
	59 Nguyen Tat Thanh, District 7, Ho Chi Minh City, Vietnam
主题:	有关合成纤维面料产品的进口
品名:	Cotton Spandex Fabric
规格:	Single Jersey Knitted
	95% Cotton 5% Spandex
	Weight: 138 gsm Width: 155 cm
原产国:	越南
数量:	50000 kgs
包装:	120米一卷 唛头由卖方决定 共3个40英尺整箱
价格:	USD 6.3/kg FOB Ho Chi Minh City INCOTERMS 2010
装运:	不迟于2011年5月20日 不允许分批装运
起运港:	胡志明市
目的港:	上海
付款:	不可撤销见票后60天付款信用证 2011年4月20前开出
保险:	由买方负责

进口商订单：

上海立信国际贸易有限公司
SHANGHAI LIXIN INTERNATIONAL TRADING CO., LTD.
5/F, NO. 2230 WEST ZHONG SHAN ROAD, 200235, SHANGHAI, P. R. CHINA
TEL：86-21-64391520   FAX：86-21-64391530

PURCHASE ORDER（订货单）

To Messrs（致）：   Order No.（订单号）：
                                     Date（日期）：

We hereby place the order for the following goods with you on the terms and conditions set forth hereunder:

Description （品名及规格）	Quantity （数量）	Unit Price （单价）	Amount （金额）

Total Amount（合计金额）：

Packing（包装）：

Payment（付款）：

Shipment（装运）：

Port of loading（装运港）：

Port of destination（目的港）：

Partial shipments（分批装运）：

Transshipment（转运）：

Insurance（保险）：

Accepted and confirmed by（双方签章确认）：

　　　Seller（卖方）   Buyer（买方）

Discuss 4-2

请根据 Discuss4-1 中的订单,以出口商的身份,缮制以下销售确认书(编号：TK-CN-SC32,日期：2011年3月28日)。

提示：自行设计唛头。

销售确认书：

SALES CONFIRMATION

SELLER: NO.:
　　　　　DATE:
BUYER: PLACE:

This confirmation is made by and agreed between the BUYER and SELLER, in accordance with the terms and conditions stipulated below:

1. Commodity & Specification	2. Quantity	3. Unit Price & Trade Terms	4. Amount
	Total:		

With　　　More or less of quantity and amount allowed at the sellers' option

5. Total Value in Words

6. Packing

7. Shipping Marks

8. Time of Shipment & Means of Transportation

9. Port of Loading & Destination

10. Insurance

11. Terms of Payment

12. Remarks

　　　　　　　　The Seller　　　　　　　　　　　　　　　　　The Buyer
　　　　　　　　(signature)　　　　　　　　　　　　　　　　(signature)

情景模拟实训五

履行合同一——落实信用证

 LOOK——情景示范

（李新将销售合同10LX-PAS075付诸国际快递后的5天内，先后收到了来自客户的会签函E-mail和会签合同。李新将会签合同呈送王经理）

李新： 王经理，意大利客户把一份销售合同快递过来了，已经签署了。

会签函：

发件人：	f. taldelli@palmavito.com
收件人：	li_xin@lixin.com.cn
日　期：	2010-07-23
主　题：	Countersign of S/C No.10 LX-PAS075

Dear Mr. Li,

Yours Sales Contract No.10 LX-PAS 075 has been received with thanks.

We have countersigned the contract and returned one copy as you required by DHL today.

We will apply for the letter of credit as soon as possible. Please arrange shipment in time.

Yours sincerely,
Fabio Taldelli
Palmavito Articoli Sportive S. P. A.

会签合同：

销售合同
SALES CONTRACT

卖方 Seller:	上海立信国际贸易有限公司 SHANGHAI LIXIN INTERNATIONAL TRADING CO., LTD. 中国上海市中山西路 2230 号 5 楼（200235） 5/F, NO. 2230 WEST ZHONG SHAN ROAD, 200235, SHANGHAI, P. R. CHINA TEL：86-21-64391520　FAX：86-21-64391530	编号 NO.: 10LX-PAS075 日期 DATE: JUL. 21, 2010 签署地点 SIGNED IN: SHANGHAI, P. R. CHINA
买方 Buyer:	PALMAVITO ARTICOLI SPORTIVE S.P.A. VIA G. MAZZINI, 46, 20116 MILANO, ITALY TEL: 39-02-369010　FAX: 39-02-369052	

经买卖双方同意成交下列商品，订立条款如下：
This contract is made by and agreed between the BUYER and SELLER, in accordance with the terms and conditions stipulated below.

货号 Article No.	商品名称及规格 Name of Commodity and Specification	数量 Quantity	单价 Unit Price	金额 Amount
KJ2001	"MILKY WAY" ANTIBACTERIAL FINISHED DYED TWILL SPECIFICATION: 100% COTTON TWILL, 20×20, 108×58, 57/58'×120 M DETAILS AS PER THE SAMPLES DISPATCHED BY THE SELLER ON JUL. 12, 2010	26400 METERS	CIF C 5% GENOVA USD 3.06 / METER	USD 80784.00
			TOTAL:	USD 80784.00

金额和数量允许：__%上下幅度 Percentage of allowance for amount and quantity: _5_ % More or Less	总值（大写） Total Amount in Words: SAY U. S. DOLLARS EIGHTY THOUSAND SEVEN HUNDRED AND EIGHTY FOUR ONLY

包装：
Packing: 120 METERS IN ONE PIECE, 4 PIECES IN ONE BALE, TOTAL 55 BALES IN ONE 20′ FCL.

运输标志：
Shipping Marks: WILL BE INDICATED IN THE LETTER OF CREDIT.

装运：
Shipment: TO BE EFFECTED DURING SEPTEMBER 2010 FROM SHANGHAI, CHINA TO GENOVA, ITALY BY SEA WITH PARTIAL SHIPMENTS PROHIBITED AND TRANSSHIPMENT PERMITTED.

保险：
Insurance:
由 ____ 方负责，按商业发票金额 ____ %投保 ____ 险。
To be effected by the _SELLER_ for _110_ % of the invoice value covering _F.P.A. AS PER THE OCEAN MARINE CARGO CLAUSES OF P.I.C.C. DATED JAN. 1, 1981._

付款：
Payment:
☐ 买方不迟于 ____ 年 ____ 月 ____ 日前将100%的货款用即期汇票/电汇送抵卖方。
　　The buyers shall pay 100% of the sales proceeds through sight(demand) draft/by T/T remittance to the sellers not later than ____.
☑ 买方应通过 ____ 银行按合同全额开立以卖方为受益人的不可撤销 ____ 天期信用证，并于 ____ 年 ____ 月 ____ 日前开抵卖方，有效至装运日后第 ____ 天在中国议付。
　　The buyers should open through _A BANK ACCEPTABLE TO THE SELLER_ an irrevocable L/C in favor of the sellers payable at _*****_ sight for 100% of the contract value to reach the sellers before _AUGUST 15, 2010_ and valid for negotiation in China until the _15TH_ day after the date of shipment.

☐ 付款交单：买方应对卖方开具的以买方为付款人的见票后 _____ 天付款跟单汇票，付款时交单。
Documents against payment(D/P):
The buyers shall duly make the payment against documentary draft made out to the buyers at ___ sight by the sellers.

☐ 承兑交单：买方应对卖方开具的以买方为付款人的见票后 _____ 天承兑跟单汇票，承兑时交单。
Documents against acceptance(D/A):
The buyers shall duly accept the documentary draft made out to the buyers at ___ days by the sellers.

检验：
Inspection:
卖方在发货前由 _____ 对货物的品质、规格和数量进行检验，并出具检验证明书。
The sellers shall have the qualities, specifications, quantities of the goods carefully inspected by __ENTRY-EXIT INSPECTION AND QUARANTINE BUREAU OF CHINA__, which shall issue Inspection Certificate before shipment.

索赔：
Claims:
如买方提出索赔，凡属品质异议须于货到目的口岸之日起____天内提出，凡属数量异议须于货到目的口岸之日起____天内提出，并均需提供卖方认可的公证机构出具的检验证明。如责任属于卖方，则卖方应于收到异议____天内答复买方并提出处理意见。
The claims, if any regarding to the quality of the goods, shall be lodged within __30__ days after arrival of the goods at the destination, if any regarding to the quantities of the goods, shall be lodged within __15__ days after arrival of the goods at the destination. In all cases, claims must be accompanied by Survey Reports of Recognized Public Surveyors agreed to by the Sellers. Should the responsibility of the subject under claim be found to rest on the part of the Sellers, the Sellers shall, within __20__ days after receipt of the claim, send their reply to the Buyers together with suggestion for settlement.

不可抗力：
Force Majeure:
如因人力不可抗拒的原因造成本合同全部或部分不能履约，卖方概不负责，但卖方应将上述发生的情况及时通知买方。
The sellers shall not hold any responsibility for partial or total non-performance of this contract due to Force Majeure. But the sellers should advise the buyers on time of such occurrence.

仲裁：
Arbitration:
凡因执行本合同或有关本合同所发生的一切争议，双方应协商解决。如果协商不能得到解决，应提交仲裁。仲裁地点在被告方所在国内，或者在双方同意的第三国。仲裁裁决是终局的，对双方都有约束力，仲裁费用由败诉方承担。
All disputes in connection with this contract of the execution thereof shall be amicably settled through negotiation. In case no amicable settlement can be reached between the two parties, the case under dispute shall be submitted to arbitration, which shall be held in the country where the defendant resides, or in third country agreed by both parties. The decision of the arbitration shall be accepted as final and binding upon both parties. The Arbitration Fees shall be borne by the losing party.

法律适用：
Law Application:
本合同之签订地，或发生争议时货物所在地在中华人民共和国境内或被诉人为中国法人的，适用中华人民共和国法律，除此规定外，适用《联合国国际货物销售合同公约》。
It will be governed by the law of the People's Republic of China under the circumstances that the contract is signed or the goods while the disputes arising are in the People's Republic of China or the defendant is Chinese legal person, otherwise it is governed by Untied Nations Convention on Contract for the International Sale of Goods.
本合同使用的价格术语系根据国际商会《INCOTERMS 2000》。
The terms in the contract based on INCOTERMS 2000 of the International Chamber of Commerce.

文字：
Versions:
本合同中、英两种文字具有同等法律效力，在文字解释上，若有异议，以中文解释为准。
This contract is made out in both Chinese and English of which version is equally effective. Conflicts between these two languages arising therefrom, if any, shall be subject to Chinese version.
本合同一式 ___ 份，买卖双方各执一份为证，自双方代表签字（盖章）之日起生效。
This contract is made out in __TWO__ original copies, one copy to be held by each party. Both contracts are effective since being singed/sealed by both parties.

Confirmed by:

卖方 The Seller SHANGHAI LIXIN INTERNATIONAL TRADING CO., LTD. 陈弘毅 (signature)	买方 The Buyer PALMAVITO ARTICOLI SPORTIVE S.P.A. *Giuseppe Del Cassano* Giuseppe Del Cassano (signature)

王经理：好，现在这票业务的销售合同一式两份都已经生效了，我们和客户各执一份，双方都有履行依据了。小李，你觉得接下来应该怎样操作下去啊？

李新：出口合同的履行主要经历"货、证、船、款"四个阶段，我觉得接下来可以备货了。

王经理：不错，用 CIF 术语和信用证支付的业务中，履行出口合同的确要经过准备货物、落实信用证、安排装运和制单结汇四个基本环节。但在当前的实际出口业务中，出口商往往先等对方开来信用证，货款有保障了，再着手备货，这样可以进一步降低出口商的风险。

李新：我明白了，那么我们接下来要做的就是等客户把信用证开过来并且进行审核吧？

王经理：对！

［又过了忙碌的 10 天，李新收到了经中国银行上海分行（BANK OF CHINA SHANGHAI BRANCH）通知的由客户通过 BANCA INTESA SANPAOLO S. P. A. 银行开来的编号为 2010556TLCU0073 的信用证］

信用证：

```
2010AUG 4            15:32:57              LOGICAL TERMINAL 41179
MT S700                  ISSUE OF A DOCUMENTARY CREDIT    PAGE:00001
                                                          FUNC WSMP5
                                                          UMR 8133747
MSGACK HFS8715 AUTH OK, KEY N4877TD8E1028557, BKCHCNBJ BKCHGS RECORD
BASIC HEADER              F   01    BKCHCNBJ R450      7120      96593
APPLICATION HEADER        O   700   1577 100804 BISIT4RXXX 8356 782049 974 E
                              *BANCA INTESA SANPAOLO S.P.A.
                              *MILANO
                              *ITALY
USER HEADER SERVICE CODE        120:
         BANK. PRIORITY         107:
         MSG USER REF.          131:
         INFO. FROM CI          105:
SEQUENCE OF TOTAL         *27   1/1
FORM OF DOC. CREDIT       *40A  IRREVOCABLE
APPLICABLE RULES           40E  UCP LATEST VERSION
DOC. CREDIT NUMBER        *20   2010556TLCU0073
DATE OF ISSUE              31C  100804
DATE AND PLACE OF EXPIRY  *31D  DATE 101007 PLACE ITALY
APPLICANT                 *50   PALMAVITO ARTICOLI SPORTIVE S.P.A.
                                VIA G. MAZZINI, 46, 20116
                                MILANO, ITALY
```

（续上）

BENEFICIARY	*59	SHANGHAI LIXIN INTERNATIONAL TRADING CO., LTD.
		5/F, NO. 2330 WEST ZHONG SHAN ROAD, 200235, SHANGHAI, P. R. CHINA
CURRENCY CODE, AMOUNT	*32B	CURRENCY USD AMOUNT 80784,00
AVALABLE WITH/BY	*41D	ANY BANK IN CHINA BY NEGOTIATION
DRAFT AT…	42C	SIGHT FOR FULL INVOICE VALUE
DRAWEE	42A	BANCA INTESA SANPAOLO S.P.A. MILANO, ITALY
PARTIAL SHIPMENTS	43P	ALLOWED
TRANSSHIPMENT	43T	NOT ALLOWED
LOADING ON BOARD	44A	SHANGHAI, CHINA
FOR TRANSPORTATION TO…	44B	GENOVA, ITALY
LATEST DATE OF SHIP.	44C	100922
DESCRIPT. OF GOODS	45A	

"MILKY WAY" ANTIBACTERIAL FINISHED DYED TWILL OF 26600 METERS AS PER SALES CONTRACT NO.10 LX-PAS 075 DATED JUL. 21, 2010
TERMS OF DELIVERY: CIFC GENOVA INCLUDING 5 PERCENT COMMISSION
PACKING IN SEAWORTHY EXPORT CARTONS
SHIPPING MARKS: PALMASPORT
                   SC#10LX-PAS075
                   GENOVA
                   C/NOS.1-UP
ALL OF THE ABOVE MUST BE MENTIONED ON THE INVOICE AND PACKING LIST.

DOCUMENTS REQUIRED   46A

+ 2/3 OF ORIGINAL CLEAN ON BORAD OCEAN BILLS OF LADING PLUS 3 N/N COPIES MADE OUT TO ORDER OF SHIPPER AND BLANK ENDORSED AND MARKED "FREIGHT PREPAID" NOTIFY APPLICANT (WITH FULL NAME, ADDRESS AND PHONE NUMBERS).
+ SIGNED COMMERCIAL INVOICE IN THREE FOLDS INDICATING THE ORIGIN OF THE GOODS SHIPPED.
+ PACKING LIST IN THREE FOLDS INDICATING G.W., N.W., AND MEAS. OF EACH PACKAGE.
+ INSURANCE POLICY OR CERTIFICATE IN DUPLICATE ENDORSED IN BLANK, FOR 120 PCT OF THE INVOICE VALUE COVERING INSTITUTE CARGO

(续上)

- CLAUSES (C) AND CLAIMS TO BE PAYABLE AT DESTINATION IN THE CURRENCY OF THE DRAFTS.
- + CERTIFICATE OF ORIGIN G.S.P. FORM A IN ONE ORIGINAL AND ONE COPY ISSUED BY COMPETENT AUTHORITY OF THE PEOPLE'S REPUBLIC OF CHINA.
- + INSPECTION CERTIFICATE OF QUALITY IN ONE ORIGINAL AND ONE COPY ISSUED BY ENTRY-EXIT INSPECTION AND QUARANTINE BUREAU OF THE PEOPLE'S REPUBLIC OF CHINA.
- + BENEFICIARY'S CERTIFICATE STATING THAT ONE SET OF N/N SHIPPING DOCUMENTS TOGETHER WITH THE 1/3 ORIGINAL B/L HAVE BEEN SENT TO THE APPLICANT BY DHL WITHIN 24 HOURS AFTER SHIPMENT.
- + COPY OF BENEFICIARY'S FAX SENT TO APPLICANT WITHIN 24 HOURS AFTER SHIPMENT ADVISING ALL SHIPPING DETAILS.

ADDITIONAL CONDITIONS   47A
- + ALL DOCUMENTS MUST INDICATE THIS CREDIT NUMBER.
- + GOODS MUST BE SHIPPED IN 1×20′ CONTAINER FCL AND B/L MUST EVIDENCE THE COMPLIANCE.
- + THIS CREDIT IS NON-OPERATIVE UNLESS THE ISSUING BANK GAVE FURTHER ADVICE.
- + ALL DOCUMENTS TO BE SENT TO BANCA INTESA SANPAOLO S.P.A. VIA MONTE DI PIETA, 8, 20121 MILANO, ITALY TEL: 39-02-366575 FAX: 39-02-366241 IN ONE LOT BY INTERNATIONAL COURIER SERVICE.

CHARGES   71B
ALL BANKING CHARGES AND COMMISSIONS INCLUDING ISSUING FEE ARE FOR ACCOUNT OF BENEFICIARY.

PERIOD FOR PRESENTATION   48
DOCUMENTS TO BE PRESENTED WITHIN 15 DAYS AFTER THE DATE OF SHIPMENT BUT WITHIN THE VALIDITY OF THE CREDIT.

CONFIRMATION   *49   WITHOUT

INSTRUCTION   78
- + UPON RECEIPT OF THE DRAFTS AND DOCUMENTS IN ORDER, WE WILL REMIT THE PROCEEDS AS INSTRUCTED BY THE NEGOTIATION BANK.
- + A DISCREPANCY FEE OF USD50,00 WILL BE DEDUCTED FROM THE PROCEEDS IF DOCUMENTS ARE PRESENTED WITH DISCREPANCY(IES) AND ACCEPTANCE OF SUCH DISCREPANT DOCUMENTS WILL NOT IN ANY WAY ALTER THE TERMS AND CONDITIONS OF THIS CREDIT.

SENDER TO RECEIVER INFO.   72   /PHONBEN/

TRAILER   <MAC:5CDES823> <CHK:641ADE2307554>

李新：王经理，意大利客户的信用证开过来了。

王经理：（边浏览信用证边问）我又要考你啦。你觉得这份信用证是以什么形式开立的？

李新：您指的是信开还是电开吧。我觉得这份信用证是电开本，并且是目前普遍采用的 SWIFT 格式，它是由许多项目组成的，中间那列数字是项目代号，左侧是项目名称，右侧是项目内容。

王经理：不错。你再描述一下这份信用证的开立及传递过程吧。

李新：（边细看信用证边说）意大利客户 PALMAVITO ARTICOLI SPORTIVE S. P. A. 公司向 BANCA INTESA SANPAOLO S. P. A. 银行申请开立信用证，这家意大利的银行用电讯的方式把这份信用证传递给 BANK OF CHINA SHANGHAI BRANCH，当中行上海分行核对其真实性后，再把这份信用证通知我们公司。在这个过程中，客户是开证申请人，意大利的银行是开证行，中行上海分行是通知行，我们是受益人。

王经理：很好。下一步你的工作就是对这份信用证的具体内容进行审核了，说说看你的想法吧。

李新：我觉得主要审核信用证条款与销售合同条款是否相符，如果发现条款有差错、时间有矛盾、数字有错误、词义不明等与销售合同不相符合，或者是我们不能接受、无法照办的内容时，都应该通知客户，要求修改信用证。

王经理：对。根据合同审核信用证关系到出口商是否能够按照信用证要求及时、正确地向银行交单并安全收取货款。小李，你重任在肩啊！

李新：我一定尽力而为！

（李新回到工位，将销售合同 No. 10 LX – PAS 075 和信用证 No. 2010556 TLCU0073 的各条款认真细致地逐项对照审核，并将所有发现的问题汇总成一份详细的审核意见呈送王经理）

信用证审核意见：

1. 信用证条款	31D　EXPIRY PLACE ITALY
存在问题	到期地点与合同规定 valid in China 不符
修改意见	改为在中国到期，即 PLACE CHINA
2. 信用证条款	59　NO. 2330
存在问题	受益人地址与合同规定 NO. 2230 不符
修改意见	改为 NO. 2230
3. 信用证条款	32B　USD 80784,00
存在问题	金额与合同规定 Percentage of allowance for amount and quantity：5％ More or Less 不符
修改意见	在该项下增加项目 39A PERCENTAGE CREDIT AMOUNT TOLERANCE：05/05

(续上)

4. 信用证条款	45A 26600 METERS	
存在问题	货物数量与合同规定 26400 METERS 不符	
修改意见	改为 26400 METERS，并增加"溢短装"为妥，即 5 PERCENT MORE OR LESS	
5. 信用证条款	43P ALLOWED	
存在问题	分批装运与合同规定 PARTIAL SHIPMENTS PROHIBITED 不符	
修改意见	改为 NOT ALLOWED	
6. 信用证条款	43T NOT ALLOWED	
存在问题	转运与合同规定 TRANSSHIPMENT PERMITTED 不符	
修改意见	改为 ALLOWED	
7. 信用证条款	44C 100922	
存在问题	最迟装运日期与合同规定 DURING SEPTEMBER 2010 不符	
修改意见	改为 100930	
8. 信用证条款	31D EXPIRY DATE 101007	
存在问题	最迟装运日期推迟后，到期日应作相应的顺延	
修改意见	改为 101015	
9. 信用证条款	45A PACKING IN SEAWORTHY EXPORT CARTONS	
存在问题	货物外包装种类与合同规定 BALES 不符	
修改意见	删去此内容	
10. 信用证条款	46A +2/3 OF ORIGINAL CLEAN ON BORAD OCEAN BILLS OF LADING +BENEFICIARY'S CERTIFICATE STATING THAT ... 1/3 ORIGINAL B/L ... WITHIN 24 HOURS AFTER SHIPMENT.	
存在问题	装运后24小时内将1/3正本提单直接快递给客户，无法保证出口商在获得货款之前掌握货权	
修改意见	将3/3正本提单提交给议付银行，删去"受益人证明"中有关快递1/3正本提单的内容	
11. 信用证条款	46A +INSURANCE POLICY ... FOR 120 PCT OF THE INVOICE VALUE COVERING INSTITUTE CARGO CLAUSES (C)	

(续上)

存在问题	"保险加成"及"承保险别"与合同规定 for 110% of the invoice value covering F. P. A. …不符
修改意见	改为 FOR 110 PCT OF THE INVOICE VALUE COVERING F. P. A. AS PER THE OCEAN MARINE CARGO CLAUSES OF P. I. C. C. DATED JAN. 1, 1981
12. 信用证条款	47A + THIS CREDIT IS NON - OPERATIVE UNLESS THE ISSUING BANK GAVE FURTHER ADVICE.
存在问题	此条款为限制信用证生效的"软条款"
修改意见	删去此条款
13. 信用证条款	71B ALL BANKING CHARGES AND COMMISSIONS INCLUDING ISSUING FEE ARE FOR ACCOUNT OF BENEFICIARY.
存在问题	按贸易惯例,开证费用不应由受益人承担
修改意见	改为由受益人承担发生在开证国以外的银行费用和佣金,即 ALL BANKING CHARGES AND COMMISSIONS OUTSIDE ITALY ARE FOR ACCOUNT OF BENEFICIARY.

(王经理将信用证仔细复审了一遍后,找到了李新)

王经理:小李,总体上来说,你的审证质量挺高的,应该说你的基本功还是比较扎实的。我有几个问题想问你,可以吗?

李新:当然可以。

王经理:在客户开来的信用证中有这样一个问题,不知你有没有注意。通常情况下,我们表示千位以上数字时用千分号,小数点用"."。为什么在这份信用证中,千位数字没有用千分号,而小数点用","表示呢?

李新:这是 SWIFT,也就是"环球同业银行金融电讯协会"规定的惯例。根据 SWIFT 对信用证条款中符号的规定,千位以上数字不使用千分号,小数点用","表示。

王经理:是啊,的确要充分重视国际贸易的有关惯例,这样业务操作可以更规范,保证安全履约。但要注意在各种外贸单据中还是用常规符号来表示数字哦!关于你的第5、第6条意见,你是怎么想的?

李新:我看它们与合同不符,倒没怎么多想。

王经理:你遇到了新手常见的问题,记住:审核信用证的依据是合同,但这并不意味要把信用证修改成与合同完全一致。我们审证的原则是:如果信用证的要求比合同的要求更为严格,或使卖方权利受损,卖方可依据合同提出修改;如果信用证的要求比合同的要求更宽松,或对卖方履约不会造成实质性的影响,卖方一般不提出修改。现在你再想想看手头这份信用证的分批和转船条款。

李新：哦，我看出来了，信用证允许分批装运，而合同不允许，信用证要求比合同要求宽松，对我们更有利，所以分批条款不用改。但信用证不允许转船，与合同不符，这对我们不利啊，还是应该改的。

王经理：考虑到修改信用证所需要的成本和时间，如果遇到那些我们通过一定的努力可以办到，而又不增加太多费用的情况时，就尽量不要修改信用证。针对转船还是直达这个问题，我到报关运输部咨询过陈老师，热那亚属于欧洲基本港，直达运输的船期完全能满足信用证要求，所以不用修改转船条款。记住，在审证时你不是一个人，要及时与相关部门沟通啊。

李新：我记住了。

王经理：你再看看你的第11条意见。

李新：您是想提醒我"承保险别"不需要修改吧。

王经理：很好，能举一反三！信用证里投保"协会货物C险"，而合同里是"平安险"，在保险公司的实际业务中，这两种险别的承保范围相近，保险费率相同，对我们没有实质影响，所以对险别可以不用改。

李新：我又学了一招。

王经理：你第12条意见里提到了"软条款"，何以见得？

李新：信用证里说"本信用证待开证行给出进一步通知时才能生效"，我认为这是给信用证生效设置条件，是典型的置我方于不利地位的"软条款"，所以要求把它删掉。

王经理：的确如此。长期以来，"软条款"是我们出口商审核信用证时要严加提防的。和我说说你的第8条审证意见吧。

李新：我是这样想的，因为把最迟装运日推迟了，就同时要对信用证到期日作相应的顺延。根据业务惯例，最迟装运日一般比到期日早15天。

王经理：再说说看你第10条意见的思路，还有"2/3"的含义吧。

李新：2/3 OF ORIGINAL BILLS OF LADING 是指承运人一共出具3份正本提单，其中的2份正本提单。信用证要求把1/3正本提单直接快递给客户，这就对我方在收到货款前掌控货权产生了不利影响，因为如果开证银行到时拒付，客户完全可凭已收到的那一份正本提单将货提走，我方就可能面临钱货两空的局面，所以我感到要删掉"快递1/3正本提单"的要求，同时要把"向银行提交2/3正本提单"改为"3/3正本提单"。

王经理：说得好！思维严密、有条理。年轻人，好好努力，你在这一行里大有可为啊！

李新：谢谢王经理，我一定努力！

王经理：现在你去写改证函吧。

李新：好，我这就去给开证行发E-mail。

王经理：哎，你的说法有问题。卖方只能通过买方向开证行提出改证请求，不能直接向开证行提，改证函的收信人仍旧是买方哦。

李新：明白！

（李新回到自己的工位上，开始拟写改证函E-mail）

出口商改证函：

发件人：	li_xin@lixin.com.cn
收件人：	f.taldelli@palmavito.com
日　期：	2010-08-05
主　题：	L/C Amendment

Dear Mr. Taldelli,

We are glad to receive your L/C No. 2010556TLCU0073 issued by BANCA INTESA SANPAOLO S.P.A., MILANO, ITALY dated Aug. 4, 2010.

However, after checking it with our S/C No. 10 LX-PAS 075, we have found some discrepancies and therefore request you to amend as follows:

1) 31D Date and place of expiry
   The date of expiry should be extended to 101015 as contracted to be 15 days after shipment.
   The place of expiry should be China as contracted, instead of Italy.
2) 59 Beneficiary
   The address of beneficiary is No. 2230, not No. 2330.
3) Please add field 39A "Percentage credit amount tolerance: 05/05".
4) 44C Latest date of ship.
   Latest date of shipment should be 100930 as contracted, instead of 100922.
5) 45A Descript. of goods
   The quantity should be "26400 meters 5 percent more of less" as contracted, instead of 26600 meters.
   Please delete the clause about the outer packing "packing in seaworthy export cartons" as contracted.
6) 46A Documents required
   +Please amend "2/3 of original clean on board ocean bills of lading …" to "Full set (3/3) original clean on board ocean bills of lading …" and consequently delete the wording "the 1/3 original B/L" in the clause "Beneficiary's certificate stating that … sent to the applicant by DHL within 24 hours after shipment".
   +We have noticed that you increased the insurance amount to 120% of the invoice value instead of 110% as contracted. This will incur the additional premium, which is to be borne by you. Please confirm the change.
7) 47A Additional Conditions
   +Please delete the clause "This credit is non-operative unless the issuing bank gave further advice" on the basis of mutual benefit.
8) 71B Charges
   According to the usual practices, the issuing fee is to be borne by the applicant. Please amend to "All banking charges and commissions outside Italy are for account of beneficiary".

Please move fast on the above amendments to avoid the delay in shipment.

Thank yon for your cooperation and look forward to the L/C amendment duly.

Yours truly,
Shanghai Lixin International Trading Co., Ltd.
Li Xin

THINK——理论思考

Think 5-1　对于履行 CIF 条件和信用证支付方式的出口合同，卖方履约时一般要经过哪些环节？

以 CIF 价格术语成交和以信用证作为支付方式的交易条件下，出口合同的履行一般需经过① 备货；② 催证、审证、改证；③ 租船订舱、商品检验、投保、报关、装船；④ 制单、交单、结汇等环节。其中以货、证、船、款四个环节最为重要。

Think 5-2　信用证支付方式有什么作用？

信用证是指银行根据进口人的请求和指示，向出口人开立的承诺在一定期限内凭规定的单据支付一定金额的书面文件。

信用证支付方式的作用有两方面：一是银行的保证作用，信用证支付方式将进口人履行付款责任，转为由银行来履行，以此保证出口人安全迅速收到货款，进口人按时收到货运单据；二是融通资金的作用；为进出口双方提供了资金融通的便利。

Think 5-3　信用证业务中涉及哪些当事人？

信用证业务有三个基本当事人，即开证人、开证银行、受益人；此外，根据需要还会有其他当事人，如通知行、议付行、付款行、偿付行、保兑行、承兑行等。

Think 5-4　信用证与买卖合同是什么关系？如何理解信用证的独立性？

《跟单信用证统一惯例》（《UCP600》）规定"就其性质而言，信用证与可能作为其开立基础的销售合同或其他合同是相互独立的交易，即使信用证含有对此类合同的任何援引，银行也与该合同无关，且不受其约束"。因此信用证是一项独立、自足的文件，其可能由于一份买卖合同而开立，但一旦开立之后则与所依据的合同完全独立。以下分别从含义和原因两方面说明信用证的独立性。

1. 信用证独立性的含义

根据《跟单信用证统一惯例》的规定，信用证独立原则的具体含义如下：

（1）开证行对受益人的付款义务独立于受益人在买卖合同项下的履行，即使受益人违反了与开证申请人之间的买卖合同项下的义务，只要受益人提交了符合信用证规定条件的单据，开证行就必须付款。开证行的职员审查单据以决定银行是否付款，他不必也不应该到现场调查并确定基础合同是否已经履行。

（2）开证行对受益人的付款义务也独立于开证申请人对开证行的义务。例如，信用证开出后，受益人尚未签发汇票时，开证申请人破产。尽管开证申请人将无能力偿付开证行，开证行也不能以此作为抗辩事由对抗受益人，而仍应在受益人提交与信用证规定相符的单据时付款。

2. 信用证独立性的原因

（1）开证行没有义务审查基础合同的履行情况。立法、惯例及司法判例都确认开证行对买卖合同的履行不承担任何责任，因为开证行并非买卖合同的签约人，它无法控制买卖合同的内容，也无法选择和决定谁将作为信用证的受益人。

（2）开证行没有能力审查基础合同的履行情况。如果开证行在付款前，除了了解信用证条款和审核单据外，还有义务了解和处理主合同实际履行状况或争议的话，那么银行将"寸步难行"，信用证结算方式也就因此丧失了其商业价值。

Think 5-5 信用证有哪些开立形式？

信用证开立方式有"信开"和"电开"两种。"信开"是指以航邮方式将信用证的正副本寄给通知行，这种方式费用低，但时间长。"电开"是指开证行将信用证内容加注密押，用电报、电传、SWIFT等电讯方式通知受益人所在地的代理行，请其转告受益人，这种方式速度快、安全可靠，但费用高。

Think 5-6 跟单信用证有哪些主要内容？

跟单信用证的主要内容包括：① 开证人名称、受益人名称、开证行的保付文句及承诺付款范围，包括最大金额、有效期、数量及合同号码；② 对单据的要求，包括单据名称、份数及单据内容；③ 对运输条件的规定，包括运输方式、启运港（地）、目的港（地）、可否转运、可否分批及如何分批；④ 对通知行/议付行的指示，包括要不要加保兑、议付后如何索偿及如何寄单等。

Think 5-7 跟单议付信用证业务包括哪些流程？

跟单议付信用证业务需要经过以下几个环节：
（1）进口商向所在地银行申请开立信用证。
（2）开证行开出信用证。
（3）通知行将信用证通知给受益人（出口商）。
（4）出口商接受信用证后，将货物交与承运人，取得相关单据。
（5）出口商备齐信用证规定的单据和汇票向指定银行交单支款。
（6）指定银行付款、承兑或议付。
（7）指定银行将单据和汇票寄往开证行索汇。
（8）开证行或偿付行提供偿付。
（9）开证行通知开证申请人付款赎单。

Think 5-8 为什么催证、审证和改证是出口合同履行中的重要环节？

由于信用证是银行做出的有条件的付款承诺，在规定的期限内凭规定的单据承诺付款，因此，出口商作为信用证的受益人必须对信用证的交单以及付款条件进行审核，如果信用证与合同或交易要求不符，出口商应该及时提出修改信用证的意见要求。

以信用证方式结算的出口合同,卖方收到买方通过银行开来的符合合同要求的信用证,才能保证安全收汇和得到资金融通,落实信用证是卖方交货的前提。

Think 5-9　如何审核信用证?

审核信用证可以从以下几方面入手:
(1) 对信用证表面完整性进行审核。
(2) 对信用证遵循惯例进行审核。
(3) 对有关责任银行的资信进行审核。
(4) 对信用证条款进行审核。
(5) 对信用证性质进行审核。
(6) 对信用证货币和金额进行审核。
(7) 对银行责任条款进行审核。
(8) 信用证的到期日、到期地点和交单期的审查。
(9) 对信用证付款责任的审查。
(10) 对信开信用证和转让信用证等的审核要特别注意。

Think 5-10　常见的实质性不符点有哪些?

在国际贸易的实践中,常见的信用证不符点有:
(1) 汇票付款期限、付款人等内容与信用证条款不符。
(2) 汇票金额与发票不符(除非信用证另有规定)。
(3) 汇票大小写金额不一致。
(4) 发票货物的描述与信用证规定不符。
(5) 发票货物数量和金额与信用证规定不符。
(6) 发票未按信用证的要求签字、公证、认证等。
(7) 运输提单有"不清洁"批注及货装舱面批注。
(8) 运输提单收货人、被通知人、装运港和卸货港、运费支付情况等内容不符。
(9) 提单未注明承运人名称、身份及签发人身份的表述。
(10) 除非信用证另有规定,未提交全套正本提单。
(11) 提单上缺少已装船批注或批注不正确。
(12) 迟期装运。
(13) 信用证过有效期。
(14) 已过交单期。
(15) 保险单据类型与信用证规定不符。
(16) 保险的险别与信用证规定不符。
(17) 保险货币与来证货币不符。
(18) 保额不足。
(19) 保单的出单日期或保险责任生效日期迟于提单已装船日、发运日或接受监管日。

(20) 缺少信用证规定的单据。
(21) 超过信用证金额。
(22) 短装、溢装等。

Think 5-11　在审核信用证的有效期、交单期与装运期时应注意哪些问题?

信用证中均须规定一个到期日及一个付款、承兑交单地点。议付信用证尚须规定一个议付交单地点(自由议付信用证除外)。规定的付款、承兑或议付的到期日,将视为提交单据的到期日。到期日决定了信用证的效期,单据应在此日期前向信用证规定的到期地点提交,否则将被视为单证不符。

如信用证注明的有效期限为"1个月"、"6个月"或类似规定,但未指明自何日起算,则开证行开立信用证的日期即视为起算日。

到期地点应与信用证的兑付方式一致,并与信用证中指定的向其提示单据的银行所在地相符。

除规定一个交单日期外,凡要求提交运输单据的信用证,尚须规定一个在装运日后按信用证规定必须交单的特定期限。如未规定该期限,则默认交单期为装运日后 21 天,当然同时还要结合信用证的到期日考虑。不管信用证规定的交单期是多少天,无论如何单据都不得迟于信用证的到期日提交。

如信用证的到期日或交单期限,或运输单据日后交单期限的最后一天,适逢接受单据的银行因不可抗力以外的原因而中止营业,即属正常的节假日或停业日,则规定的到期日及/或装运日后一定期限内交单的最后一天,将顺延至该银行开业的第一个营业日。

信用证的议付有效到期地一般应在我国境内。

Think 5-12　如何区别可撤销和不可撤销信用证?

不可撤销信用证是指信用证一经开出,在有效期内未经信用证各有关当事人的同意,开证行不得单方面修改或撤销的信用证。只要受益人提供相符单据,开证行就必须履行其付款义务。不可撤销信用证一般在信用证中注明"不可撤销"字样,并载有开证行保证付款的文句。

可撤销信用证是指开证行对所开信用证不必征得受益人或有关当事人的同意而有权随时撤销的信用证。凡可撤销信用证,应在信用证上注明"可撤销"字样。若未注明,则视为不可撤销信用证。

Think 5-13　为什么有时信用证要加保兑?

保兑信用证意味着该信用证不但有开证行不可撤销的付款保证,而且有保兑行的兑付保证。两者的付款人都是负第一性的付款责任,所以对出口商最为有利。

Think 5-14　远期信用证对双方各有哪些利弊?

采用远期信用证的利弊:对进口商来说,其好处是可以利用出口商的资金,便于其本身资金的周转;对出口商来说,便于成交,可以扩大出口,收汇也较托收方式安全。但是,延期付款信用证不要求出口商开立汇票,所以出口商不能利用贴现市场资金,只能自行垫款或向银行借款。因此在出口业务中使用这种信用证,货价应比银行承兑远期信用证高一些。另有一种买方远期信用证,它规定受益人开立远期汇票,由付款行负责贴现,并规定一切利息和费用由进口人负担。该信用证下,进口人要待远期汇票到期时才付款给付款行,但出口人却可以即期收到完全的货款。

Think 5-15 修改信用证的流程是怎样的?

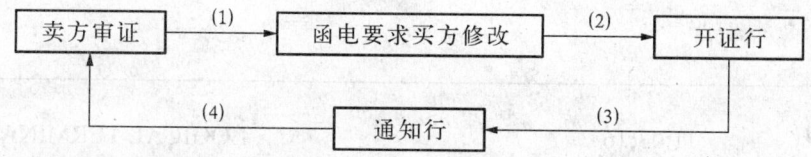

(1) 卖方审证后发现不符点,要求买方修改信用证。
(2) 买方接受,则通知开证行据其指示修改信用证。
(3) 开证行通过通知行向卖方发出信用证修改通知书。
(4) 卖方如未在合适的期限内表示异议,则表示接受。

Think 5-16 修改信用证要注意哪些问题?

经审证后,发现有不符合,或不能接受之处,即应请开证申请人通过开证行进行修改。并在收到改证通知确定无误后发货。改证时应注意以下事项:

(1) 修改的各项内容,应尽量一次性提出,避免多次修改,以免增加双方的手续和费用,浪费双方的时间。
(2) 凡能办到而又不增加费用的,应尽量不修改。例如,合同允许分批装运,而来证不准分批,如果此时货已全部备妥,能一次出运,就无须改证。
(3) 修改应及时提出,以避免因拖延时间过长,造成银行认为我方已接受的误解。
(4) 对信用证的修改书也应认真审核,防止国外客户趁机修改、添加、删除一些重要内容。
(5) 修改书应由原通知行传递。
(6) 对通知行转来的同一修改通知书,如修改内容有两处以上,出口企业只能全部接受或全部拒绝,不能只接受其中的一部分,部分接受修改内容当属无效。

Think 5-17 信用证改证函撰写有哪些要点?

出口方审核信用证,发现有不符合买卖合同或不利于出口方安全收汇的条款,可及时联系进口方通过开证行对信用证进行修改。一封规范的改证函,通常包括以下几个方面的内容:

(1) 感谢对方通过银行开来的信用证。
(2) 列明证中不符点、不能接受的条款,并说明如何改正。
(3) 感谢对方的合作,提醒信用证修改书应于某日前到达,以便按时装运等。

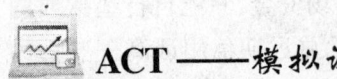 ACT——模拟训练

Act 5-1 出口商审核信用证

2010年11月20日,钱晓俊收到经中国银行上海分行通知的由客户通过 CHASE MANHATTAN BANK 银行开来的信用证。

信用证:

```
2010NOV19           11:03:16                    LOGICAL TERMINAL P012
MT S700                       ISSUE OF A DOCUMENTARY CREDIT   PAGE:00001
                                                              FUNC HJWR47
                                                              UMR 2548401

MSGACK ERV2040 AUTH OK, KEY Q18728BTE1085972, BKCHCNBJ DKLRGM RECORD
BASIC HEADER                F    01   BKCHCNBJ P280    55702   284307
APPLICATION HEADER          O    700  4200 852410 WMIY7XXX 4330 824100 251 N
                                      CHASE MANHATTAN BANK
                                      147 PETITE STATON AVENUE
                                      HOUSTON TX 40132
                                      U.S.A.
USER HEADER SERVICE CODE         105:
         BANK. PRIORITY          114:
         MSG USER REF.           102:
         INFO. FROM CI           117:
SEQUENCE OF TOTAL           *27       1/1
FORM OF DOC. CREDIT         *40A      IRREVOCABLE
APPLICABLE RULES            40E       UCP LATEST VERSION
DOC. CREDIT NUMBER          *20       CHASEMBKLC72075359
DATE OF ISSUE               31C       101119
DATE AND PLACE OF EXPIRY    *31D      DATE   110105      PLACE  CHINA
APPLICANT                   *50       GULFLAND DAINECESS INC.
                                      404 BRENNIN ST., SUITE 255, HOUSTON, TX
                                      75013, UNITED STATES
BENEFICIARY                 *59       SHANGHAI HAINA IMPORT & EXPORT
                                      COMPANY LIMITED
                                      RM. 905 YONG AN MANSION, NO. 12
                                      HUASHAN RD., SHANGHAI, P. R. CHINA
```

（续上）

CURRENCY CODE, AMOUNT	*32B	CURRENCY USD AMOUNT 82977,80
MAX. CREDIT AMOUNT	39B	NOT EXCEEDING
AVALABLE WITH/BY	*41D	ADVISING BANK ONLY BY NEGOTIATION
DRAFT AT…	42C	30 DAYS AFTER BILL OF LADING DATE FOR FULL INVOICE VALUE
DRAWEE	42A	OURSELVES
PARTIAL SHIPMENTS	43P	NOT ALLOWED
TRANSSHIPMENT	43T	ALLOWED
LOADING ON BOARD	44A	SHANGHAI, CHINA
FOR TRANSPORTATION TO…	44B	SAN ANTONIO, TX, US
LATEST DATE OF SHIP.	44C	101231
DESCRIPT. OF GOODS	45A	

    VACUUM FLASK
    AS PER SALES CONFIRMATION NO. SCHN-GD10147 DATED NOV. 6, 2010

ARTICLE NO.	COMMODITY	QUANTITY	UNIT PRICE
CWS3-50	SPORT TYPE VACUUM FLASK	16120PCS	USD2,21
CWT2-100	TRAVEL TYPE VACUUM FLASK	14220PCS	USD3,33

    PRICE TERM: CIF SAN ANTONIO
    SHIPPING MARKS: GULFDAINE
                                  S/CNO.SCHN-GD10147
                                  SAN ANTONIO
                                  C/NOS.1-UP

DOCUMENTS REQUIRED   46A

1. SIGNED COMMERCIAL INVOICE IN DUPLICATE SHOWING SHIPPING MARKS AND STATING THAT COMMODITY IS IN ACCORDANCE WITH APPLICANT'S ORDER NO. GD-PO-CNSHA129 INDICATING FOB VALUE, FREIGHT AND INSURANCE CHARGES.
2. PACKING LIST IN DUPLICATE INDICATING GROSS WEIGHT, NET WEIGHT, AND MEASUREMENT OF EACH ARTICLE NO. AND EACH PACKAGE.
3. COMPLETE SET OF ORIGINAL CLEAN ON BOARD STRAIGHT OCEAN BILLS OF LADING MADE OUT TO APPLICANT AND BLANK ENDORSED AND MARKED "FREIGHT TO COLLECT".
4. CERTIFICATE OF ORIGIN IN DUPLICATE STATING THAT THE GOODS ARE OF CHINESE ORIGIN.
5. INSURANCE POLICY OR CERTIFICATE IN DUPLICATE, ENDORSED IN BLANK, FOR 110 PCT OF THE INVOICE VALUE, STIPULATING THAT CLAIMS ARE PAYABLE IN THE CURRENCY OF THE DRAFT AND SHOWING THE

(续上)

	INSURANCE COVERAGE AS: ALL RISKS AND WAR RISKS AS PER OCEAN MARINE CARGO CLAUSES OF P. I. C. C. DATED 1/1/1981.	
ADDITIONAL COND.	47B	
1	B/L MUST INDICATE THE NUMBERS OF THE CONTAINERS BEING SHIPPED TOGETHER WITH THE CONTAINER AND SEAL NUMBERS.	
2	THREE ADDITIONAL COPIES OF THE COMMERCIAL INVOICES AND TRANSPORT DOCUMENTS ARE REQUESTED TO BE PRESENTED TOGETHER WITH THE DOCUMENTS FOR THE ISSUING BANK'S REFERENCE ONLY.	
3	BENEFICIARY SHOULD SEND SHIPPING ADVICE TO APPLICANT WITHIN 48 HOURS AFTER THE SHIPMENT INDICATING VESSEL'S NAME, SHIPMENT DATE, NUMBER OF PACKAGES, SHIPPING MARKS, L/C NO. AND AMOUNT. ONE COPY OF SUCH ADVICE MUST ACCOMPANY THE DOCUMENTS.	
4	DRAFT SHOULD BEAR A CLAUSE DRAWN UNDER DOCUMENTARY CREDIT NO. CHASEMBKLC72075359 OF CHASE MANHATTAN BANK DATED 101119.	
5	ALL DOCUMENTS MUST MENTION NAME OF ISSUING BANK AND L/C NO. AND S/C NO., DOCUMENTS ISSUED PRIOR TO THE ISSURANCE OF THIS L/C ARE NOT ACCEPTABLE.	
6	THE CARRYING VESSEL SHOULD BELONG TO CONFERENCE LINE AND NOT MORE THAN 20 YEARS OLD. A CERTIFICATE TO THIS EFFECT ISSUED BY THE SHIPPING COMPANY TO BE PRESENTED WITH THE L/C DOCUMENTS UPON NEGOTIATION.	
7	THE ISSUING BANK IS OBLIGED TO PAYMENT ONLY AFTER GOODS ARE SHIPPED TO THE PORT OF DESTINATION.	
DETAILS OF CHARGES	71B	
	ALL BANKING CHARGES INCLUDING ADVISING, NEGOTIATION AND REIMBURSEMENT ARE FOR THE ACCOUNT OF BENEFICIARY.	
PRESENTATION PERIOD	48	
	DOCUMENTS TO BE PRESENTED WITHIN 5 DAYS AFTER THE DATE OF SHIPMENT BUT WITHIN THE VALIDITY OF THE CREDIT.	
CONFIRMATION	*49	WITHOUT
INSTRUCTION	78	
1	T/T REIMBURSEMENT IS NOT ACCEPTABLE.	
2	IN REIMBURSEMENT, NEGOTIATION BANK MUST DISPATCH ALL DOCUMENTS BY REGISTERED AIRMAIL OR AIR COURIER TO US IN ONE LOT.	
3	A DISCREPANCY FEE OF USD50,00 WILL BE DEDUCTED FROM THE PROCEEDS IF DOCUMENTS ARE PRESENTED WITH DISCREPANCY(IES) AND ACCEPTANCE OF SUCH DISCREPANT DOCUMENTS WILL NOT IN ANY WAY ALTER THE TERMS AND CONDITIONS OF THIS CREDIT.	
4	UPON RECEIPT OF FULL SET OF DOCUMENTS IN ORDER, WE SHALL REIMBURSE YOU ACCORDING TO YOUR INSTRUCTIONS.	
SEND. TO REC. INFO.	72	/PHONBEN/
TRAILER	MAC:	7LM53E74
	CHK:	1427GRAC452420711

请以钱晓俊的身份审核信用证。

Act 5-2　出口商撰写改证函

钱晓俊将信用证审核意见书交经理复核后，准备给客户写一封改证函E-mail。
请以钱晓俊的身份，撰写该改证E-mail。

出口商改证函：

发件人：	damonchan@hainaco.com.cn
收件人：	ray.sinclair@gulfday.com
日　期：	2010-11-20
主　题：	Amendment of L/C

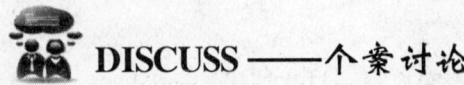 **DISCUSS——个案讨论**

Discuss 5

延续实训四 DISCUSS 环节,2011 年 3 月 31 日,李新收到了来自越南供应商的销售确认书(编号:TK-CN-SC 32,日期:2011 年 3 月 28 日)。根据 Discuss4-2 中已缮制完成的该销售确认书及以下信用证开证要求,李新该如何缮制开证申请书(日期:2011 年 4 月 1 日)?

信用证开证要求

开证银行:中国银行上海分行
开证方式:SWIFT
单据要求:
(1) 商业发票一式四份。
(2) 装箱单一式四份。
(3) 权威机构出具的原产地证明一式二份。
(4) 全套海运提单,做成凭开证银行指示抬头。
(5) 保险单一式二份,按发票金额加 10% 投保一切险和偷窃、提货不着险(THEFT, PILFERAGE AND NON-DELIVERY RISK)。
(6) 瑞士通用公证行(SOCIETE GENERALE DE SURVEILLANCE S.A.)出具的品质证明一式二份。
(7) 装船后 24 小时内发出的装运通知副本。
(8) 交单期为运输单据出单日后 15 天。

信用证开证申请书：

IRREVOCABLE DOCUMENTARY CREDIT APPLICATION	
To:	Issued by Date:
Applicant (Full name and address)	Credit No. Date and place of expiry
Beneficiary (Full name and address)	Amount (both in figures and words)
Partial shipments ☐allowed ☐not allowed	Transshipment ☐allowed ☐not allowed	Credit available with By ☐sight payment ☐acceptance ☐negotiation ☐deferred payment at against the documents detailed herein ☐and beneficiary's draft(s) for _____ % of invoice value
Loading on board/dispatch/taking in charge at/from not later than For transportation to: ☐FOB ☐CFR ☐CIF ☐or other terms	at_____ sight drawn on_____ Price term: _____

Documents required: (marked with ☑)
1. ☐ Signed commercial invoice in _____ copies indicating L/C No. and Contract No._____
2. ☐ Full set of clean on board Bills of Lading made out to _____ and blank endorsed, marked "freight ☐ to collect / ☐ prepaid ☐ showing freight amount" notifying _____
3. ☐ Airway bills/cargo receipt/copy of railway bills issued by _____ showing "freight ☐ to collect / ☐ prepaid ☐ indicating freight amount" and consigned to_____.
4. ☐ Insurance Policy/Certificate in _____ copies for _____ % of the invoice value showing claims payable at destination in currency of the draft, blank endorsed, covering_____
5. ☐ Packing List/Weight Memo in _____ copies indicating quantity, gross and net weights of each package.
6. ☐ Certificate of Quantity/Weight in _____ copies issued by _____.
7. ☐ Certificate of Quality in _____ copies issued by ☐ manufacturer/ ☐ public recognized surveyor _____
8. ☐ Certificate of Origin in _____ copies issued by_____
9. ☐ Beneficiary's certified copy of fax / telex dispatched to the applicant within _____ hours after shipment advising L/C No., name of vessel, date of shipment, name, quantity, weight and value of goods.
Other documents, if any

Description of goods:

Additional instructions:
1. ☐ All banking charges outside the opening bank are for beneficiary's account.
2. ☐ Documents must be presented within _____ days after date of issuance of the transport documents but within the validity of this credit.
3. ☐ Third party as shipper is not acceptable, Short Form/Blank back B/L is not acceptable.
4. ☐ Both quantity and credit amount_____% more or less are allowed.
5. ☐ All documents must be sent to issuing bank by courier/speed post in one lot.
   ☐ Other terms, if any

Account No.:_____ with _____ (name of bank)
Transacted by:_____
Telephone No.:_____

(Applicant: name, signature of authorized person)

情景模拟实训六

履行合同二——托运订舱和报检

 LOOK——情景示范

（10 天后，李新接中国银行上海分行通知，收到了 BANCA INTESA SANPAOLO S. P. A. 银行开来的信用证修改书，立刻转呈王经理）

信用证修改书：

```
2010AUG 15           09:47:21                    LOGICAL TERMINAL 41179
MT S707           AMENDMENT OF A DOCUMENTARY CREDIT      PAGE:00001
                                                         FUNC WSMP5
                                                         UMR 8133747
MSGACK HFS8715 AUTH OK, KEY N48210U7519R1741, BKCHCNBJ BOCSHAG RECORD
BASIC HEADER             F    01   BKCHCNBJ R450    1142    37420
APPLICATION HEADER       O   707   7851 100815 BISIT37XXX 4285 301732   582  E
                             *BANCA INTESA SANPAOLO S.P.A.
                             *MILANO
                             *ITALY
USER HEADER SERVICE CODE         120:
         BANK. PRIORITY          107:
         MSG USER REF.           131:
         INFO. FROM CI           105:
SENDER'S REFERENCE       *20    2010556TLCU0073
RECEIVER'S REFERENCE     *21    NONREF
NUMBER OF AMENDMENT      26E    1
DATE OF AMENDMENT        30     100815
DATE OF ISSUE            31C    100804
BENEFICIARY (BEFORE THIS AMENDMENT)    *59  SHANGHAI LIXIN INTERNATIONAL
                                            TRADING CO., LTD.
```

(续上)

```
                                        5/F, NO. 2330 WEST ZHONG SHAN
                                        ROAD, 200235, SHANGHAI, P. R. CHINA
NARRATIVE                        79
    ++   UNDER FIELD 31D
         AMEND "DATE 101007" TO "DATE 101015" AND "PLACE ITALY" TO "PLACE CHINA"
    ++   UNDER FIELD 59
         AMEND "NO. 2330" TO "NO. 2230"
    ++   ADD FIELD 39A PERCENTAGE CREDIT AMOUNT TOLERANCE: 05/05
    ++   UNDER FIELD 44C
         AMEND TO READ:          100930
    ++   UNDER FIELD 45A
         AMEND "26 600 METERS" TO "26 400 METERS 5 PERCENT MORE OF LESS" AND
         DELETE THE CLAUSE "PACKING IN SEAWORTHY EXPORT CARTONS"
    ++   UNDER FIELD 46A
         AMEND "2/3 OF ORIGINAL CLEAN ON BOARD OCEAN BILLS OF LADING…" TO
         "FULL SET 3/3 ORIGINAL CLEAN ON BOARD OCEAN BILLS OF LADING…"
    ++   UNDER FIELD 46A
         AMEND "INSURANCE POLICY OR CERTIFICATE…FOR 120 PCT OF THE INVOICE
         VALUE…" TO "INSURANCE POLICY OR CERTIFICATE…FOR 110 PCT OF THE INVOICE
         VALUE…"
    ++   UNDER FIELD 46A
         DELETE THE WORDING "TOGETHER WITH THE 1/3 ORIGINAL B/L" IN THE CLAUSE
         "BENEFICIARY'S CERTIFICATE STATING THAT…WITHIN 24 HOURS AFTER
         SHIPMENT"
    ++   UNDER FIELD 47A
         DELETE THE CLAUSE "THIS CREDIT IS NON-OPERATIVE UNLESS THE ISSUING
         BANK GAVE FURTHER ADVICE"
    ++   UNDER FIELD 71B
         AMEND TO READ:
         ALL BANKING CHARGES AND COMMISSIONS OUTSIDE ITALY ARE FOR ACCOUNT
         OF BENEFICIARY
ALL OTHER TERMS AND CONDITIONS REMAIN UNCHANGED
SEND. TO REC. INFO.             72       /PHONBEN/
TRAILER         <MAC:5CDES823> <CHK:5927PL577H1W3>
```

李新：王经理，意大利客户通过开证银行把信用证修改书开过来了。

王经理：上面对保险加成率怎么说？

李新：（边细看信用证修改书边说）把20%修改为10%了。

王经理：好，原先在信用证中这个问题悬而未决，现在可以定下来了。

李新：我请教您一个问题，开证行为什么不是重开一份信用证，而只是开一份修改书呢？

王经理：我问你：这份信用证是可撤销的还是不可撤销的？

李新：哦，我明白了，您这一问就回答了我的问题了。根据《UCP600》，现在银行开出的都是不可撤销信用证，就是IRREVOCABLE，所以开证行修改信用证的时候只能另开一份修改书了。

王经理：好一个活学活用啊。接下来你把这份信用证修改书好好审核一下，然后转给我复核。如果没有问题的话，就能把它和原先的信用证订在一起了，这叫"锁证"。到时候我们向银行提交单据时，也要把信用证和修改书一起提交。

李新：明白！

（李新回到工位，将信用证修改书对照信用证和销售合同进行了认真审核，并经王经理复核，该修改书已符合公司的改证要求）

（又过了忙碌的10天，货源部张经理找到李新）

张经理：小李，我刚接到绍兴轻纺开发公司的通知，意大利客户的货物已经生产出来了，现在在他们的仓库里进行外包装了。

李新：谢谢张经理通知，接下来我应该为这票货办理托运了吧？

张经理：对啊，有关托运订舱的具体问题，你得向报关运输部的陈老师多请教了。

李新：我知道了。

（李新通过请教报关运输部的同事及上网查询中远集装箱运输有限公司、航运交易公报电子公报等多家航运网站，多方了解从上海到意大利热那亚的船期、运价等情况。在委托国际货运代理公司出运之前，李新向陈老师请教）

李新：陈老师，我想请教您，经过我的了解，我们公司到地中海地区去的货物基本上都委托上海速捷国际货运公司向中远集运订舱，我手上的这票货物也不例外吧？

陈老师：我想先听你说说看货代公司在货物出口方面的作用。

李新：货代公司在货物出口方面的主营业务是接受货主的委托，为货主代办各种国际运输手续，把货物顺利运出我国关境，最终运抵收货人处。从我正在做的这票业务看，我们公司是货主，也是托运人，意大利PALMAVITO ARTICOLI SPORTIVE S.P.A.公司是收货人，如果向中远集运订舱的话，中远集运就是承运人，货代公司则相当于沟通我们公司和中远的桥梁。

陈老师：回答得不错啊。目前我们公司凡是向中远订舱，都是委托速捷货代做的。接下来你要去制作订舱文件了，我再问你，你觉得在订舱时要做哪几张单据啊？提醒你一下，我们公司自己负责出口报关。

李新：按照这票业务目前的进展，我觉得至少要做订舱委托书、商业发票、装箱单，如果把出口报关一起委托货代的话，还要做报关委托书、手写报关单、出口收汇核销单。

陈老师：挺熟的。订舱委托书是我们公司委托货代的详细托运要求，商业发票和装箱单是对货物的详细说明，这两张单据在你接下来办理各项履约手续时都会用到，同时也是做其他单据的依据，你都要认真制作哦。

李新：是！

（李新回到工位上，打开电脑中的专业制单软件，开始了细致的制单工作……半小时后，李新拿着打印输出的三份单据请陈老师审核）

海运出口订舱委托书：

上海立信国际贸易有限公司
SHANGHAI LIXIN INTERNATIONAL TRADING CO., LTD.
5/F, NO. 2230 WEST ZHONG SHAN ROAD, 200235, SHANGHAI, P. R. CHINA
TEL：86-21-64391520　　FAX：86-21-64391530

海运出口订舱委托书

发货人： Shipper:	SHANGHAI LIXIN INTERNATIONAL TRADING CO., LTD. 5/F, NO. 2230 WEST ZHONG SHAN ROAD, 200235, SHANGHAI, P. R. CHINA TEL：86-21-64391520　FAX：86-21-64391530		编号	LX-PAS100247		
			日期	2010/08/25		
收货人： Consignee:	TO ORDER OF SHIPPER		合同号	10LX-PAS075		
通知人： Notify Party:	PALMAVITO ARTICOLI SPORTIVE S.P.A. VIA G. MAZZINI, 46, 20116 MILANO, ITALY TEL: 39-02-369010　FAX: 39-02-369052		信用证号	2010556TLCU0073		
			贸易国别	ITALY		
运费支付方式	FREIGHT PREPAID	是否要求代报关	☐ 是　☑ 否		提单份数	3正3副
起运港	SHANGHAI, CHINA	目的港	GENOVA, ITALY	可否转运	NOT ALLOWED	可否分批	ALLOWED
标记唛码	总件数及包装名称	货物描述		总毛重	总体积	成交条件
AS PER INVOICE NO. LX-PAS10075	55 BALES	100% COTTON DYED TWILL		7425.00 KGS	24.75 CBM	CIF
装箱方式	☑ FCL ☐ LCL	门点装箱地点	闵行区华漕镇纪诸公路 1073 号			
箱型箱量	1×20′GP		电话	51802633	联系人	李飞翰
货物备妥日期	2010/08/30	特种集装箱要求		☐ 冷藏货		☐ 危险品
备注	1. 请配 COSCON 2010/09/10 2. 提单须标注 FREIGHT PREPAID 3. 提单须标注信用证号 2010556TLCU0073 4. 提单须标注 1×20′GP FCL					

商业发票:

SHANGHAI LIXIN INTERNATIONAL TRADING CO., LTD.
5/F, NO. 2230 WEST ZHONG SHAN ROAD, 200235, SHANGHAI, P. R. CHINA
TEL：86-21-64391520　FAX：86-21-64391530

COMMERCIAL INVOICE

TO: PALMAVITO ARTICOLI SPORTIVE S.P.A.
VIA G. MAZZINI, 46, 20116 MILANO, ITALY
TEL: 39-02-369010　FAX: 39-02-369052

INVOICE NO: LX-PAS10075
INVOICE DATE: AUG. 25, 2010
S/C NO: 10LX-PAS075
L/C NO: 2010556TLCU0073

FROM: SHANGHAI, CHINA　　**TO:** GENOVA, ITALY

MARKS & NOS.	DESCRIPTION OF GOODS	QUANTITY	UNIT PRICE	AMOUNT
PALMASPORT SC#10LX-PAS075 GENOVA C/NOS.1-55	100% COTTON DYED TWILL "MILKY WAY" ANTIBACTERIAL FINISHED DYED TWILL ART. NO. KJ2001	 26400 METERS	CIFC5% GENOVA USD3.06/METER TOTAL:	 USD 80 784.00 USD 80 784.00

AS PER SALES CONTRACT NO. 10LX-PAS075 DATED JUL. 21, 2010

TERMS OF DELIVERY: CIFC GENOVA INCLUDING 5 PERCENT COMMISSION

ORIGIN OF THE GOODS: P. R. CHINA

TOTAL AMOUNT IN WORDS:　SAY U. S. DOLLARS EIGHTY THOUSAND SEVEN HUNDRED
　　　　　　　　　　　　　　AND EIGHTY FOUR ONLY

TOTAL G.W. / TOTAL N.W.:　7425.00 KGS / 7150.00 KGS
TOTAL PACKAGES:　55 BALES

SHANGHAI LIXIN INTERNATIONAL TRADING CO., LTD.

陈弘毅
(signature)

装箱单：

SHANGHAI LIXIN INTERNATIONAL TRADING CO., LTD.
5/F, NO. 2230 WEST ZHONG SHAN ROAD, 200235, SHANGHAI, P. R. CHINA
TEL：86-21-64391520　FAX：86-21-64391530

PACKING LIST

TO:　PALMAVITO ARTICOLI SPORTIVE S.P.A.　　　　INVOICE NO:　　LX-PAS10075
　　　VIA G. MAZZINI, 46, 20116 MILANO, ITALY　　　INVOICE DATE:　AUG. 25, 2010
　　　TEL: 39-02-369010　FAX: 39-02-369052　　　　S/C NO:　　　　10LX-PAS075
　　　　　　　　　　　　　　　　　　　　　　　　　L/C NO:　　　　2010556TLCU0073

FROM: SHANGHAI, CHINA　　　　TO: GENOVA, ITALY

MARKS & NOS.	DESCRIPTION OF GOODS	PACKAGE	QUANTITY	G.W. (KGS)	N.W. (KGS)	MEAS. (CBM)
PALMASPORT SC#10LX-PAS075 GENOVA C/NOS.1-55	100% COTTON DYED TWILL ART. NO. KJ2001	55 BALES	26400 METERS	@135.00/7425.00	@130.00/7150.00	@0.45/24.75

PACKING: 120 METERS IN ONE PIECE,
　　　　　4 PIECES IN ONE BALE,
　　　　　TOTAL 55 BALES.

TOTAL:　55 BALES　26400 METERS　　7425.00 KGS　7150.00 KGS　24.75 CBM

AS PER SALES CONTRACT NO. 10LX-PAS075 DATED JUL. 21, 2010

TERMS OF DELIVERY: CIFC GENOVA INCLUDING 5 PERCENT COMMISSION

TOTAL PACKAGES IN WORDS:　SAY FIFTY FIVE BALES ONLY

SHANGHAI LIXIN INTERNATIONAL TRADING CO., LTD.

陈弘毅
(signature)

陈老师：(边来回细看三份单据边问)你制作这几份单据的依据是什么？

李新：主要是两个"一致"：单据要和信用证及其修改书保持一致，各单据之间要保持一致。另外我也上网查询了中远集运的船期表，并且电话询问了绍兴轻纺开发公司目前的出货进度，之后在订舱委托书中要求装船日期是9月10日，绍兴轻纺公司要在8月30日前把货物运抵我们公司在闵行华漕镇的仓库。

陈老师：不错，单据没什么问题。记得在收到配舱回单后务必再和绍兴轻纺公司确认一下进仓时间哦。

李新：谢谢陈老师！

(李新将订舱委托书传真给速捷货代公司，并将商业发票、装箱单一并快递了过去)

［第二天，李新收到了速捷公司传真来的"配舱回单"等五联(见第121~125页)，呈送陈老师］

李新：陈老师，速捷货代把配舱回单传真过来了。

陈老师：你对这些单据熟悉吗？

李新：这些单据的学名是"集装箱货物托运单"俗称"十联单"，是货代向船公司订舱用的。对我们货主来说，十联单中核心的几联包括配舱回单、装货单和场站收据。现在货代把这几联传真给我们，主要是让我们审核并确认后留存，以便办理以后各项手续。我还想问您一下，配舱回单右下角为什么是"外轮代理公司"签章，而不是"中远集运"呢？

陈老师：外代公司是家船务代理公司，俗称"船代公司"，主营业务是代理中远集运船公司对外销售舱位，所以速捷货代得向外代订中远的舱位，自然是外代公司出配舱回单。你再想想，从配舱回单中的几处地方能看出货代订舱成功了？

李新：(边细看配舱回单边说)D/R No.、船名、航次和装船日期章。

陈老师：当然，货物还未实际装船，船代敲装船日期章只是方便我们办理之后的手续。

李新：接下来要办理报检了吧？

陈老师：That's right. Keep moving!

(李新与绍兴轻纺开发公司电话确认务必将货物在8月30日前通过公路运抵立信公司在闵行华漕镇的仓库。得到绍兴轻纺公司肯定能在8月29日下午运达仓库的答复后，李新立即电告速捷货代公司，和其确认8月30日到华漕仓库装集装箱。随后，李新在报关运输部报检员林质平的指导下，使用专业报检软件，制作"出境货物报检单")(见第126页)

李新：陈老师，我把报检单制作好了，连同换证凭单、商业发票、装箱单(见第127~129页)一起请您审核。

陈老师：(边细看各份单据边问)你能解释一下换证凭单的作用吗？

李新：换证凭单主要用于产地和报关地不一致的出境货物。比如我们这批纺织品面料，产地是绍兴，但报关地在上海，绍兴商检局对货物施行检验后，出具换证凭单，之后随着货物一起流转到上海商检局，上海局不再重新检验，直接凭这张单据换发"出境货物通关单"和商检证书，这样能避免重复检验，提高办事效率，加快出境速度。

陈老师：不错，解释得挺完整。报检单没什么问题，你跟着小林去现场报检吧。

(李新备齐出境报检单、出境换证凭单、商业发票和装箱单等单据，跟随报检员林质平至洋山出入境检验检疫局办理现场报检手续……)

集装箱货物托运单第九联——配舱回单(1)：

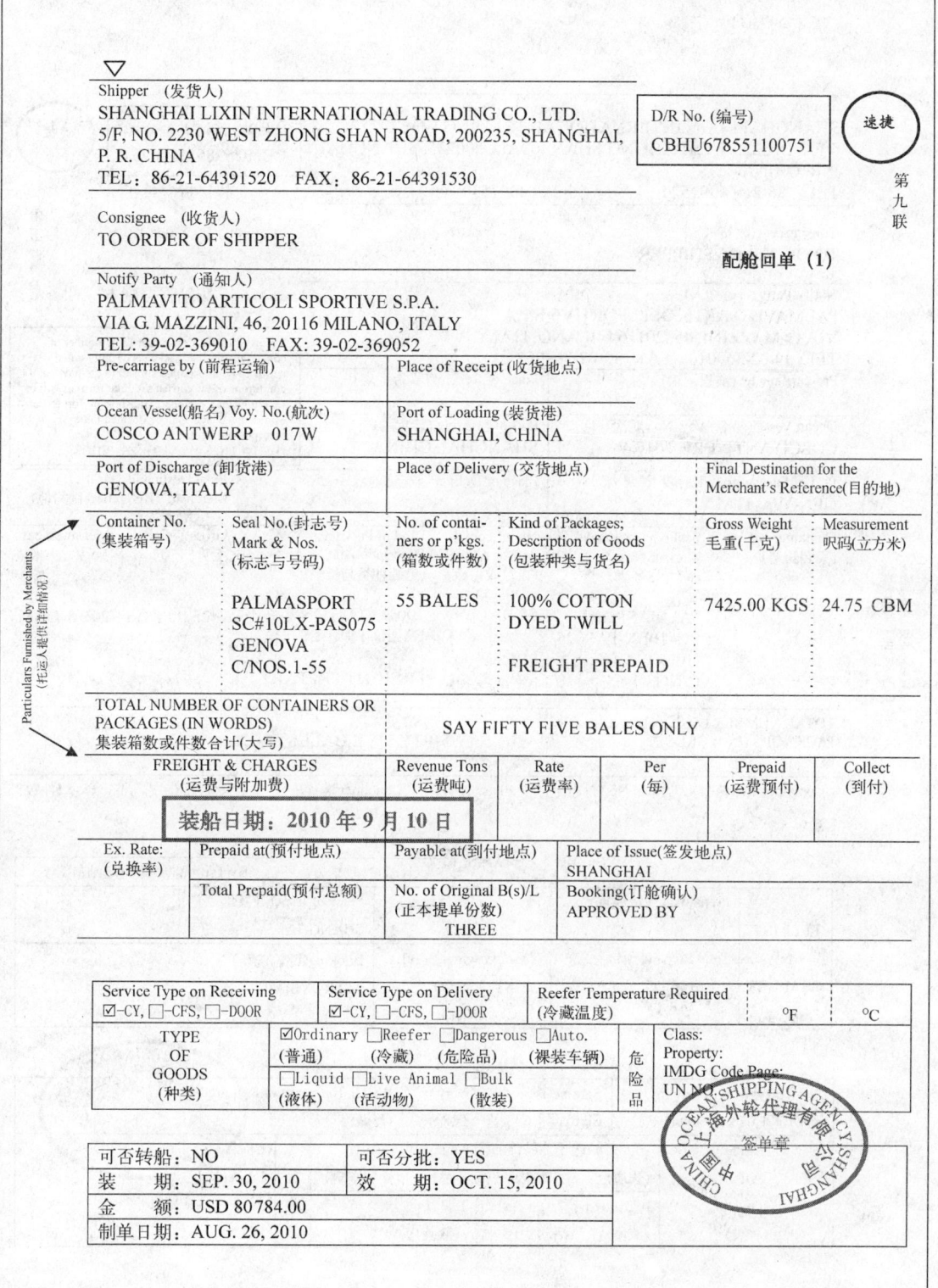

集装箱货物托运单第五联——装货单（场站收据副本）：

Shipper (发货人) SHANGHAI LIXIN INTERNATIONAL TRADING CO., LTD. 5/F, NO. 2230 WEST ZHONG SHAN ROAD, 200235, SHANGHAI, P. R. CHINA TEL：86-21-64391520 FAX：86-21-64391530	D/R No. (编号) CBHU678551100751 装 货 单	速捷 第五联
Consignee (收货人) TO ORDER OF SHIPPER	场站收据副本	
Notify Party (通知人) PALMAVITO ARTICOLI SPORTIVE S.P.A. VIA G. MAZZINI, 46, 20116 MILANO, ITALY TEL：39-02-369010 FAX: 39-02-369052	Received by the Carrier the Total number of containers or other packages or units stated below to be transported subject to the terms and conditions of the carrier's regular form of Bill of Loading (for Combined Transport or Port to Port Shipment) which shall be deemed to be incorporated herein.	

Pre-carriage by (前程运输)	Place of Receipt (收货地点)	
Ocean Vessel(船名) Voy. No.(航次) COSCO ANTWERP 017W	Port of Loading (装货港) SHANGHAI, CHINA	Date (日期)： AUG. 26, 2010
Port of Discharge (卸货港) GENOVA, ITALY	Place of Delivery (交货地点)	Final Destination for the Merchant's Reference(目的地)

Container No. (集装箱号)	Seal No.(封志号) Mark & Nos. (标志与号码)	No. of containers or p'kgs. (箱数或件数)	Kind of Packages; Description of Goods (包装种类与货名)	Gross Weight 毛重(千克)	Measurement 呎码(立方米)
	PALMASPORT SC#10LX-PAS075 GENOVA C/NOS.1-55	55 BALES	100% COTTON DYED TWILL FREIGHT PREPAID	7425.00 KGS	24.75 CBM
TOTAL NUMBER OF CONTAINERS OR PACKAGES (IN WORDS) 集装箱数或件数合计(大写)		SAY FIFTY FIVE BALES ONLY			

Particulars Furnished by Merchants (托运人提供详细情况)

Container No.(箱号)	Seal No.(封志号)	Pkgs.(件数)	Container No.(箱号)	Seal No.(封志号)	Pkgs.(件数)

Received (实收)   By Terminal Clerk (场站员签字)

FREIGHT & CHARGES	Prepaid at(预付地点)	Payable at(到付地点)	Place of Issue(签发地点) SHANGHAI
	Total Prepaid(预付总额)	No. of Original B(s)/L (正本提单份数) THREE	Booking (订舱确认) APPROVED BY

Service Type on Receiving ☑-CY, ☐-CFS, ☐-DOOR	Service Type on Delivery ☑-CY, ☐-CFS, ☐-DOOR	Reefer Temperature Required (冷藏温度)		签单章
TYPE OF GOODS (种类)	☑Ordinary ☐Reefer ☐Dangerous ☐Auto. (普通) (冷藏) (危险品) (裸装车辆) ☐Liquid ☐Live Animal ☐Bulk (液体) (活动物) (散装)		危 险 品	Class: Property: IMDG Code Page: UN NO.

集装箱货物托运单第六联——场站收据副本(大副联):

Shipper (发货人) SHANGHAI LIXIN INTERNATIONAL TRADING CO., LTD. 5/F, NO. 2230 WEST ZHONG SHAN ROAD, 200235, SHANGHAI, P. R. CHINA TEL: 86-21-64391520 FAX: 86-21-64391530	D/R No. (编号) CBHU678551100751 场站收据副本 大副联
Consignee (收货人) TO ORDER OF SHIPPER	速捷
Notify Party (通知人) PALMAVITO ARTICOLI SPORTIVE S.P.A. VIA G. MAZZINI, 46, 20116 MILANO, ITALY TEL: 39-02-369010 FAX: 39-02-369052	COPY OF DOCK RECEIPT (FOR CHIEF OFFICER)

Pre-carriage by (前程运输)	Place of Receipt (收货地点)	Received by the Carrier the Total number of containers or other packages or units stated below to be transported subject to the terms and conditions of the carrier's regular form of Bill of Loading (for Combined Transport or Port to Port Shipment) which shall be deemed to be incorporated herein. Date (日期): AUG. 26, 2010
Ocean Vessel (船名) Voy. No.(航次) COSCO ANTWERP 017W	Port of Loading (装货港) SHANGHAI, CHINA	
Port of Discharge (卸货港) GENOVA, ITALY	Place of Delivery (交货地点)	Final Destination for the Merchant's Reference (目的地)

Container No. (集装箱号)	Seal No.(封志号) Mark & Nos. (标志与号码)	No. of containers or p'kgs. (箱数或件数)	Kind of Packages; Description of Goods (包装种类与货名)	Gross Weight 毛重(千克)	Measurement 呎码(立方米)
	PALMASPORT SC#10LX-PAS075 GENOVA C/NOS.1-55	55 BALES	100% COTTON DYED TWILL FREIGHT PREPAID	7425.00 KGS	24.75 CBM
TOTAL NUMBER OF CONTAINERS OR PACKAGES (IN WORDS) 集装箱数或件数合计(大写)		SAY FIFTY FIVE BALES ONLY			

Particulars Furnished by Merchants (托运人提供详细情况)

Container No.(箱号)	Seal No.(封志号)	Pkgs.(件数)	Container No.(箱号)	Seal No.(封志号)	Pkgs.(件数)

			Received (实收)	By Terminal Clerk (场站员签字)
FREIGHT & CHARGES	Prepaid at(预付地点)	Payable at(到付地点)	Place of Issue(签发地点) SHANGHAI	
	Total Prepaid(预付总额)	No. of Original B(s)/L (正本提单份数) THREE	Booking(订舱确认) APPROVED BY	

Service Type on Receiving ☑-CY, ☐-CFS, ☐-DOOR	Service Type on Delivery ☑-CY, ☐-CFS, ☐-DOOR	Reefer Temperature Required (冷藏温度)	°F	°C
TYPE OF GOODS (种类)	☑Ordinary ☐Reefer ☐Dangerous ☐Auto. (普通) (冷藏) (危险品) (裸装车辆) ☐Liquid ☐Live Animal ☐Bulk (液体) (活动物) (散装)		危 险 品	Class: Property: IMDG Code Page: UN NO.

第六联

集装箱货物托运单第七联——场站收据：

Shipper (发货人) SHANGHAI LIXIN INTERNATIONAL TRADING CO., LTD. 5/F, NO. 2230 WEST ZHONG SHAN ROAD, 200235, SHANGHAI, P. R. CHINA TEL：86-21-64391520　FAX：86-21-64391530	D/R No. (编号) CBHU678551100751　　速捷 场站收据
Consignee (收货人) TO ORDER OF SHIPPER	第七联
Notify Party (通知人) PALMAVITO ARTICOLI SPORTIVE S.P.A. VIA G. MAZZINI, 46, 20116 MILANO, ITALY TEL: 39-02-369010　FAX: 39-02-369052	**DOCK RECEIPT** Received by the Carrier the Total number of containers or other packages or units stated below to be transported subject to the terms and conditions of the carrier's regular form of Bill of Loading (for Combined Transport or Port to Port Shipment) which shall be deemed to be incorporated herein. Date(日期):　AUG. 26, 2010

Pre-carriage by (前程运输)	Place of Receipt (收货地点)
Ocean Vessel (船名) Voy. No.(航次) COSCO ANTWERP　017W	Port of Loading (装货港) SHANGHAI, CHINA
Port of Discharge (卸货港) GENOVA, ITALY	Place of Delivery (交货地点)	Final Destination for the Merchant's Reference(目的地)

Particulars Furnished by Merchants (托运人提供详细情况)

Container No. (集装箱号)	Seal No.(封志号) Mark & Nos. (标志与号码)	No. of containers or p'kgs. (箱数或件数)	Kind of Packages; Description of Goods (包装种类与货名)	Gross Weight 毛重(千克)	Measurement 呎码(立方米)
	PALMASPORT SC#10LX-PAS075 GENOVA C/NOS.1-55	55 BALES	100% COTTON DYED TWILL FREIGHT PREPAID	7425.00 KGS	24.75 CBM
TOTAL NUMBER OF CONTAINERS OR PACKAGES (IN WORDS) 集装箱数或件数合计(大写)		SAY FIFTY FIVE BALES ONLY			

Container No.(箱号)	Seal No.(封志号)	Pkgs.(件数)	Container No.(箱号)	Seal No.(封志号)	Pkgs.(件数)

Received (实收)　　　By Terminal Clerk (场站员签字)

FREIGHT & CHARGES	Prepaid at(预付地点)	Payable at(到付地点)	Place of Issue(签发地点) SHANGHAI
	Total Prepaid(预付总额)	No. of Original B(s)/L (正本提单份数) THREE	Booking(订舱确认) APPROVED BY

	Service Type on Receiving ☑-CY, ☐-CFS, ☐-DOOR	Service Type on Delivery ☑-CY, ☐-CFS, ☐-DOOR	Reefer Temperature Required (冷藏温度)	°F	°C
TYPE OF GOODS (种类)	☑Ordinary (普通) ☐Reefer (冷藏) ☐Dangerous (危险品) ☐Auto. (裸装车辆) ☐Liquid (液体) ☐Live Animal (活动物) ☐Bulk (散装)			危险品	Class: Property: IMDG Code Page: UN NO.

集装箱货物托运单第十联——配舱回单(2)：

Shipper （发货人） SHANGHAI LIXIN INTERNATIONAL TRADING CO., LTD. 5/F, NO. 2230 WEST ZHONG SHAN ROAD, 200235, SHANGHAI, P. R. CHINA TEL：86-21-64391520 FAX：86-21-64391530		D/R No. (编号) CBHU678551100751	速捷 第十联
Consignee （收货人） TO ORDER OF SHIPPER			配舱回单（2）
Notify Party （通知人） PALMAVITO ARTICOLI SPORTIVE S.P.A. VIA G. MAZZINI, 46, 20116 MILANO, ITALY TEL: 39-02-369010 FAX: 39-02-369052			
Pre-carriage by (前程运输)	Place of Receipt (收货地点)		
Ocean Vessel(船名) Voy. No.(航次) COSCO ANTWERP 017W	Port of Loading (装货港) SHANGHAI, CHINA		
Port of Discharge (卸货港) GENOVA, ITALY	Place of Delivery (交货地点)	Final Destination for the Merchant's Reference(目的地)	
Container No. (集装箱号)	Seal No.(封志号) Mark & Nos. (标志与号码)	No. of containers or p'kgs. (箱数或件数)	Kind of Packages; Description of Goods (包装种类与货名)	Gross Weight 毛重(千克)	Measurement 呎码(立方米)
	PALMASPORT SC#10LX-PAS075 GENOVA C/NOS.1-55	55 BALES	100% COTTON DYED TWILL FREIGHT PREPAID	7425.00 KGS	24.75 CBM
TOTAL NUMBER OF CONTAINERS OR PACKAGES (IN WORDS) 集装箱数或件数合计(大写)		SAY FIFTY FIVE BALES ONLY			
FREIGHT & CHARGES (运费与附加费)	Revenue Tons (运费吨)	Rate (运费率)	Per (每)	Prepaid (运费预付)	Collect (到付)
Ex. Rate: (兑换率)	Prepaid at(预付地点) Total Prepaid(预付总额)	Payable at(到付地点) No. of Original B(s)/L (正本提单份数) THREE	Place of Issue(签发地点) SHANGHAI Booking(订舱确认) APPROVED BY		

Particulars Furnished by Merchants (托运人填供详细情况)

Service Type on Receiving ☑-CY, ☐-CFS, ☐-DOOR	Service Type on Delivery ☑-CY, ☐-CFS, ☐-DOOR	Reefer Temperature Required (冷藏温度) °F °C
TYPE OF GOODS (种类)	☑Ordinary ☐Reefer ☐Dangerous ☐Auto. (普通) (冷藏) (危险品) (裸装车辆) ☐Liquid ☐Live Animal ☐Bulk (液体) (活动物) (散装)	危险品	Class: Property: IMDG Code Page: UN NO.

可否转船：NO   可否分批：YES
装　　期：SEP. 30, 2010   效　　期：OCT. 15, 2010
金　　额：USD 80 784.00
制单日期：AUG. 26, 2010

出境货物报检单：

中华人民共和国出入境检验检疫出境货物报检单

报检单位（加盖公章）：	上海立信国际贸易有限公司		*编　号	
报检单位登记号：	3100701626	联系人：林质平　电话：64392478		报检日期：2010年8月28日

发货人	（中文）	上海立信国际贸易有限公司
	（外文）	SHANGHAI LIXIN INTERNATIONAL TRADING CO., LTD.
收货人	（中文）	***
	（外文）	PALMAVITO ARTICOLI SPORTIVE S.P.A.

货物名称(中/外文)	H.S.编码	产地	数/重量	货物总值	包装种类及数量
全棉染色布	52083300.00	浙江省绍兴市	26400米	80784.00美元	55包

运输工具名称号码	船舶 COSCO ANTWERP/017W	贸易方式	一般贸易	货物存放地点	***
合同号	10LX-PAS075	信用证号	2010556TLCU0073	用途	***
发货日期	***	输往国家(地区)	意大利	许可证/审批号	***
启运地	上海口岸	到达口岸	热那亚	生产单位注册号	***
集装箱规格、数量及号码		1个海运20尺普通箱			

合同、信用证订立的检验检疫条款或特殊要求	标记及号码	随附单据（划"✓"或补填）	
检验证书须注明下列内容： CREDIT NUMBER: 2010556TLCU0073	参见发票 LX-PAS10075	☐合同 ☐信用证 ☑发票 ☑换证凭单 ☑装箱单 ☐厂检单	☐包装性能结果单 ☐许可/审批文件 ☐ ☐ ☐ ☐

需要证单名称（划"✓"或补填）				*检验检疫费
☑品质证书	1正1副	☐植物检疫证书	_正_副	总金额（人民币元）
☐重量证书	_正_副	☐熏蒸/消毒证书	_正_副	
☐数量证书	_正_副	☐出境货物换证凭单	_正_副	计费人
☐兽医卫生证书	_正_副	☑出境货物通关单	1正2副	
☐健康证书	_正_副	☐		收费人
☐卫生证书	_正_副	☐		
☐动物卫生证书	_正_副			

报检人郑重声明： 1. 本人被授权报检。 2. 上列填写内容正确属实，货物无伪造或冒用他人的厂名、标志、认证标志，并承担货物质量责任。 签名：林质平	领取证单	
	日期	
	签名	

注：有"*"号栏由出入境检验检疫机关填写　　◆国家出入境检验检疫局制
[1-2 (2000.1.1)]

出境货物换证凭单：

中华人民共和国出入境检验检疫
出境货物换证凭单

类别：	口岸申报换证		编号	330600242716909
发货人	上海立信国际贸易有限公司		标记及号码	
收货人	***			暂无
品 名	全棉染色布			
H.S.编码	52083300.00			
报检数/重量	-26400-米			
包装种类及数量	包-430-			
申报总值	-80784.00-美元			
产 地	浙江省绍兴市	生产单位（注册号）	绍兴轻纺开发公司	
生产日期	2010.8	生产批号	10SXQF0821083	
包装性能检验结果单号	***	合同/信用证号	10LX-PAS075/***	
		运输工具名称及编号	船舶	
输往国家或地区	意大利	集装箱规格及数量	*** ***	
发货日期	***	检验依据	FZ61002-91标准及销售合同	
检验检疫结果	本批货物共55包/26400米，经按FZ61002-91标准，在仓库随机抽取代表性样品3包/1440米，根据检验依据要求进行检验，结果合格。******** 签字：赵邦道　　　　　　　　　　　日期：2010年8月23日			
本单有效期	截止于 2011 年 8 月 22 日			
备注	纺织品标识查验合格			

分批出境核销栏	日期	出境数/重量	结存数/重量	核销人	日期	出境数/重量	结存数/重量	核销人

说明：1. 货物出境时，经口岸检验检疫机关查验货证相符，且符合检验检疫要求的予以签发通关单或换发检验检疫证书；2. 本单不作为国内贸易的品质或其它证明；3. 涂改无效。

A 5432818　　　　　　①办理换证　　　　[5-3（2001.1.1）*1]

商业发票：

SHANGHAI LIXIN INTERNATIONAL TRADING CO., LTD.
5/F, NO. 2230 WEST ZHONG SHAN ROAD, 200235, SHANGHAI, P. R. CHINA
TEL：86-21-64391520　FAX：86-21-64391530

COMMERCIAL INVOICE

TO: PALMAVITO ARTICOLI SPORTIVE S.P.A. VIA G. MAZZINI, 46, 20116 MILANO, ITALY TEL: 39-02-369010　FAX: 39-02-369052	**INVOICE NO:** LX-PAS10075 **INVOICE DATE:** AUG. 25, 2010 **S/C NO:** 10LX-PAS075 **L/C NO:** 2010556TLCU0073
FROM: SHANGHAI, CHINA	**TO:** GENOVA, ITALY

MARKS & NOS.	DESCRIPTION OF GOODS	QUANTITY	UNIT PRICE	AMOUNT
PALMASPORT SC#10LX-PAS075 GENOVA C/NOS.1-55	100% COTTON DYED TWILL "MILKY WAY" ANTIBACTERIAL FINISHED DYED TWILL ART. NO. KJ2001	26400 METERS	CIFC5% GENOVA USD 3.06/METER	 USD 80784.00 TOTAL: USD 80784.00

AS PER SALES CONTRACT NO. 10LX-PAS075 DATED JUL. 21, 2010

TERMS OF DELIVERY: CIFC GENOVA INCLUDING 5 PERCENT COMMISSION

ORIGIN OF THE GOODS: P. R. CHINA

TOTAL AMOUNT IN WORDS: SAY U. S. DOLLARS EIGHTY THOUSAND SEVEN HUNDRED AND EIGHTY FOUR ONLY

TOTAL G.W. / TOTAL N.W.: 7425.00 KGS / 7150.00 KGS
TOTAL PACKAGES: 55 BALES

SHANGHAI LIXIN INTERNATIONAL TRADING CO., LTD.

陈弘毅

(signature)

装箱单：

SHANGHAI LIXIN INTERNATIONAL TRADING CO., LTD.
5/F, NO. 2230 WEST ZHONG SHAN ROAD, 200235, SHANGHAI, P. R. CHINA
TEL：86-21-64391520   FAX：86-21-64391530

PACKING LIST

TO: PALMAVITO ARTICOLI SPORTIVE S.P.A.　　**INVOICE NO:** LX-PAS10075
　　　VIA G. MAZZINI, 46, 20116 MILANO, ITALY　　**INVOICE DATE:** AUG. 25, 2010
　　　TEL: 39-02-369010   FAX: 39-02-369052　　**S/C NO:** 10LX-PAS075
　　　　　　　　　　　　　　　　　　　　　　　L/C NO: 2010556TLCU0073

FROM: SHANGHAI, CHINA　　　**TO:** GENOVA, ITALY

MARKS & NOS.	DESCRIPTION OF GOODS	PACKAGE	QUANTITY	G.W. (KGS)	N.W. (KGS)	MEAS. (CBM)

PALMASPORT　　100% COTTON DYED TWILL
SC#10LX-PAS075
GENOVA
C/NOS.1-55　　ART. NO. KJ2001　 55 BALES 26400 METERS @135.00/7425.00   @130.00/7150.00   @0.45/24.75

　　　　　　　PACKING: 120 METERS IN ONE PIECE,
　　　　　　　　　　　 4 PIECES IN ONE BALE,
　　　　　　　　　　　 TOTAL 55 BALES.

　　　　　　　TOTAL: 55 BALES 26400 METERS   7425.00 KGS   7150.00 KGS   24.75 CBM

　　　　　　　AS PER SALES CONTRACT NO. 10LX-PAS075 DATED JUL. 21, 2010

　　　　　　　TERMS OF DELIVERY: CIFC GENOVA INCLUDING 5 PERCENT COMMISSION

TOTAL PACKAGES IN WORDS: SAY FIFTY FIVE BALES ONLY

SHANGHAI LIXIN INTERNATIONAL TRADING CO., LTD.
　　　　　　　　　　　陈弘毅

　　　　　　　　　　　　(signature)

出境货物通关单：

中华人民共和国出入境检验检疫
出境货物通关单

编号： 310834042802273

1. 发货人 上海立信国际贸易有限公司 ***			5. 标记及唛码 PALMASPORT SC#10LX-PAS075 GENOVA C/NOS.1-55
2. 收货人 ***			
3. 合同/信用证号 10LX-PAS075 / 2010556TLCU0073		4. 输往国家或地区 意大利	
6. 运输工具名称及号码 船舶 COSCO ANTWERP / 017W		7. 发货日期 ***	8. 集装箱规格及数量 1个海运20尺普通箱
9. 货物名称及规格	10. H.S.编码	11. 申报总值	12. 数/重量、包装数量及种类
全棉染色布 *** （以下空白）	52083300.00 *** （以下空白）	*80 784.00 美元 *** （以下空白）	*26 400 米 *55 包 *** （以下空白）

13. 证明

上述货物业经检验检疫，请海关予以放行

本通关单有效期至 二〇一〇 年 九 月 二十 日

签字：岳清风　　　　　　　　　　日期：2010年 8 月 30 日

14. 备注
***

品质检验证书：

中华人民共和国出入境检验检疫
ENTRY-EXIT INSPECTION AND QUARANTINE OF THE PEOPLE'S REPUBLIC OF CHINA

第 1 页共 1 页 Page 1 of 1

编号 No.: 042552078010624

QUALITY INSPECTION CERTIFICATE

发货人 Consignor	SHANGHAI LIXIN INTERNATIONAL TRADING CO., LTD.	
收货人 Consignee	PALMAVITO ARTICOLI SPORTIVE S.P.A.	
品名 Description of Goods	100% COTTON DYED TWILL	标记及号码 Mark & No.
报检数量/重量 Quantity/Weight Declared	-26 400-METERS / -7425-KGS	PALMASPORT SC#10LX-PAS075
包装种类及数量 Number and Type of Packages	-55-BALES	GENOVA C/NOS.1-55
运输工具 Means of Conveyance	COSCO ANTWERP / 017W	

检验结果：
RESULTS OF INSPECTION:

At the request of consignor, our inspectors attended at the warehouse of the consignment on 2010/8/29. In accordance with FZ61002-91 and the relevant state stipulations GB2541 and GB5523, 2 bales were taken and opened at random for visual inspection, from which representative samples were drawn and inspected according to the stipulation mentioned above. The results are as follows:
 Appearance: Pass
 Specifications: Pass
 Quantity: -26 400-METERS, -55-BALES
 Safety: Pass
 Hygienics: Pass

印章 Official Stamp　　签发地点 Place of Issue **SHANGHAI**　　签证日期 Date of Issue **AUG. 30, 2010**

授权签字人 Authorized Officer **XIA SIYU**　　签名 Signature 夏斯语

我们已尽所知和最大能力实施上述检验，不能因我们签发本证书而免除卖方或其他方面根据合同和法律所承担的产品责任和其他责任。
All inspections are carried out conscientiously to the best of our knowledge and ability. This certificate does not in any respect absolve the seller and other related parties from his contractual and legal obligations especially when product quality is concerned.

［洋山商检局根据报检单上"需要证单"的相关要求,当场向立信公司出具了"出境货物通关单"(见第130页),并于两天后签发了"品质检验证书"(见第131页)］

(速捷货代公司的集卡拉着空集装箱至立信公司在闵行华漕镇的仓库装箱后,载着整箱货驶往洋山深水港区的集装箱堆场……)

THINK——理论思考

Think 6-1 在哪些贸易条件下出口商需要办理租船订舱手续?

在 CIF 或 CFR 条件下,租船订舱是卖方的责任之一。如出口货物数量较大,需要整船载运的,则要对外办理租船手续;对出口货物数量不大,不需整船装运的,则安排班轮或租订部分舱位运输。

Think 6-2 出口集装箱货物托运和订舱的流程是怎样的?

(1) 出口商(货主)缮制"出口货物订舱委托书"、商业发票和装箱单,一并交给货运代理委托其向船公司订舱。

(2) 货运代理收到出口商的委托书后,缮制"集装箱货物海运托运单"(俗称"十联单"),向船公司订舱。

(3) 船公司接受订舱后,在"十联单"上标注船名、航次和 D/R 编号,加盖船公司签单章并作装船日期批注(或电告装船日期),然后将"十联单"中第五至第十联返还给货运代理。

(4) 货运代理留存"十联单"的第八联后,将第五、第六、第七、第九、第十联交给出口商。

"集装箱货物海运托运单",一式十联,因而又被称为"十联单",各联的名称分别为:

第一联:集装箱货物托运单(货主留底);
第二联:集装箱货物托运单(船代留底);
第三联:运费通知(1);
第四联:运费通知(2);
第五联:装货单 场站收据副本(SHIPPING ORDER, S/O);
        附页   缴纳出口货物港务申请书;
第六联:场站收据副本 大副联;
第七联:场站收据(DOCK RECEIPT, D/R);
第八联:货代留底;
第九联:配舱回单(1);
第十联:配舱回单(2)。

"十联单"虽有多联,然而对于出口商而言,其核心单据为配舱回单、装货单和场站收据,分别说明如下:

第九联配舱回单,是对订舱委托的反馈,船公司完成配载后会在配舱回单上注明船名、航次和提单号码返还货运代理。

第五联装货单(Shipping Order, S/O)又称关单,是船公司或其代理向船上负责人(船长或大副)和集装箱装卸作业区签发的一种通知其接受装货的指示文件。在准备装货前,托运人必须先向海关办理出口报关手续。装货单是报关时必须向海关提交的单据之一。经海关查验后,在装货单上加盖放行章,托运人才能凭此装货单要求装货。这也是装货单习称关单的缘由。

第七联场站收据(Dock Receipt, D/R),是指承运人委托集装箱堆场、集装箱货运站或内陆站在收到整箱货或拼箱货后签发的收据。场站收据的作用类似于传统运输(件杂货、散货运输)中的大副收据(Mate's Receipt, M/R),托运人可凭经签收的 D/R 向船公司或其代理换取正本提单。

第六联场站收据副本大副联,供港区配载使用,由港区或由大副留存。

Think 6-3 出口货物订舱委托书缮制有哪些要点?

出口企业在备妥货物、落实信用证后,即可根据合同和信用证的规定,结合船公司的船期表选择合适的船公司(承运人)填写海运出口托运单(又称订舱委托书),列明出口货物的名称、件数、包装、唛头、毛重、尺码、目的港和最后装运日期等内容,作为订舱的依据。该托运单一式数份,分别用于外轮代理公司留存、装货单、收货单、配舱回单、运费通知、托运人和外运公司留底等。

海洋运输有两种方式:传统散货运输、现代集装箱运输。两种运输方式有不同格式托运单。

(一) 散货运输托运单

散货运输托运单是在装货单和收货单(大副收据)基础上发展而成的一种多功能单据,其内容及填制方法如下:

(1) SHIPPER(托运人)。此处一般填写出口合同的卖方,信用证支付方式下应与信用证受益人的名称、地址一致。

(2) NO S/S(编号、船名)。此为托运单的顺序编号,船名可留给船方安排船只舱位后填写。

(3) FOR(目的港)。按合同/信用证规定填写目的港具体名称,遇世界重名港口时,应在港口名称后面加注国名。

(4) MARKS & NOS (标记及号码)。本栏应按合同或信用证规定的内容和形式填写,如没有规定,可由出口商自己编制,没有唛头则填"N/M"。

(5) QUANTITY(件数)。按最大包装实际件数填写,应与唛头中的件数一致。

(6) DESCRIPTION OF GOODS(货名):本栏填写货物大类名称或统称,与发票(信用证)中的货名一致。运费到付(FREIGHT TO COLLECT)或运费预付(FREIGHT PREPAID)也可借用此栏加以注明。

(7) WEIGHT(重量)。本栏内容是计算船只受载吨位和运费的基础资料,以千克为单位,须分别填写整批货物的毛重和净重。

(8) MEASUREMENT(尺码)。本栏填写整批货物的体积实数,以立方米为单位,是计算运费的主要依据之一,计算应务求准确。

(9) PARTIAL SHIPMENT,TRANSSHIPMENT(分批转船)。本栏应严格按合同或信用证填写"允许"或"不允许"。

(10) DATE OF SHIPMENT,DATE OF EXPIRY(装运期、有效期)。本栏根据信用证规定的最迟装运期和议付有效期分别填写。

(11) CONSIGNEE(收货人)。本栏一般根据信用证要求填写"TO ORDER/TO ORDER OF SHIPPER"。

(12) NOTIFY(通知人)。本栏填写接受船方发出货到通知的人的名称与地址。

(13) 备注。本栏填写信用证中有关运输方面的特殊要求。

(二) 集装箱货物托运单

集装箱货物托运单与海运散货出口托运单基本相同,发货人在办理集装箱货物托运时,除应填写与海运散货出口托运单相似栏目内容外,还应标明托运货物的交接方式,如 CY—CY、CFS—CFS 等和集装箱货物的种类如普通、冷藏、液体等。

Think 6-4 商业发票缮制要点有哪些?

商业发票简称发票是出口商对进口商开立的发货价目清单,它全面反映合同内容,是装运货物的总说明。主要供进口商凭以收货、支付货款和进出口双方记账、报关、纳税的依据,它是各种单据的核心。

商业发票无统一的格式,但所需填制的内容却大体相同。

(一) 商业发票的结构

发票在结构上分三部分:

(1) 首文。包括出口商的名称地址、"INVOICE"发票字样、合同/信用证号码、发票号码、签发日期、发票抬头人、起运地、目的地等。这些内容一般都是印好的固定格式,后面留有空格以便填写。

(2) 主文。即发票的主要部分,主要描述商品的全面情况,如商品名称、规格、数量、包装、价格及其条件、货物的总值、唛头等。

(3) 结尾。据来证所需列明进口许可证号、买方有关参考号、特殊证明条款受益人签章等。

(二) 商业发票的缮制方法

(1) 出口商的名称地址。一般在发票的正上方表示,多事先印好无需另行填写。

(2) 发票名称。一般多事先印好"INVOICE"字样,无需在它的前面加"商业"(COMMERCIAL)字样(来证要求"详细发票"、"证实发票"时,则需在 INVOICE 前加"详细"、"证实"字样)。

(3) 出票日期、地点。发票是全套单据中出票最早的,其日期只要在合同签订之后,提单签发日期之前即可;出票地点为受益人所在地(议付所在地)。

(4) 发票号码。一般由出口公司自行编制。汇票、装箱单、托运单等出口商出具的单据一般都使用发票号码。为结汇方便,也可使用银行编制的统一编号(BP 号)。

(5) 起运地、目的地(FROM … TO …)。按货物运输的实际情况填写(与信用证一致),如 FROM TIANJIN TO LONDON。

(6) 抬头人。一般填写买方(信用证申请人)名称地址。

(7) 唛头及编码(MARKS AND NOS)。按合同、信用证规定填制,合同、信用证规定无规定时,由受益人自定(收货人代号、目的港、件数等组成),没有唛头时,填写无唛头("N/M")字样。

(8) 品名及货物描述(DESCRIPTION)。本栏包括货物的名称、品质、规格、数量包装等内容,应严格与合同/信用证一致。信用证未规定的内容尽量少打,以免画蛇添足。

(9) 价格(PRICE)。包括术语、单价和总值,是发票的主要内容,须正确填写。发票上有两项或两项以上商品时,须分别列出每一项的金额小计,最后列出总额。信用证要求列明折扣或佣金时,须在有关小计或总金额下列出所扣除折扣或佣金的百分率和金额,然后列出净值。

(10) 自由处理区。自由处理区位于发票格式的下方,用于表达其他栏目不能表达的内容。如:要求在发票上注明生产厂家名称、许可证号,其他文件的参考号或对发票内容正确性、真实性及货物原产地声明等。来证有此要求,必须照办,但缮打的文字一般应根据需要予以适当编写,不可完全照抄原文。

(11) 签发人的签字盖章。国外来证常要求出口商提供签署的商业发票,如果来证有此要求,出口商提供的发票商必须有出口商的签字盖章。

Think 6-5 装箱单缮制要点有哪些?

装箱单又称包装单,是表明出口货物的包装形式、包装内容、数量、重量、体积或件数的单据。其主要用途作为海关、进出口商等验货的凭据和商业发票的补充,装箱单须按装箱情况详细列明商品包装的具体情况,如名称、数量、花色品种搭配、商品包装尺码、毛净重等,其他项目内容填写与发票相同。

Think 6-6 如何理解出口货物报检在进出口贸易中的重要性?

按《进出口商品检验法》规定,凡属于《实行检验商品种类表》中需要法定检验和合同或信用证规定由商检机构检验出证的出口商品,出口单位在装运前必须到商检机构申请检验。检验合格者,商检机构在出口货物报关单上加盖放行章,海关凭以放行,非法定检验但须商检出证的商品,没有经过商检机构检验和发放相应证书,银行不予结汇。可见商品检验在进出口贸易中的重要。

Think 6-7 出口货物报检主要经过哪些流程?

(1) 出口商填写"出口商品检验申请表",以书面方式向商检部门提出商品检验申请(报检)。

(2) 商检部门接受出口商商品检验申请,对出口商品进行检验。

(3) 商检部门按照检验结果进行出证。

Think 6-8 出口报检需提供哪些资料和单据?

出口商品报检时,一般需提供以下单证、资料:

(1) 出口销售合同或销售确认书。

(2) 信用证及或有关函电。

(3) 厂检结果单、出口商品预检结果单、出口商品检验检疫换证凭单等。

Think 6-9　出口货物报检单缮制要点有哪些?

出口商品检验申请单由各口岸进出口商品检验局统一印发,是出口商申请出口商品检验和商检部门接受检验的依据。出口商品检验申请单一般用中文填写(特别要求的除外)。填写时凡未作说明的栏目按实际情况填写或打"对号",具体如下:

(1) 报检单位。填写报检单位全称并加盖公章或报检专用章(或附单位介绍信)。

(2) 报检日期。填写报检当天日期。

(3) 报检号。商检机构受理报检的编号,由商检机构受理报检人员填写。

(4) 联系人及电话。按实际填写。

(5) 发货人。填写合同上卖方或信用证受益人名称(全称并中英文对照)。

(6) 受货人。填写合同上的买方或信用证的开证人名称(全称并中英文对照)。

(7) 商品品名。按合同、信用证中所列的名称填写(中英文对照)。

(8) 报检重量毛/净:填写实际报检商品总的毛重和净重。

(9) 报检数量。按实际申请检验数量填写并注明计量单位,如××件。

(10) 包装情况。按实际情况填写使用的包装材料及包装情况是否良好,如"纸箱包装,包装完好"。

(11) 贸易方式。在"正常贸易"或"三来一补"下划"√"或在其他贸易方式下填写其他具体贸易方式。

(12) 商品编码。按《商品分类及编码协调制度》8位数字填写。

(13) 合同/发票总值。按实际情况填写。

(14) 输往国别。填写出口货物的最终销售国。

(15) 卫生注册/质量许可证号。只在出口需要卫生注册/质量许可商品时按实际填写。

(16) 合同号、信用证号、存货地点。按实际情况填写。

(17) 需要商检单证。需要单证后划"√"。

(18) 合同信用证对商检条款的特殊要求。合同信用证有特殊要求时按实际要求填写,例如:信用证中要求不列明收货人或收货人栏需以敬启者(To Whom It May Concern)、凭指示(To Order)出证的,都应填写在此栏内,以便商检机构出证时参考,使报检人顺利结汇。

(19) 标记及号码。按实际情况填写。

Think 6-10　缮制商检证书时需要注意哪些问题?

缮制商检证书时需要注意:

(1) 出具的商检证书应符合信用证规定。在信用证未规定商检证书的出具人时,可以由任何人包括信用证的受益人出具,但如果信用证规定了由指定的人出具,则出具人必须要与信用证规定一致。

(2) 证书内容符合信用证规定,并且与发票或其他单据的记载一致。检验证书上的货物品名、规格、数量、包装单位等都要和信用证、商业发票及其他单据的记载相符,特别要注意货物描述的填写必须一致。在检验结果一栏中,除非信用证授权,否则不能有对货物、规格、品质、包装等内容的不良记载。

(3) 注意发货人与收货人的填写。一般情况下,检验证书中的"发货人"应是信用证的受益人。但是,当实际发货人不是受益人而是第三方时,证书中的发货人一栏应与提单中的"托运人"栏相同。收货人的填写应该和提单上的"收货人"名称相同。如果提单上的收货人是银行、空白抬头(to order)或凭开证行指示(to order of the issuing bank),依惯例可将收货人填写为"to whom it may concern"。

(4) 检验证书的签发日期最好早于提单日期。检验证书必须要有签发的日期。尽管该日期表明的是证书的出具时间,但是为了避免纠纷,该日期最好不迟于提单的装运日期。在实际业务中,为了保险起见,当检验证书的签发日期迟于提单日期时,应当在证书中加注检验行为发生于装运日之前或装运日当天的文字表述。

如果信用证要求提交"装运前检验证书",则所出具的单据要通过标题或内容来表明检验行为是发生在装运日之前或装运日当天。

一般检验证书的签发日期早于提单日期,但是要注意检验证书的有效期。如果检验日期太早,超过了有效期才装船,会遭到收货人的异议,甚至会要求重新检验。

(5) 证书的签字要与信用证规定一致。检验证书自身的性质要求其必须签字。如果信用证对签字的方式、指定的签字人有具体规定,所提交的单据应予照办。如果出口方不能接受这些规定,应在审证时提出修改。

Think 6-11 如何掌握出口商品报检的时间?

出口商品报检时间,最迟于报关或装运出口前10天向商检机构办理。对检验周期较长的商品如羊绒等应加上相应的抽样、检验、化验等工作的时间。

ACT——模拟训练

Act 6-1 出口商缮制订舱单据

2010年11月30日,钱晓俊收到CHASE MANHATTAN BANK银行开来的信用证修改书,经审核,符合海纳公司的改证要求,并且保险险别由"一切险加战争险"改为"平安险"。12月10日,钱晓俊接到永康采薇杯业公司通知货物已生产完毕,遂委托上海众联国际货运有限公司向船公司订舱。

请以钱晓俊的身份,缮制以下订舱单据:
(1) 海运出口订舱委托书(编号:BNHN-GD10203、货物备妥日期:12月15日、预订船公司:SINOTRANS、预订装船时间:12月25日)。
(2) 商业发票(编号:INVHN-GD10174)。
(3) 装箱单。

海运出口订舱委托书：

上海海纳进出口有限公司
SHANGHAI HAINA IMPORT & EXPORT COMPANY LIMITED
RM. 905 YONG AN MANSION, NO. 12 HUASHAN RD., SHANGHAI, P. R. CHINA
TEL: 0086-21-54105623   FAX: 0086-21-54742511   E-MAIL：SALES@HAINACO.COM

海运出口订舱委托书

发货人： Shipper:			编　号	
			日　期	
收货人： Consignee:			合同号	
通知人： Notify Party:			信用证号	
			贸易国别	

运费支付方式		是否要求代报关	□ 是　☑ 否	提单份数	
起运港		目的港		可否转运		可否分批	

标记唛码	总件数及包装名称	货物描述	总毛重	总体积	成交条件

装箱方式	□ FCL □ LCL	门点装箱地点	宝山区杨行镇杨鑫路 836 号甲		
箱型箱量			电话	36121494	联系人	韩音德
货物备妥日期		特种集装箱要求		□ 冷藏货	□ 危险品
备注					

商业发票：

SHANGHAI HAINA IMPORT & EXPORT COMPANY LIMITED
RM. 905 YONG AN MANSION, NO. 12 HUASHAN RD., SHANGHAI, P. R. CHINA
TEL: 0086-21-54105623   FAX: 0086-21-54742511   E-MAIL：SALES@HAINACO.COM

COMMERCIAL INVOICE

TO:

INVOICE NO:
INVOICE DATE:
S/C NO:
L/C NO:
L/C ISSUED BY:

FROM: TO:

MARKS & NOS.	DESCRIPTION OF GOODS	QUANTITY	UNIT PRICE	AMOUNT

TOTAL AMOUNT IN WORDS:

TOTAL G.W. / TOTAL N.W.:
TOTAL PACKAGES:

SHANGHAI HAINA IMPORT & EXPORT COMPANY LIMITED
周致君

(signature)

装箱单：

SHANGHAI HAINA IMPORT & EXPORT COMPANY LIMITED
RM. 905 YONG AN MANSION, NO. 12 HUASHAN RD., SHANGHAI, P. R. CHINA
TEL: 0086-21-54105623   FAX: 0086-21-54742511   E-MAIL：SALES@HAINACO.COM

PACKING LIST

TO:

INVOICE NO:
INVOICE DATE:
S/C NO:
L/C NO:
L/C ISSUED BY:

FROM: TO:

MARKS & NOS.	DESCRIPTION OF GOODS	PACKAGE	QUANTITY	G.W. (KGS)	N.W. (KGS)	MEAS. (CBM)

TOTAL PACKAGES IN WORDS:

SHANGHAI HAINA IMPORT & EXPORT COMPANY LIMITED
周致君
(signature)

Act 6-2　出口商缮制报检单据

12月13日，钱晓俊收到众联货代公司返还的配舱回单后，即向出入境检验检疫局办理出口货物报检手续。

请以钱晓俊的身份，缮制出境货物报检单（H. S. 编码：96170090.00、船名/航次：SINOTRANS SEATTLE/045E）。

出境货物报检单：

中华人民共和国出入境检验检疫
出境货物报检单

报检单位（加盖公章）： 上海海纳进出口有限公司　　　*编　号　_____

报检单位登记号： 3100022150　联系人： 徐可彤　电话： 54107535　报检日期：　年　月　日

发货人	（中文）	
	（外文）	
收货人	（中文）	
	（外文）	

货物名称(中/外文)	H.S.编码	产地	数/重量	货物总值	包装种类及数量

运输工具名称号码		贸易方式		货物存放地点	
合同号		信用证号		用途	
发货日期		输往国家(地区)		许可证/审批号	
启运地		到达口岸		生产单位注册号	

集装箱规格、数量及号码

合同、信用证订立的检验检疫条款或特殊要求	标记及号码	随附单据（划"✓"或补填）	
		□合同	□包装性能结果单
		□信用证	□许可/审批文件
		□发票	□
		□换证凭单	□
		□装箱单	□
		□厂检单	□

需要证单名称（划"✓"或补填）		*检验检疫费	
□品质证书　　　正　副 □重量证书　　　正　副 □数量证书　　　正　副 □兽医卫生证书　正　副 □健康证书　　　正　副 □卫生证书　　　正　副 □动物卫生证书　正　副	□植物检疫证书　　　正　副 □熏蒸/消毒证书　　正　副 □出境货物换证凭单　正　副 □出境货物通关单　　正　副 □	总金额 （人民币元）	
		计费人	
		收费人	

报检人郑重声明： 1. 本人被授权报检。 2. 上列填写内容正确属实，货物无伪造或冒用他人的厂名、标志、认证标志，并承担货物质量责任。 签名：*徐可彤*	领取证单
	日期
	签名

注：有"*"号栏由出入境检验检疫机关填写　　　　　　◆国家出入境检验检疫局制

[1-2 (2000.1.1)]

DISCUSS——个案讨论

Discuss 6-1

在本实训 ACT 环节中,12月11日,当众联货代公司收到海纳公司的订舱委托后,缮制"集装箱货物海运托运单"(十联单),向"中外运集装箱运输有限公司"(SINOTRANS)订舱。根据 Act 6-1 中的订舱单据,货代公司该如何缮制十联单(编号:SNLU3743520522,船公司已标注船名、航次,集装箱交接方式: CY/CY)?

集装箱货物托运单第九联——配舱回单(1):

Shipper (发货人)				D/R No. (编号)		众联
Consignee (收货人)				配舱回单(1)		第九联
Notify Party (通知人)						
Pre-carriage by (前程运输)		Place of Receipt (收货地点)				
Ocean Vessel(船名) Voy. No.(航次)		Port of Loading (装货港)				
Port of Discharge (卸货港)		Place of Delivery (交货地点)		Final Destination for the Merchant's Reference(目的地)		
Container No. (集装箱号)	Seal No.(封志号) Mark & Nos. (标志与号码)	No. of containers or p'kgs. (箱数或件数)	Kind of Packages; Description of Goods (包装种类及货名)	Gross Weight 毛重(千克)		Measurement 呎码(立方米)
TOTAL NUMBER OF CONTAINERS OR PACKAGES (IN WORDS) 集装箱数或件数合计(大写)						
FREIGHT & CHARGES (运费与附加费)		Revenue Tons (运费吨)	Rate (运费率)	Per (每)	Prepaid (运费预付)	Collect (到付)
Ex. Rate: (兑换率)	Prepaid at(预付地点)	Payable at(到付地点)		Place of Issue(签发地点)		
	Total Prepaid(预付总额)	No. of Original B(s)/L (正本提单份数)		Booking(订舱确认) APPROVED BY		
Service Type on Receiving □-CY, □-CFS, □-DOOR		Service Type on Delivery □-CY, □-CFS, □-DOOR		Reefer Temperature Required (冷藏温度)	°F	°C
TYPE OF GOODS (种类)	□Ordinary (普通) □Liquid (液体)	□Reefer (冷藏) □Live Animal (活动物)	□Dangerous (危险品) □Bulk (散装)	□Auto. (裸装车辆)	危险品	Class: Property: IMDG Code Page: UN NO.
可否转船: 装 期: 金 额: 制单日期:		可否分批: 效 期:				

Discuss 6-2

在本实训 ACT 环节中,12 月 13 日,出入境检验检疫局收到海纳公司的出境报检单据,经审核后于 12 月 15 日签发"出境货物通关单"。根据 Act 6-2 中的出境货物报检单,商检局该如何缮制出境通关单(编号:310233480059197)?

出境货物通关单:

中华人民共和国出入境检验检疫 出境货物通关单			
		编号:	
1. 发货人		5. 标记及唛码	
2. 收货人			
3. 合同/信用证号		4. 输往国家或地区	
6. 运输工具名称及号码		7. 发货日期	8. 集装箱规格及数量
9. 货物名称及规格	10. H.S.编码	11. 申报总值	12. 数/重量、包装数量及种类
13. 证明 上述货物业经检验检疫,请海关予以放行。 本通关单有效期至　　　年　　月　　日 签字:陈怀德　　　　　　　　　日期:　年　月　日			
14. 备注			

· 143 ·

情景模拟实训七

履行合同三——投保与原产地认证

 LOOK——情景示范

（李新协助完成出境报检手续，取得"出境货物通关单"和"品质检验证书"后，向王经理请教）

李新：王经理，我们公司与意大利客户的销售合同中采用的是 CIF 术语，接下来我应该去办理投保手续了吧？

王经理：货物到码头仓库了吗？

李新：我刚接到货代的通知，集装箱已经进入洋山港区的码头堆场了。

王经理：我问你，保险公司对保险责任的起讫，一般是怎么规定的？

李新：一般采用 Warehouse to Warehouse Clause——仓到仓条款，也就是说，保险单从货物运离起运地仓库时开始生效，直到货物运抵目的地仓库时效力终止，其中的整个时段都属于保险公司的责任期间。

王经理：对集装箱货物来说，进堆场就相当于进入起运地仓库，现在的确应该抓紧去办理投保手续啦，你快去制作投保单吧！

李新：遵命！

[20 分钟后，李新将制作完成的投保单连同商业发票(见第 145、第 146 页)呈送王经理审核]

王经理：我问你，投保单中的"投保金额"88863 美元是怎么得出来的？

李新：根据信用证要求，投保金额是把商业发票金额乘以投保加成 110%，得到 88862.4 美元，为了符合保险公司的惯例，再用"进一取整"的方法进到 88863 美元。

王经理：还有，"提单号"从哪儿得来？

李新：哦，配舱回单右上角的 D/R No. 通常就是今后的海运提单编号。

王经理：很好！你去保险公司办理投保吧。

李新：Yes sir！

[李新备齐投保单及商业发票，至中国人民财产保险公司上海分公司办理投保手续……第二天，李新收到了保险公司签发的保险单(见第 147 页)，立即呈送王经理]

王经理：好的，接下来你的工作是申办"原产地证明"。我又要考你了，原产地证明有什么作用啊？

货物运输保险投保单：

PICC 中国人民财产保险股份有限公司　上海市分公司
PICC Property and Casualty Company Limited, Shanghai Branch

地址：中国上海市中山南路 700 号　　　　　　　　　　　　电话(TEL)：021-63773000
ADD: No. 700 Zhongshan Road(S) Shanghai, China　　　　传真(FAX)：021-63764678
邮编(Post Code)：200010

货物运输保险投保单
APPLICATION FORM FOR CARGO TRANSPORTATION INSURANCE

被保险人： INSURED:	SHANGHAI LIXIN INTERNATIONAL TRADING CO., LTD.
发票号(INVOICE NO.)	LX-PAS10075
合同号(CONTRACT NO.)	10LX-PAS075
信用证号(L/C NO.)	2010556TLCU0073
发票金额(INVOICE AMOUNT)	USD 80 784.00　　　投保加成(PLUS)　　10 %

兹有下列物品向中国人民财产保险股份有限公司　上海分　公司投保。(INSURANCE IS REQUIRED ON THE FOLLOWING COMMODITIES:)

标　记 MARKS & NOS.	包装及数量 QUANTITY	保险货物项目 DESCRIPTION OF GOODS	保险金额 AMOUNT INSURED
AS PER INVOICE NO. LX-PAS10075	55 BALES	100% COTTON DYED TWILL	USD88863.00

启运日期： DATE OF COMMENCEMENT:	SEP. 10, 2010	装载运输工具： PER CONVEYANCE:	COSCO ANTWERP 017W
自 FROM	SHANGHAI, CHINA	经 VIA　　　　　至 　　　　　　　TO	GENOVA, ITALY
提单号： B/L NO.:	CBHU678551100751	赔款偿付地点： CLAIM PAYMENT AT:	GENOVA

投保险别：(PLEASE INDICATE THE CONDITIONS &/OR SPECIAL COVERAGES)
COVERING INSTITUTE CARGO CLAUSES (C)

备注：(REMARKS)
1）须两份正本保单
2）保单须注明信用证号码 2010556TLCU0073

请如实告知下列情况：(如"是"在[ ]中打"×") IF ANY, PLEASE MARK "×":

1、货物种类　普通[×]　散装[ ]　冷藏[ ]　液体[ ]　活动物[ ]　机器/汽车[ ]　危险品等级[ ]
　　GOODS　　ORDINARY　BULK　REEFER　LIQUID　LIVE ANIMAL　MACHINE/AUTO　DANGEROUS CLASS
2、集装箱种类　普通[×]　开顶[ ]　框架[ ]　平板[ ]　冷藏[ ]
　　CONTAINER　ORDINARY　OPEN　FRAME　FLAT　REFRIGERATOR
3、转运工具　海轮[ ]　飞机[ ]　驳船[ ]　火车[ ]　汽车[ ]
　　BY TRANSIT　SHIP　PLANE　BARGE　TRAIN　TRUCK
4、船舶资料　船籍[ ]　　　　　　　　船龄[ ]
　　PARTICULAR OF SHIP　REGISTRY　　　　AGE

备注：被保险人确认本保险合同条款和内容已经完全了解　　投保人(签名盖章)APPLICANT'S SIGNATURE
THE ASSURED CONFIRMS HEREWITH THE TERMS AND
CONDITIONS OF THESE INSURANCE CONTRACT FULLY　　　李新
UNDERSTOOD.

投保日期：(DATE)　SEP. 1, 2010　　　　　电话：(TEL) 021-64391520
　　　　　　　　　　　　　　　　　　　　　地址：(ADD) 5/F, NO. 2230 WEST ZHONG SHAN
　　　　　　　　　　　　　　　　　　　　　　　　　　ROAD, 200235, SHANGHAI, P. R. CHINA

本公司自用(FOR OFFICE USE ONLY)

经办人　　　　　　　　　　　核保人　　　　　　　　　　NO.: PICC 0729638
Made By　　　　　　　　　　Checked By

商业发票：

SHANGHAI LIXIN INTERNATIONAL TRADING CO., LTD.
5/F, NO. 2230 WEST ZHONG SHAN ROAD, 200235, SHANGHAI, P. R. CHINA
TEL：86-21-64391520　FAX：86-21-64391530

COMMERCIAL INVOICE

TO: PALMAVITO ARTICOLI SPORTIVE S.P.A.   **INVOICE NO:** LX-PAS10075
VIA G. MAZZINI, 46, 20116 MILANO, ITALY   **INVOICE DATE:** AUG. 25, 2010
TEL: 39-02-369010　FAX: 39-02-369052   **S/C NO:** 10LX-PAS075
                                                                      L/C NO: 2010556TLCU0073

FROM: SHANGHAI, CHINA   **TO:** GENOVA, ITALY

MARKS & NOS.	DESCRIPTION OF GOODS	QUANTITY	UNIT PRICE	AMOUNT
PALMASPORT SC#10LX-PAS075 GENOVA C/NOS.1-55	100% COTTON DYED TWILL "MILKY WAY" ANTIBACTERIAL FINISHED DYED TWILL ART. NO. KJ2001	 26400 METERS	CIFC 5% GENOVA USD 3.06/METER	 USD 80784.00
			TOTAL:	USD 80784.00

AS PER SALES CONTRACT NO. 10LX-PAS075 DATED JUL. 21, 2010

TERMS OF DELIVERY: CIFC GENOVA INCLUDING 5 PERCENT COMMISSION

ORIGIN OF THE GOODS: P. R. CHINA

TOTAL AMOUNT IN WORDS: SAY U. S. DOLLARS EIGHTY THOUSAND SEVEN HUNDRED
                                          AND EIGHTY FOUR ONLY

TOTAL G.W. / TOTAL N.W.:   7425.00 KGS / 7150.00 KGS
TOTAL PACKAGES: 55 BALES

SHANGHAI LIXIN INTERNATIONAL TRADING CO., LTD.
陈弘毅
(signature)

货物运输保险单：

PICC
中国人保财险

货物运输保险单
CARGO TRANSPORTATION INSURANCE POLICY

总公司设于北京　　一九四九年创立
Head Office Beijing　　Established in 1949

发票号(INVOICE NO.) LX-PAS10075	保单号次 POLICY NO. PYIE201014258770335917
合同号(CONTRACT NO.) 10LX-PAS075	
信用证号(L/C NO.) 2010556TLCU0073	
被保险人： INSURED: SHANGHAI LIXIN INTERNATIONAL TRADING CO., LTD.	

中国人民财产保险股份有限公司(以下简称公司)根据被保险人的要求，由被保险人向本公司缴付约定的保险费，按照本保险单承保险别和背面所载条款与下列特款承保下述货物运输保险，特立本保险单。
THIS POLICY OF INSURANCE WITNESSES THAT PICC PROPERTY AND CASUALTY COMPANY LIMITED (HEREINAFTER CALLED "THE COMPANY") AT THE REQUEST OF THE INSURED AND IN CONSIDERATION OF THE AGREED PREMIUM PAID TO THE COMPANY BY THE INSURED, UNDERTAKES TO INSURE THE UNDERMENTIONED GOODS IN TRANSPORTATION SUBJECT TO THE CONDITIONS OF THIS POLICY AS PER THE CLAUSES PRINTED OVERLEAF AND OTHER SPECIAL CLAUSES ATTACHED HEREON.

标记 MARKS & NOS	包装及数量 QUANTITY	保险货物项目 DESCRIPTION OF GOODS	保险金额 AMOUNT INSURED
AS PER INVOICE NO. LX-PAS10075	55 BALES	100% COTTON DYED TWILL	USD88863.00
		CREDIT NUMBER: 2010556TLCU0073	

总保险金额 TOTAL AMOUNT INSURED: SAY U.S. DOLLARS EIGHTY EIGHT THOUSAND EIGHT HUNDRED AND SIXTY THREE ONLY

保费： PERMIUM: AS ARRANGED	启运日期 DATE OF COMMENCEMENT: AS PER B/L	装载运输工具： PER CONVEYANCE: COSCO ANTWERP/ 017W
自 FROM: SHANGHAI, CHINA	经 VIA	至 TO: GENOVA, ITALY

承保险别：
CONDITIONS:

COVERING INSTITUTE CARGO CLAUSES (C)

所保货物，如发生保险单项下可能引起索赔的损失或损坏，应立即通知本公司下述代理人查勘。如有索赔，应向本公司提交保单正本(本保险单共有 **贰** 份正本)及有关文件。如一份正本已用于索赔，其余正本自动失效。
IN THE EVENT OF LOSS OR DAMAGE WITCH MAY RESULT IN A CLAIM UNDER THIS POLICY, IMMEDIATE NOTICE MUST BE GIVEN TO THE COMPANY'S AGENT AS MENTIONED HEREUNDER. CLAIMS, IF ANY, ONE OF THE ORIGINAL POLICY WHICH HAS BEEN ISSUED IN **2** ORIGINAL(S) TOGETHER WITH THE RELEVANT DOCUMENTS SHALL BE SURRENDERED TO THE COMPANY. IF ONE OF THE ORIGINAL POLICY HAS BEEN ACCOMPLISHED. THE OTHERS TO BE VOID.

中国人民财产保险股份有限公司 上海市分公司
PICC Property and Casualty Company Limited,
Shanghai Branch

赔款偿付地点
CLAIM PAYABLE AT/IN　GENOVA IN USD

出单日期
ISSUING DATE　SEP. 2, 2010

钟退思

GENERAL MANAGER

李新：原产地证明相当于货物的"户籍证"，因为各国对进口商品普遍实行差别关税，所以进口国海关要求出口商出具货物的原产地证明已经成为国际惯例。

王经理：我国哪几种原产地证明比较常用啊，签发机关分别是哪里啊？

李新：我国比较常用的原产地证明有两种：一是由出入境检验检疫局或中国国际贸易促进委员会签发的一般原产地证明，简写为 C/O；二是由出入境检验检疫局签发的普惠制原产地证明格式 A，简写为 GSP Form A。

王经理：好，深得吾意。我们这笔业务的信用证要求出 Form A，是因为意大利是全球三十多个给予中国普遍优惠制的国家之一，所以这份 Form A 能让我们享受进口的优惠关税。小李，你去制作 Form A 申请书和 Form A 吧。

李新：At your service!

[半小时后，李新将制作完成的 Form A 申请书、Form A，连同商业发票(见第 149~151 页)呈送王经理审核]

王经理：做得挺到位。我有个问题要问你。在 Form A 申请书中，你是怎么得出"商品 FOB 总值"的？

李新：我把 CIF 总值减去海运费总值和保险费总值，就能得到 FOB 总值。具体来说，这笔合同的 CIF 总值是 80784 美元，一个 20 英尺集装箱的包箱费是 1800 美元，所以海运费就是 1800 美元，保险费的计算过程是 $3.06 \times 26400 \times (1+10\%) \times 0.15\%$，等于 133.29 美元。因此，FOB 总值是 $80784-1800-133.29=78850.71$ 美元。

王经理：正确。

李新：王经理，我对 Form A 第 9 格不是很确定，想请教您一下。

王经理：说说看你的想法。

李新：第 9 格填"毛重或其他数量"，我觉得如果照这个字面表述，往往不容易确定何时填毛重，何时填其他数量。我是根据商业发票中的计量单位来确定的，比如这笔业务的计量单位是"米"，Form A 第 9 格的数量也填"米"。不知道我的想法对不对？

王经理：完全正确，说得非常好！你一直挺会动脑筋，好好干，你一定能成为一名优秀的外贸业务员！

李新：多谢王经理的鼓励！我从你身上学到了很多啊。

王经理：准备去商检局申办 Form A 吧。

李新：明白！

[李新备齐 Form A 申请书、Form A 及商业发票，至出入境检验检疫局申请办理认证手续……

第二天，李新收到了出入境检验检疫局签章的 Form A(见第 152 页)，立即呈送王经理]

王经理：原产地证明认证之后就要准备出口报关了，你要多向报关运输部的陈老师学习啊！

李新：知道了。

普惠制原产地证明书申请书：

普惠制原产地证明书申请书

申请单位（加盖公章）：　　　　　　　　　　　　证书号：G10/248101/L640
申请人郑重声明：　　　　　　　　　　　　　　　注册号：248101
　　本人是被正式授权代表本企业办理和签署本申请书的。
　　本申请书及普惠制原产地证明书格式A所列内容正确无误，如发现弄虚作假，冒充格式A所列货物，擅改证书，自愿接受签发机构的处罚并承担法律责任。现将有关情况申报如下：

生产单位	绍兴轻纺开发公司	生产单位联系人电话	0575-85780676
商品名称 （中英文）	全棉染色布 / 100% COTTON DYED TWILL	H.S.税目号 （以八位数码计）	5208.3300
商品FOB总值（以美元计）	78850.71美元	发票号	LX-PAS10075
最终销售国	意大利	证书种类划"√"	（　）加急证书　　（√）普通证书
货物拟出运日期			SEP. 10, 2010

贸易方式和企业性质（请在适用处划"√"）

正常贸易 C	来进料加工 L	补偿贸易 B	其他	中外合资 H	中外合作 Z	外商独资 D	其他
√							√

	包装数量或毛重或其他数量	55包 / 7425千克 / 26400米

原产地标准：
本项商品系在中国生产，完全符合该给惠国给惠方案规定，其原产地情况符合以下第（1）条：
　（1）"P"（完全国产，未使用任何进口原材料）；
　（2）"W"其H.S.税目号为＿＿＿＿＿＿＿＿＿＿（含进口成分）；
　（3）"F"（对加拿大出口产品，其进口成分不超过产品出厂价值的40%）。
本批产品系：　1. 直接运输从　　中国　　到　　意大利　　；
　　　　　　　2. 转口运输从＿＿＿＿＿　中转国（地区）＿＿＿＿＿到＿＿＿＿＿。

申请人说明	领证人（签名）　李新
	电话：021-64391520
	日期：2010年9月3日

　　现提交中国出口商业发票副本一份，普惠制产地证明书格式A（FORM A）一正二副，以及其他附件 *** 份，请予审核签证。
　　注：凡有进口成分的商品，必须要求提交《含进口成分受惠商品成本明细单》。

检验检疫局联系记录

上海出入境检验检疫局制

普惠制原产地证明书格式 A：

ORIGINAL	
1. Goods consigned from (Exporter's business name, address, country) SHANGHAI LIXIN INTERNATIONAL TRADING CO., LTD. 5/F, NO. 2230 WEST ZHONG SHAN ROAD, 200235, SHANGHAI, P. R. CHINA TEL：86-21-64391520　FAX：86-21-64391530	Reference No.　　G10/248101/L640 GENERALIZED SYSTEM OF PREFERENCES CERTIFICATE OF ORIGIN (Combined declaration and certificate) FORM A Issued in THE PEOPLE'S REPUBLIC OF CHINA (country)
2. Goods consigned to (Consignee's name, address, country) PALMAVITO ARTICOLI SPORTIVE S.P.A. VIA G. MAZZINI, 46, 20116 MILANO, ITALY TEL: 39-02-369010　FAX: 39-02-369052	See Notes overleaf
3. Means of transport and route (as far as known) FROM SHANGHAI, CHINA TO GENOVA, ITALY BY SEA	4. For official use

5. Item number	6. Marks and numbers of packages	7. Number and kind of packages; description of goods	8. Origin criterion (see Notes overleaf)	9. Gross weight or other quantity	10. Number and date of invoices
01	PALMASPORT SC#10LX-PAS075 GENOVA C/NOS.1-55	55(FIFTY FIVE) BALES OF 100% COTTON DYED TWILL ********************************** CREDIT NUMBER: 2010556TLCU0073	"P"	26400 METERS	LX-PAS10075 AUG. 25, 2010

11. Certification It is hereby certified, on the basis of control carried out, that the declaration by the exporter is correct.	12. Declaration by the exporter The undersigned hereby declares that the above details and statements are correct, that all the goods were produced in　　　　　　CHINA 　　　　　　　　　　　(country) and that they comply with the origin requirements specified for those goods in the Generalized System of Preferences for goods exported to 　　　　　　　　　　ITALY 　　　　　　　　(importing country) SHANGHAI, CHINA　SEP. 3, 2010
Place and date, signature and stamp of certifying authority	Place and date, signature and stamp of authorized signatory

商业发票：

SHANGHAI LIXIN INTERNATIONAL TRADING CO., LTD.
5/F, NO. 2230 WEST ZHONG SHAN ROAD, 200235, SHANGHAI, P. R. CHINA
TEL：86-21-64391520 FAX：86-21-64391530

COMMERCIAL INVOICE

TO: PALMAVITO ARTICOLI SPORTIVE S.P.A.
VIA G. MAZZINI, 46, 20116 MILANO, ITALY
TEL: 39-02-369010 FAX: 39-02-369052

INVOICE NO: LX-PAS10075
INVOICE DATE: AUG. 25, 2010
S/C NO: 10LX-PAS075
L/C NO: 2010556TLCU0073

FROM: SHANGHAI, CHINA   **TO:** GENOVA, ITALY

MARKS & NOS.	DESCRIPTION OF GOODS	QUANTITY	UNIT PRICE	AMOUNT
PALMASPORT SC#10LX-PAS075 GENOVA C/NOS.1-55	100% COTTON DYED TWILL "MILKY WAY" ANTIBACTERIAL FINISHED DYED TWILL ART. NO. KJ2001	26400 METERS	CIF C5% GENOVA USD 3.06/METER	USD 80784.00 TOTAL: USD 80784.00

AS PER SALES CONTRACT NO. 10LX-PAS075 DATED JUL. 21, 2010

TERMS OF DELIVERY: CIFC GENOVA INCLUDING 5 PERCENT COMMISSION

ORIGIN OF THE GOODS: P. R. CHINA

TOTAL AMOUNT IN WORDS: SAY U. S. DOLLARS EIGHTY THOUSAND SEVEN HUNDRED AND EIGHTY FOUR ONLY

TOTAL G.W. / TOTAL N.W.: 7425.00 KGS / 7150.00 KGS
TOTAL PACKAGES: 55 BALES

SHANGHAI LIXIN INTERNATIONAL TRADING CO., LTD.

陈弘毅

(signature)

经签章的普惠制原产地证明书格式 A：

ORIGINAL

1. Goods consigned from (Exporter's business name, address, country) SHANGHAI LIXIN INTERNATIONAL TRADING CO., LTD. 5/F, NO. 2230 WEST ZHONG SHAN ROAD, 200235, SHANGHAI, P. R. CHINA TEL：86-21-64391520　FAX：86-21-64391530	Reference No.　G10/248101/L640 GENERALIZED SYSTEM OF PREFERENCES CERTIFICATE OF ORIGIN (Combined declaration and certificate) FORM A Issued in THE PEOPLE'S REPUBLIC OF CHINA (country)
2. Goods consigned to (Consignee's name, address, country) PALMAVITO ARTICOLI SPORTIVE S.P.A. VIA G. MAZZINI, 46, 20116 MILANO, ITALY TEL: 39-02-369010　FAX: 39-02-369052	See Notes overleaf
3. Means of transport and route (as far as known) FROM SHANGHAI, CHINA TO GENOVA, ITALY BY SEA	4. For official use

5. Item number	6. Marks and numbers of packages	7. Number and kind of packages; description of goods	8. Origin criterion (see Notes overleaf)	9. Gross weight or other quantity	10. Number and date of invoices
01	PALMASPORT SC#10LX-PAS075 GENOVA C/NOS.1-55	55(FIFTY FIVE) BALES OF 100% COTTON DYED TWILL ********************************** CREDIT NUMBER: 2010556TLCU0073	"P"	26400 METERS	LX-PAS10075 AUG. 25, 2010

11. Certification It is hereby certified, on the basis of control carried out, that the declaration by the exporter is correct. SHANGHAI, CHINA　SEP. 4, 2010　宋子玲 Place and date, signature and stamp of certifying authority	12. Declaration by the exporter The undersigned hereby declares that the above details and statements are correct, that all the goods were produced in .... CHINA .... 　　　　　　　　　(country) and that they comply with the origin requirements specified for those goods in the Generalized System of Preferences for goods exported to .... ITALY .... 　　　　　　(importing country) SHANGHAI, CHINA　SEP. 3, 2010　李新 Place and date, signature and stamp of authorized signatory

THINK——理论思考

Think 7-1　李新为什么需要办理出口货物投保手续?

出口贸易中如果以 CIF 或 CIP 方式成交,由出口方向保险公司投保。我国出口货物保险采用逐笔投保方式。由于出口货物采用"仓至仓条款",因此投保手续应在完成托运手续取得配舱回单后且在货物离开发货人仓库发往装运地之前办理,以避免运输途中货物由于"漏保"使出口公司遭受不应有的损失。

Think 7-2　国际货物运输保险条款主要包括哪些内容?

保险条款的内容主要包括:保险金额、投保险别、保险费率、保险费的负担以及所援引保险条款的版本和生效日期。

Think 7-3　我国海洋运输货物保险的险别主要有哪些?

(1) 我国海运保险的基本险别有平安险、水渍险和一切险。

(2) 附加险有一般附加险(碰损、破碎险、串味险、渗漏险、受潮受热险等 11 种)和特殊附加险(战争险、罢工险、舱面险、进口关税险等 8 种)。

Think 7-4　出口货物运输投保经过哪些流程?

在办理投保手续时,投保人(出口公司)备齐提单、发票等复印件,填制"投保单"一式两份,并在投保单上加盖公章。其中一份由保险公司签署后交投保人作为接受投保的凭证,另一份由保险公司留存作为缮制保险单的依据。如果是信用证付款,最好将信用证中对保险单有特殊要求的部分复印一份作为投保单的附件。

保险公司核保人员将审核保单,根据投保内容与投保人协商承保条件,约定费率、免赔额和特约责任、除外责任等,协商一致后签发保险单或保险凭证,并计算保险费。保险单一式五份,其中一份留存。投保人付款,外币保单要求用相应币种支付,根据国家外汇管理局有关规定应使用支票或转账方式付款。付清保险费后投保人取得四份正本保单,投保即告完成。

Think 7-5　出口货运投保单缮制要点有哪些?

货物运输投保单是保险公司接受投保人(被保险人)的投保申请和开立保险单的依据。投保单内容正确与否,不仅影响保险公司出具的保险单内容的正确性,同时还会影响出口商的顺利结汇。货物运输投保单用英文填写,方法如下:

(1) 被保险人(INSURED)。此栏填写投保人(外贸公司),一般与合同卖方或信用证受益人一致。信用证有要求时应按信用证要求填写。

(2) 发票、合同、信用证号码(INVOICE NO/CONTRACT NO/LC NO)。此处按实际情况如实填写。

(3) 发票金额(INVOICE AMOUNT)。发票金额应按发票实际金额填写(不超过信用证规定的额度)。

(4) 投保加成(PLUS)。一般情况下按合同或信用证填写 10%。

(5) 标记(MARKS & NOS)。填写实际发运货物包装唛头,应与发票、提单保持一致。

(6) 数量及包装(QUANTITY)。填写实际发运货物的(最大)包装及件数。

(7) 保险货物项目(DESCRIPTION OF GOODS)。此处可以使用大类货物名称,但应与提单、发票保持一致(与信用证相符)。

(8) 保险金额(AMOUNT INSURED)。此处一般按合同或信用证规定的发票金额 110%计打(小数点后尾数进为整数,使用货币与信用证币种相同)。

(9) 启运日期、装载运输工具、运输起讫地、提单号码(DATE OF COMMENCEMENT, PER CONVEYANCE, FROM TO B/L NO)。按实际填写,与提单保持一致。

(10) 赔款偿付地点(CLAIM PAYABLE AT)。一般为货物最终目的地。

(11) 投保险别(CONDITION)。按合同/信用证填写。

(12) 货物、集装箱、运输工具种类和船舶资料。按所给选项及实际情况划"√"。

Think 7-6 出口货物保险单据有哪些作用?主要形式有哪些?

出口货物保险单据是保险人对被保险人之间的契约。它具体规定了保险人与被保险人的权利和义务,在保险标的物遭受险别责任范围内的损失时,它是被保险人索赔和保险人理赔的主要依据。在 CIF 和 CIP 等交货条件中,它又是卖方必须向买方提供的出口单据之一。

常用的出口货物保险单据有:保险单;保险凭证;联合凭证;预约保单;批单。

Think 7-7 一般原产地证明的申领经过哪些程序?

原产地证签发程序如下:

(1) 进出口公司根据合同或信用证填写原产地证书及其申请书。

(2) 货物装运出口(报关)前(最迟报关出运前三天),外贸公司持填好的原产地证书、原产地证书申请书及其他必要单据资料到商检局或贸促会办理原产地证书签发手续。

(3) 商检局或贸促会按外贸公司的申请,对公司提交的原产地证书、原产地证书申请书以及其他资料进行审核,如无误,在原产地证书上签字盖章,将其还给外贸公司。

Think 7-8 申领原产地证书需要提供哪些资料与单据?

外贸公司向商检局或贸促会申请签发原产地证明书时,须向签发机关提供如下单据:

(1) 原产地证明书申请书一份。

(2) 原产地证明(Certificate of Origin)一套。

(3) 商业发票、装箱单各一份。

Think 7-9 一般原产地证明书缮制要点有哪些?

原产地证明书用英文填写,填写方法具体如下:

(1) EXPORTER(出口方)。本栏一般填写合同的卖方或发票出票人(包括其详细名称和地址),不得使用印章或留空。

(2) CONSIGNEE(收货方)。本栏填写最终收货人(合同的买方或信用证规定的收货人)的名称、地址。在信用证规定或其他贸易需要时也可打"TO ORDER"或"TO WHOM IT MAY CONCERN"。

(3) MEANS OF TRANSPORT AND ROUTE(运输方式和路线)。此栏填写实际的运输方式及路线。如陆海联运由北京经香港到新加坡,可填"SHIPMENT FROM BEIJING TO SINGAPORE VIA HONGKONG BY LAND/SEA",应与提单一致。

(4) DESTINATION PORT(目的港)。此处指货物最终运抵港,不能填写中间商国家名称。这里的最终港,即最终进口国,一般与最终收货人或最终目的港所在国一致。

(5) FOR CERTIFYING AUTHORITY USE ONLY(仅供签证机构使用)。此栏出口申报人免填。一般由签证机构根据需要加注如:"证书丢失,重新补发;声明××号证书作废"等内容。

(6) MARKS AND NUMBERS OF PACKAGES(运输标志)。此栏应按发票或提单所列运输标志(唛头)填写。运输标志过长填不下时,可占用7～10栏空白处。无运输标志填N/M。

(7) NUMBER AND KIND OF PACKAGES, DESCRIPTION OF GOODS(包装种类、件数,货物的描述)。此栏填两项内容:① 包装种类和件数。一般先用数字再用英文表示。② 商品名称。填写货物具体名称,应同发票一致。

(8) H. S. CODE(商品编码)。一般填打4位数的H. S.编码(商品分类和编码协调制度税目号)。该编码须准确无误,与报关单保持一致。

(9) QUANTITY OR WEIGHT(数量或重量)。此栏应以商品的计量单位填打(连用)。以重量计算的,可打重量(需注明毛重或净重)。

(10) NUMBER AND DATE OF INVOICES(发票号和发票日期)。此栏应按发票照抄有关日期和号码,不能留空,有关日期须用英文表示。

(11) DECLARATION BY THE EXPORTER(出口方声明)。此处出口商声明早已印好,无须填写。但须由申请单位的法人代表手签并加盖中英文对照的公章,签字与公章不得重合,同时签注申报日期和地点。其中,申报日期不得早于发票日期(也不得晚于提单日期)。

(12) CERTIFICATION(签证机构证明)。签证机构证明文句也是印好的,无须现打。它只是在签证机构审核无误后,由授权的签证人进行手签,加盖签证机构印章,并注明签署地点、时间(此栏日期不得早于第11栏的申报日期)。

此外,证书右上角的CERTIFICATE NO.(证书号),应填写签证当局所编号码。

Think 7-10 什么叫普遍优惠制?

普遍优惠制简称普惠制,是发达国家给予发展中国家出口的制成品和半制成品(包括初级产品)的普遍的、非歧视的、非互惠的关税优惠待遇。

Think 7-11　普惠制原产地证明的申领经过哪些程序?

我国普惠制原产地证书(FORM A)的签发机关是进出口商品检验局。进出口商品检验局根据外贸进出口公司的申请,签发普惠制原产地证书。商检局签发普惠制原产地证书的基本程序如下:

(1) 进出口公司根据合同或信用证填写普惠制原产地证书(FORM A)及其申请书。

(2) 货物装运出口(报关)前,外贸公司持填好的普惠制原产地证书、普惠制原产地证书申请书以及其他必要单据资料到商检局办理普惠制原产地证书签发手续。

(3) 商检局按外贸公司的申请,对公司提交的普惠制原产地证书、普惠制原产地证书申请书以及其他资料进行审核,如无误,即在普惠制原产地证书上签字盖章,将其退给外贸公司。

Think 7-12　申请签发普惠制原产地证明书应提供哪些单证和资料?

外贸业务中,外贸公司向商检局申请签发普惠制原产地证明书除须向商检局提供填好的普惠制原产地证书和普惠制原产地证书申请书外,还需根据情况提供下列单证资料:

(1) 正式的出口商业发票、装箱单各一份。

(2) 《产品成本明细单》(出口含有进口成分的产品时提供)。

(3) 《来料凭证》(出口以来料加工方式生产的产品时提供)。

(4) 出口合同、信用证、提单等(商检机构认为必要时提供)。

Think 7-13　普惠制原产地证明书缮制要点有哪些?

普惠制产地证明书 FORM A 共12栏。其中,第4栏、第11栏由签证当局签署,其余各栏由出口公司填制,填证须用英文缮打,不得涂改。普惠制产地证明书各栏的填写方法如下:

(1) GOODS CONSIGNED FROM(出口商品名称、地址和所在国家)。本栏带有强制性,必须填写外贸出口公司(信用证受益人)详细的名称和地址(包括街道、门牌号码、城市名称及国名)。

(2) GOODS CONSIGNED TO(收货人名称、地址、国家)。本栏一般应填写给惠国最终收货人(信用证指定收货人)的名称和地址。如收货人不明确,可填写发票抬头人或提单被通知人的名称和地址(不得填写中间转口商的名称和地址)。

(3) MEANS OF TRANSPORT AND ROUTE(运输工具及线路)。本栏一般填写三项内容:① 提单或其他运输单据的签发日期;② 运输方式;③ 起运地,转运地,目的地。

(4) FOR OFFICIAL USE(官方填写)。此栏正常情况下空白。需要时由签证当局根据情况填写。

(5) ITEM NUMBER(项目编号)。如本证书下货物有不同品种,可按不同品种分别填写1~4等。如只有单项商品,此栏只填"1"(不能空白不填)。

(6) MARKS AND NUMBERS OF PACKAGES(唛头及包装号码)。本栏填写内容须

与发票上的唛头及包装号一致。如无唛头,填 N/M。如运输标志(唛头)过多填写不下,可占用 7~10 栏的空白处,也可另附纸(须打上原证号,加盖公章并签字)。

(7) NUMBER AND KIND OF PACKAGES; DESCRIPTION OF GOODS(包装件数、种类及商品名称)。此栏填写两项内容:① 最大包装及件数。须用大小写两种方式表示。如(100)ONE HUNDRED CARTONS;② 商品名称。此处应填写商品具体的品种名称及规格,但商品的商标、牌号、货号可以不填。此栏内容填完后,应在次行加上表示结束的符号,如"＊＊＊＊＊"等,以防被别人添加其他内容。国外信用证如要求注明合同、信用证号码等,也可加在此栏空白处。

(8) ORIGIN CRITERION(原产地标准)。此栏是国外海关审核的重点项目,必须按规定如实填写,具体要求如下:① 完全自产,无进口成分,填"P"。② 含有进口成分,但仍符合原产地标准填"W"。出口到挪威、瑞士、芬兰、瑞典、奥地利等欧盟成员国及日本的含有进口原料成分的产品都填"W",并在"W"下方表明产品的 CECN 税则号。③ 对加拿大出口,产品含有进口成分占产品出口厂价 40% 以下填"F"。④ 出口到澳大利亚、新西兰的产品此栏可空白。

(9) GROSS WEIGHT OR OTHER QUANTITY(毛重或其他数量)。本栏填写商品的正常数量,以重量计算的,只填毛重(与提单一致);没有毛重只有净重时,填净重,但要标明 N.W.(NET WEIGHT),并在次行打上结束的符号。

(10) NUMBER AND DATE OF INVOICE(发票号及日期)。此栏应按正式发票填写,不得空白。

(11) CERTIFICATION(签证当局证明)。此栏由商检局加盖公章,并由授权的签证人手签。商检局原则上只签一份,副本概不签章。本栏签发日期不得早于第 10 栏发票日期和第 12 栏申报日期,并早于提单日期。

(12) DECLARATION BY THE EXPORTER(出口商声明)。本栏生产国(PRODUCED IN)横线上填"CHINA",进口国(EXPORTED TO)横线上填的进口国应与收货人和目的港的国别一致,进口国应是给惠国。本栏底部盖出口公司印章,并由公司指派的专人手签,手签人的名单应先在商检局备案,正副本均需有签章。最后填写出口人所在地及出单日期,日期不得迟于第 11 栏商检局签发日期,也不得早于提单日期。

此外,证书右上角的 REFERENCE NO.(证书号),应填写签证当局所编号码;证书号码下面"ISSUED IN"横线上填写"中华人民共和国"即 ISSUED IN "THE PEOPLE'S REPUBLIC OF CHINA"。

ACT——模拟训练

Act 7-1 出口商缮制投保单据

2010 年 12 月 15 日,钱晓俊收到出入境检验检疫局签发的出境货物通关单。12 月 17 日,钱晓俊向中国人民财产保险股份有限公司上海分公司办理投保手续。

请以钱晓俊的身份,缮制投保单。

货物运输保险投保单:

PICC 中国人民财产保险股份有限公司 上海市分公司
PICC Property and Casualty Company Limited, Shanghai Branch

地址：中国上海市中山南路 700 号　　　　　　　　　　　电话(TEL)：021-63773000
ADD: No. 700 Zhongshan Road(S) Shanghai, China　　　　传真(FAX)：021-63764678
邮编(Post Code)：200010

货物运输保险投保单
APPLICATION FORM FOR CARGO TRANSPORTATION INSURANCE

被保险人：
INSURED:
发票号(INVOICE NO.)
合同号(CONTRACT NO.)
信用证号(L/C NO.)
发票金额(INVOICE AMOUNT)_____　　　　投保加成(PLUS) _____ %

兹有下列物品向中国人民财产保险股份有限公司 **上海分** 公司投保。(INSURANCE IS REQUIRED ON THE FOLLOWING COMMODITIES:)

标 记 MARKS & NOS.	包装及数量 QUANTITY	保险货物项目 DESCRIPTION OF GOODS	保险金额 AMOUNT INSURED

启运日期：　　　　　　　　　　　　　　　　装载运输工具：
DATE OF COMMENCEMENT: _____　PER CONVEYANCE: _____
自 _____ 经 _____ VIA _____ 至 _____ TO _____
FROM
提单号：　　　　　　　　　　　　　　　　　赔款偿付地点：
B/L NO.: _____　CLAIM PAYMENT AT: _____
投保险别：(PLEASE INDICATE THE CONDITIONS &/OR SPECIAL COVERAGES)

备注：(REMARKS)

请如实告知下列情况：(如"是"在[ ]中打"×") IF ANY, PLEASE MARK "×":
1、货物种类　普通[ ]　散装[ ]　冷藏[ ]　液体[ ]　活动物[ ]　机器/汽车[ ]　危险品等级[ ]
　　GOODS　　ORDINARY BULK　　REEFER　LIQUID　LIVE ANIMAL　MACHINE/AUTO　DANGEROUS CLASS
2、集装箱种类　普通[ ]　开顶[ ]　框架[ ]　平板[ ]　冷藏[ ]
　　CONTAINER　ORDINARY　OPEN　FRAME　FLAT　REFRIGERATOR
3、转运工具　海轮[ ]　飞机[ ]　驳船[ ]　火车[ ]　汽车[ ]
　　BY TRANSIT SHIP　PLANE　BARGE　TRAIN　TRUCK
4、船舶资料　船籍[ ]　　　　　　　　　　船龄[ ]
　　PARTICULAR OF SHIP　REGISTRY　　　　AGE

备注：被保险人确认本保险合同条款和内容已经完全了解　　投保人(签名盖章)APPLICANT'S SIGNATURE
THE ASSURED CONFIRMS HEREWITH THE TERMS AND
CONDITIONS OF THESE INSURANCE CONTRACT FULLY
UNDERSTOOD.　　　　　　　　　　　　　　　　　　　　　*钱晓俊*
投保日期：(DATE)_____
　　　　　　　　　　　　　　　　　　　　　　　电话：(TEL) 021-54105623
　　　　　　　　　　　　　　　　　　　　　　　地址：(ADD) RM. 905 YONG AN MANSION, NO. 12
　　　　　　　　　　　　　　　　　　　　　　　　　HUASHAN RD., SHANGHAI, P. R. CHINA

本公司自用(FOR OFFICE USE ONLY)

经办人　　　　　　　　　　　　核保人　　　　　　　　　　NO.: PICC 0817554
Made By _____　Checked By _____

Act 7-2 出口商缮制原产地认证单据

12月19日,钱晓俊收到保险公司签发的保险单后,即向出入境检验检疫局申请办理原产地认证手续。

请以钱晓俊的身份,缮制"一般原产地证明书申请书"(证书号:D03/182041/L916、企业性质:国内合资)和"一般原产地证明书"。

一般原产地证明书申请书:

中国贸促会上海市分会
中国国际商会上海商会
一般原产地证明书/加工装配证明书
申　请　书

申请单位注册号: **072150**	证书号: _____	全部国产填上 P	"P"
申请人郑重声明:	发票号: _____	含进口成分填上 W	

申请人郑重声明:

　　本人被授权代表本企业办理和签署本申请书。
　　本申请书及一般原产地证书/加工装配证明书所列内容正确无误,如发现弄虚作假,冒充证书所列货物,擅改证书、愿按《中华人民共和国出口货物原产地规则》有关规定接受惩处并承担法律责任,现将有关情况申报如下:

商品名称		H.S.编码(八位数)	
商品生产、制造、加工单位、地点			
含进口成分产品主要制造加工工序			
商品FOB总值(以美元计)		最终目的地国/地区	
拟出运日期		转口国(地区)	
包装数量或毛重或其他数量			
贸易方式和企业性质			
贸易方式		企业性质	

　　现提交中国出口货物商业发票一份、一般原产地证明书/加工装配证明书一正三副,以及其他附件 *** 份,请予审核签证。

申领人(签名) 钱晓俊
电话:021-54105623
申请单位盖章:
日期:　　年　　月　　日

如有补发、重发或更改 C.O.证书,请填写背面申请单。

一般原产地证明书：

ORIGINAL	
1.Exporter	Certificate No.
	CERTIFICATE OF ORIGIN OF THE PEOPLE'S REPUBLIC OF CHINA
2.Consignee	
3.Means of transport and route	5.For certifying authority use only
4.Country / region of destination	

6.Marks and numbers	7.Number and kind of packages; description of goods	8.H.S.Code	9.Quantity	10.Number and date of Invoices

| 11.Declaration by the exporter
    The undersigned hereby declares that the above details and statements are correct, that all the goods were produced in China and that they comply with the Rules of Origin of the People's Republic of China.

钱晓俊

Place and date, signature and stamp of authorized signatory | 12.Certification
    It is hereby certified that the declaration by the exporter is correct.

Place and date, signature and stamp of certifying authority |

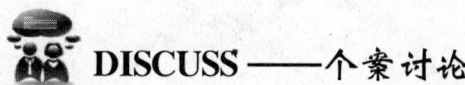

Discuss 7

在本实训ACT环节中,12月17日,中国人民财产保险公司收到海纳公司的投保单据,经审核后于12月18日签发保险单。根据Act 7-1中的投保单,保险公司该如何缮制保险单(保单号次:PYIE2010168912170 76823)?

货物运输保险单:

	货物运输保险单
PICC	CARGO TRANSPORTATION INSURANCE POLICY
中国人保财险	总公司设于北京 一九四九年创立 Head Office Beijing Established in 1949

发票号(INVOICE NO.)
合同号(CONTRACT NO.)   保单号次
信用证号(L/C NO.)   POLICY NO.
被保险人:
INSURED:

中国人民财产保险股份有限公司(以下简称公司)根据被保险人的要求,由被保险人向本公司缴付约定的保险费,按照本保险单承保险别和背面所载条款与下列特款承保下述货物运输保险,特立本保险单。
THIS POLICY OF INSURANCE WITNESSES THAT PICC PROPERTY AND CASUALTY COMPANY LIMITED (HEREINAFTER CALLED "THE COMPANY") AT THE REQUEST OF THE INSURED AND IN CONSIDERATION OF THE AGREED PREMIUM PAID TO THE COMPANY BY THE INSURED, UNDERTAKES TO INSURE THE UNDERMENTIONED GOODS IN TRANSPORTATION SUBJECT TO THE CONDITIONS OF THIS POLICY AS PER THE CLAUSES PRINTED OVERLEAF AND OTHER SPECIAL CLAUSES ATTACHED HEREON.

标 记 MARKS & NOS	包装及数量 QUANTITY	保险货物项目 DESCRIPTION OF GOODS	保险金额 AMOUNT INSURED

总保险金额
TOTAL AMOUNT INSURED:
保费   启运日期   装载运输工具:
PERMIUM: **AS ARRANGED** DATE OF COMMENCEMENT: PER CONVEYANCE:
自   经   至
FROM: VIA   TO
承保险别:
CONDITIONS:

所保货物,如发生保险单项下可能引起索赔的损失或损坏,应立即通知本公司下述代理人查勘。如有索赔,应向本公司提交保险单正本(本保险单共有____份正本)及有关文件。如一份正本已用于索赔,其余正本自动失效。
IN THE EVENT OF LOSS OR DAMAGE WITCH MAY RESULT IN A CLAIM UNDER THIS POLICY, IMMEDIATE NOTICE MUST BE GIVEN TO THE COMPANY'S AGENT AS MENTIONED HEREUNDER. CLAIMS, IF ANY, ONE OF THE ORIGINAL POLICY WHICH HAS BEEN ISSUED IN ____ ORIGINAL(S) TOGETHER WITH THE RELEVANT DOCUMENTS SHALL BE SURRENDERED TO THE COMPANY. IF ONE OF THE ORIGINAL POLICY HAS BEEN ACCOMPLISHED. THE OTHERS TO BE VOID.

中国人民财产保险股份有限公司 上海市分公司
PICC Property and Casualty Company Limited,
Shanghai Branch

赔款偿付地点
CLAIM PAYABLE AT/IN

出单日期
ISSUING DATE   GENERAL MANAGER

情景模拟实训八

履行合同四——报关与装运

 LOOK——情景示范

（经过了忙碌的3天，李新来到报关运输部，向陈老师请教）

李新：陈老师，根据我手头这笔意大利客户业务的进度，现在应该推进到出口报关了吧？

陈老师：对，你觉得办理出口报关时，除了报关单外，还应该随附些什么单据啊？

李新：就这笔业务看，我觉得至少还应该随附商业发票、装箱单、十联单第五联装货单、第六联场站收据副本大副联、第七联场站收据、出境货物通关单和出口收汇核销单等单据。

陈老师：（边将一份"出口收汇核销单"递给李新边问）这是我们公司的核销员刚从国家外汇管理局上海市分局领取的"出口收汇核销单"，说说看这份单据的使用场合吧。

李新：哦，在后续几步业务手续中需要用到这份单据，包括向海关办理出口报关、向银行办理出口收汇、向外汇管理局办理出口收汇核销和向税务局办理出口退税申报等手续。

陈老师：答得挺完整，你去制作单据吧，这是对你的一大考验哦。

李新：我一定尽力而为！

（李新回到自己的工位上，在报关运输部报关员张闻信的指导下，使用专业报关软件，制作"出口货物报关单"）（见第163页）

李新：陈老师，我把报关单、核销单制作好了，连同其他的各随附单据一起请您审核。

陈老师：（边细看各份单据边问）报关单中的"集装箱号"，你是从何处得来的？

李新："集装箱号"这一栏填的"CBHU4261027/20/2275"中的集装箱号CBHU4261027和20英尺集装箱的自重2275千克都来自速捷货代公司之前返还给我们的"集装箱装箱单"。

陈老师：不错，单据方面没什么问题了，你跟着小张去现场报关吧。

李新：谢谢陈老师！

［李新备齐出口报关单、商业发票、装箱单、十联单第五联、第六联、第七联、出境通关单和出口收汇核销单等单据（见第163～170页），跟随报关员张闻信至洋山海关办理现场报关手续……］

出口货物报关单：

中华人民共和国海关出口货物报关单

预录入编号：224820100493215380　　　　海关编号：224820100493215380

出口口岸 洋山海关（港区）	备案号		出口日期	申报日期 2010-09-08
经营单位 上海立信国际贸易有限公司 3103070520	运输方式 江海运输	运输工具名称 COSCO ANTWERP/017W		提运单号 CBHU678551100751
发货单位 上海立信国际贸易有限公司 3103070520	贸易方式 一般贸易		征免性质 一般征税	结汇方式 信用证
许可证号	运抵国（地区） 意大利	指运港 热那亚		境内货源地 闵行其他
批准文号 017336422	成交方式 CIF	运费 502/1800.0000/3	保费 502/133.2945/3	杂费 000//
合同协议号 10LX-PAS075	件数 55	包装种类 BALES	毛重(千克) 7425	净重(千克) 7150
集装箱号 CBHU4261027 / 20 / 2275	随附单据	出境货物通关单：310834042802273		生产厂家
标记唛码及备注 PALMASPORT SC#10LX-PAS075 GENOVA C/NOS.1-55				

项号	商品编号	商品名称、规格型号	数量及单位	最终目的国(地区)	单价	总价	币制	征免
1	52083300 00	全棉染色布 100% COTTON DYED TWILL KJ2001	26400.000 米 7425.000 千克	意大利	3.0600	80784.00	USD	照章

税费征收情况

录入员　　录入单位	兹声明以上申报无讹并承担法律责任	海关审单批注及放行日期(签章)
报关员 3192714518236750 报关员 张闻信	（上海立信国际贸易有限公司 报关专用章）	审单　　审价 征税　　统计 查验　　放行
单位地址 上海市中山西路2230号5楼		
邮编 200235　电话 021-64391520	填制日期 2010-09-08	

商业发票：

SHANGHAI LIXIN INTERNATIONAL TRADING CO., LTD.
5/F, NO. 2230 WEST ZHONG SHAN ROAD, 200235, SHANGHAI, P. R. CHINA
TEL：86-21-64391520 FAX：86-21-64391530

COMMERCIAL INVOICE

TO: PALMAVITO ARTICOLI SPORTIVE S.P.A.
VIA G. MAZZINI, 46, 20116 MILANO, ITALY
TEL: 39-02-369010 FAX: 39-02-369052

INVOICE NO: LX-PAS10075
INVOICE DATE: AUG. 25, 2010
S/C NO: 10LX-PAS075
L/C NO: 2010556TLCU0073

FROM: SHANGHAI, CHINA **TO:** GENOVA, ITALY

MARKS & NOS.	DESCRIPTION OF GOODS	QUANTITY	UNIT PRICE	AMOUNT
PALMASPORT SC#10LX-PAS075 GENOVA C/NOS.1-55	100% COTTON DYED TWILL "MILKY WAY" ANTIBACTERIAL FINISHED DYED TWILL ART. NO. KJ2001	26400 METERS	CIFC5% GENOVA USD 3.06/METER TOTAL:	 USD 80784.00 USD 80784.00

AS PER SALES CONTRACT NO. 10LX-PAS075 DATED JUL. 21, 2010

TERMS OF DELIVERY: CIFC GENOVA INCLUDING 5 PERCENT COMMISSION

ORIGIN OF THE GOODS: P. R. CHINA

TOTAL AMOUNT IN WORDS: SAY U. S. DOLLARS EIGHTY THOUSAND SEVEN HUNDRED AND EIGHTY FOUR ONLY

TOTAL G.W. / TOTAL N.W.: 7425.00 KGS / 7150.00 KGS
TOTAL PACKAGES: 55 BALES

SHANGHAI LIXIN INTERNATIONAL TRADING CO., LTD.

陈弘毅
(signature)

装箱单：

SHANGHAI LIXIN INTERNATIONAL TRADING CO., LTD.
5/F, NO. 2230 WEST ZHONG SHAN ROAD, 200235, SHANGHAI, P. R. CHINA
TEL：86-21-64391520 FAX：86-21-64391530

PACKING LIST

TO: PALMAVITO ARTICOLI SPORTIVE S.P.A.
    VIA G. MAZZINI, 46, 20116 MILANO, ITALY
    TEL: 39-02-369010 FAX: 39-02-369052

INVOICE NO: LX-PAS10075
INVOICE DATE: AUG. 25, 2010
S/C NO: 10LX-PAS075
L/C NO: 2010556TLCU0073

FROM: SHANGHAI, CHINA   **TO:** GENOVA, ITALY

MARKS & NOS.	DESCRIPTION OF GOODS	PACKAGE	QUANTITY	G.W. (KGS)	N.W. (KGS)	MEAS. (CBM)

PALMASPORT   100% COTTON DYED TWILL

SC#10LX-PAS075

GENOVA
C/NOS.1-55   ART. NO. KJ2001   55 BALES   26400 METERS   @135.00/7425.00   @130.00/7150.00   @0.45/24.75

    PACKING: 120 METERS IN ONE PIECE,
               4 PIECES IN ONE BALE,
               TOTAL 55 BALES.

    TOTAL: 55 BALES   26400 METERS   7425.00 KGS   7150.00 KGS   24.75 CBM

    AS PER SALES CONTRACT NO. 10LX-PAS075 DATED JUL. 21, 2010

    TERMS OF DELIVERY: CIFC GENOVA INCLUDING 5 PERCENT COMMISSION

TOTAL PACKAGES IN WORDS: SAY FIFTY FIVE BALES ONLY

                              SHANGHAI LIXIN INTERNATIONAL TRADING CO., LTD.

                                                   陈弘毅
                                                   (signature)

集装箱货物托运单第五联——装货单(场站收据副本):

Shipper (发货人)	D/R No. (编号)	
SHANGHAI LIXIN INTERNATIONAL TRADING CO., LTD. 5/F, NO. 2230 WEST ZHONG SHAN ROAD, 200235, SHANGHAI, P. R. CHINA TEL: 86-21-64391520 FAX: 86-21-64391530	CBHU678551100751 装 货 单	速捷
Consignee (收货人) TO ORDER OF SHIPPER		第五联
Notify Party (通知人) PALMAVITO ARTICOLI SPORTIVE S.P.A. VIA G. MAZZINI, 46, 20116 MILANO, ITALY TEL: 39-02-369010 FAX: 39-02-369052	场站收据副本	

Pre-carriage by (前程运输)	Place of Receipt (收货地点)	Received by the Carrier the Total number of containers or other packages or units stated below to be transported subject to the terms and conditions of the carrier's regular form of Bill of Loading (for Combined Transport or Port to Port Shipment) which shall be deemed to be incorporated herein.
Ocean Vessel(船名) Voy. No.(航次) COSCO ANTWERP 017W	Port of Loading (装货港) SHANGHAI, CHINA	Date (日期): AUG. 26, 2010
Port of Discharge (卸货港) GENOVA, ITALY	Place of Delivery (交货地点)	Final Destination for the Merchant's Reference(目的地)

Container No. (集装箱号)	Seal No.(封志号) Mark & Nos. (标志与号码)	No. of containers or p'kgs. (箱数或件数)	Kind of Packages; Description of Goods (包装种类与货名)	Gross Weight 毛重(千克)	Measurement 呎码(立方米)
	PALMASPORT SC#10LX-PAS075 GENOVA C/NOS.1-55	55 BALES	100% COTTON DYED TWILL FREIGHT PREPAID	7425.00 KGS	24.75 CBM

Particulars Furnished by Merchants (托运人提供详细情况)

TOTAL NUMBER OF CONTAINERS OR PACKAGES (IN WORDS) 集装箱数或件数合计(大写)	SAY FIFTY FIVE BALES ONLY

Container No.(箱号)	Seal No.(封志号)	Pkgs.(件数)	Container No.(箱号)	Seal No.(封志号)	Pkgs.(件数)

	Received (实收)	By Terminal Clerk (场站员签字)

FREIGHT & CHARGES	Prepaid at(预付地点)	Payable at(到付地点)	Place of Issue(签发地点) SHANGHAI
	Total Prepaid(预付总额)	No. of Original B(s)/L (正本提单份数) THREE	Booking(订舱确认) APPROVED BY

Service Type on Receiving ☑-CY, ☐-CFS, ☐-DOOR	Service Type on Delivery ☑-CY, ☐-CFS, ☐-DOOR	Reefer Temperature Required (冷藏温度)	签单章
TYPE OF GOODS (种类)	☑Ordinary ☐Reefer ☐Dangerous ☐Auto. (普通) (冷藏) (危险品) (裸装车辆) ☐Liquid ☐Live Animal ☐Bulk (液体) (活动物) (散装)	Class Property IMDG Code Page: UN NO.	危险品

(CHINA OCEAN SHIPPING AGENCY SHANGHAI 上海外轮代理有限公司 中国)

集装箱货物托运单第六联——场站收据副本(大副联):

Shipper (发货人)
SHANGHAI LIXIN INTERNATIONAL TRADING CO., LTD.
5/F, NO. 2230 WEST ZHONG SHAN ROAD, 200235, SHANGHAI, P. R. CHINA
TEL: 86-21-64391520 FAX: 86-21-64391530

D/R No. (编号)
CBHU678551100751

速捷
场站收据副本
大副联

第六联

Consignee (收货人)
TO ORDER OF SHIPPER

Notify Party (通知人)
PALMAVITO ARTICOLI SPORTIVE S.P.A.
VIA G. MAZZINI, 46, 20116 MILANO, ITALY
TEL: 39-02-369010 FAX: 39-02-369052

COPY OF DOCK RECEIPT (FOR CHIEF OFFICER)
Received by the Carrier the Total number of containers or other packages or units stated below to be transported subject to the terms and conditions of the carrier's regular form of Bill of Loading (for Combined Transport or Port to Port Shipment) which shall be deemed to be incorporated herein.
Date (日期): AUG. 26, 2010

Pre-carriage by (前程运输)	Place of Receipt (收货地点)
Ocean Vessel(船名) Voy. No.(航次) COSCO ANTWERP 017W	Port of Loading (装货港) SHANGHAI, CHINA
Port of Discharge (卸货港) GENOVA, ITALY	Place of Delivery (交货地点)	Final Destination for the Merchant's Reference(目的地)

Container No. (集装箱号)	Seal No.(封志号) Mark & Nos. (标志与号码)	No. of containers or p'kgs. (箱数或件数)	Kind of Packages; Description of Goods (包装种类与货名)	Gross Weight 毛重(千克)	Measurement 呎码(立方米)
	PALMASPORT SC#10LX-PAS075 GENOVA C/NOS.1-55	55 BALES	100% COTTON DYED TWILL FREIGHT PREPAID	7425.00 KGS	24.75 CBM

Particulars Furnished by Merchants (托运人提供详细情况)

TOTAL NUMBER OF CONTAINERS OR PACKAGES (IN WORDS) 集装箱数或件数合计(大写)	SAY FIFTY FIVE BALES ONLY

Container No.(箱号)	Seal No.(封志号)	Pkgs.(件数)	Container No.(箱号)	Seal No.(封志号)	Pkgs.(件数)

Received (实收)   By Terminal Clerk (场站员签字)

FREIGHT & CHARGES	Prepaid at(预付地点)	Payable at(到付地点)	Place of Issue(签发地点) SHANGHAI
	Total Prepaid(预付总额)	No. of Original B(s)/L (正本提单份数) THREE	Booking(订舱确认) APPROVED BY

Service Type on Receiving ☑-CY, ☐-CFS, ☐-DOOR	Service Type on Delivery ☑-CY, ☐-CFS, ☐-DOOR	Reefer Temperature Required (冷藏温度) °F °C
TYPE OF GOODS (种类)	☑Ordinary ☐Reefer ☐Dangerous ☐Auto. (普通) (冷藏) (危险品) (裸装车辆) ☐Liquid ☐Live Animal ☐Bulk (液体) (活动物) (散装)	危险品	Class: Property: IMDG Code Page: UN NO.

集装箱货物托运单第七联——场站收据：

Shipper (发货人) SHANGHAI LIXIN INTERNATIONAL TRADING CO., LTD. 5/F, NO. 2230 WEST ZHONG SHAN ROAD, 200235, SHANGHAI, P. R. CHINA TEL: 86-21-64391520　FAX: 86-21-64391530	D/R No. (编号) CBHU678551100751 场站收据　　速捷
Consignee (收货人) TO ORDER OF SHIPPER	第七联
Notify Party (通知人) PALMAVITO ARTICOLI SPORTIVE S.P.A. VIA G. MAZZINI, 46, 20116 MILANO, ITALY TEL: 39-02-369010　FAX: 39-02-369052	**DOCK RECEIPT** Received by the Carrier the Total number of containers or other packages or units stated below to be transported subject to the terms and conditions of the carrier's regular form of Bill of Loading (for Combined Transport or Port to Port Shipment) which shall be deemed to be incorporated herein. Date (日期): AUG. 26, 2010

Pre-carriage by (前程运输)	Place of Receipt (收货地点)	
Ocean Vessel (船名) Voy. No. (航次) COSCO ANTWERP　017W	Port of Loading (装货港) SHANGHAI, CHINA	
Port of Discharge (卸货港) GENOVA, ITALY	Place of Delivery (交货地点)	Final Destination for the Merchant's Reference (目的地)

Container No. (集装箱号)	Seal No. (封志号) Mark & Nos. (标志与号码)	No. of containers or p'kgs. (箱数或件数)	Kind of Packages; Description of Goods (包装种类与货名)	Gross Weight 毛重(千克)	Measurement 呎码(立方米)
	PALMASPORT SC#10LX-PAS075 GENOVA C/NOS.1-55	55 BALES	100% COTTON DYED TWILL FREIGHT PREPAID	7425.00 KGS	24.75 CBM

TOTAL NUMBER OF CONTAINERS OR PACKAGES (IN WORDS) 集装箱数或件数合计(大写)	SAY FIFTY FIVE BALES ONLY

Container No.(箱号)	Seal No.(封志号)	Pkgs.(件数)	Container No.(箱号)	Seal No.(封志号)	Pkgs.(件数)

Received (实收)　　By Terminal Clerk (场站员签字)

FREIGHT & CHARGES	Prepaid at (预付地点)	Payable at (到付地点)	Place of Issue (签发地点) SHANGHAI
	Total Prepaid (预付总额)	No. of Original B(s)/L (正本提单份数) THREE	Booking (订舱确认) APPROVED BY

Service Type on Receiving ☑-CY, ☐-CFS, ☐-DOOR	Service Type on Delivery ☑-CY, ☐-CFS, ☐-DOOR	Reefer Temperature Required (冷藏温度)　　°F　　°C	
TYPE OF GOODS (种类)	☑Ordinary ☐Reefer ☐Dangerous ☐Auto. (普通)　(冷藏)　(危险品)　(裸装车辆) ☐Liquid ☐Live Animal ☐Bulk (液体)　(活动物)　(散装)	危险品	Class: Property: IMDG Code Page: UN NO.

出境货物通关单：

中华人民共和国出入境检验检疫
出境货物通关单

编号：310834042802273

1. 发货人 上海立信国际贸易有限公司 ***		5. 标记及唛码 PALMASPORT SC#10LX-PAS075 GENOVA C/NOS.1-55
2. 收货人 ***		
3. 合同／信用证号 10LX-PAS075 / 2010556TLCU0073	4. 输往国家或地区 意大利	
6. 运输工具名称及号码 船舶 COSCO ANTWERP / 017W	7. 发货日期 ***	8. 集装箱规格及数量 1个海运20尺普通箱
9. 货物名称及规格 全棉染色布 *** （以下空白）	10. H.S.编码 52083300.00 *** （以下空白）	11. 申报总值 *80784.00 美元 *** （以下空白）	12. 数／重量、包装数量及种类 *26400 米 *55 包 *** （以下空白）

13. 证明

上述货物业经检验检疫，请海关予以放行

本通关单有效期至　二〇一〇 年　九 月　二十 日

签字：岳清风　　　　　　　　　　　日期：2010 年 8 月 30 日

14. 备注
***

出口收汇核销单：

出口收汇核销单存根	出口收汇核销单	出口收汇核销单 出口退税专用	
编号：017336422	监制章编号：017336422	监制章编号：017336422	
出口单位：上海立信国际贸易有限公司	出口单位：上海立信国际贸易有限公司	出口单位：上海立信国际贸易有限公司	未经核销此联不得撕开
单位代码：18747627	单位代码：18747627	单位代码：18747627	
出口币种总价：USD80784.00	银行签注栏：类别/币种金额/日期/盖章	货物名称：全棉染色布　数量：26400米　币种总价：USD80784.00	
收汇方式：信用证			
预计收款日期：2010年10月20日		（海关盖章）	
报关日期：2010年9月8日	海关签注栏：	报关单编号：224820100493215380	
备注：			
此单报关有效期截止到2010年9月10日	外汇局签注栏：　年　月　日（盖章）	外汇局签注栏　年　月　日（盖章）	

[洋山海关在十联单第五联装货单上加盖"海关放行章"（见第171页），以示放行货物，并将该联及第六联、第七联退还给张闻信]

（李新将海关加盖放行章的十联单第五联装货单及第六联、第七联呈送陈老师）

李新：陈老师，这票货物顺利通关了吧？

陈老师：可以这么说。不过在装货船舶离境后，海关还会签发出口报关单的"收汇核销联"和"出口退税专用"联，并退还加盖"海关验讫章"的出口收汇核销单。

李新：我记住了。

陈老师：哦，信用证对"最迟装运日期"是怎样规定的？

李新：在9月30日之前。

陈老师：好，一切尽在我们的掌握中！现在你把十联单的三联交给速捷货代公司，指示他们操作装船事宜吧。

李新：知道了。

（李新将十联单第五联装货单、第六联场站收据副本大副联、第七联场站收据提交给速捷货代公司，货代公司将该三联单据流转给洋山港区的码头堆场，堆场审核无误后，在第七联上签章并退回。9月10日，集装箱顺利装船。同日，李新凭之前从货代公司退回的第七联场站收据向中远集运船公司换领海运提单三正三副）

[李新将全套海运提单（见第172页）呈送陈老师]

陈老师：小李，信用证对提单有些什么要求？

李新：（拿出信用证细看相关条款）清洁、已装船、收货人做成"凭托运人指示"、标注"运费预付"、通知人是信用证申请人、标注信用证号，还有标注集装箱箱型箱类和流转形态。

陈老师：何以见得？

经海关加盖放行章的装货单：

Shipper (发货人) SHANGHAI LIXIN INTERNATIONAL TRADING CO., LTD. 5/F, NO. 2230 WEST ZHONG SHAN ROAD, 200235, SHANGHAI, P. R. CHINA TEL：86-21-64391520 FAX：86-21-64391530	D/R No. (编号) CBHU678551100751 **装 货 单** (速捷 stamp) 第五联
Consignee (收货人) TO ORDER OF SHIPPER	
Notify Party (通知人) PALMAVITO ARTICOLI SPORTIVE S.P.A. VIA G. MAZZINI, 46, 20116 MILANO, ITALY TEL: 39-02-369010 FAX: 39-02-369052	**场站收据副本**

Pre-carriage by (前程运输)	Place of Receipt (收货地点)	Received by the Carrier the Total number of containers or other packages or units stated below to be transported subject to the terms and conditions of the carrier's regular form of Bill of Loading (for Combined Transport or Port to Port Shipment) which shall be deemed to be incorporated herein. Date (日期)：AUG. 26, 2010
Ocean Vessel(船名) Voy. No.(航次) COSCO ANTWERP 017W	Port of Loading (装货港) SHANGHAI, CHINA	
Port of Discharge (卸货港) GENOVA, ITALY	Place of Delivery (交货地点)	Final Destination for the Merchant's Reference(目的地)

Container No. (集装箱号)	Seal No.(封志号) Mark & Nos. (标志与号码)	No. of containers or p'kgs. (箱数或件数)	Kind of Packages; Description of Goods (包装种类与货名)	Gross Weight 毛重(千克)	Measurement 呎码(立方米)
	PALMASPORT SC#10LX-PAS075 GENOVA C/NOS.1-55	55 BALES	100% COTTON DYED TWILL FREIGHT PREPAID	7425.00 KGS	24.75 CBM
TOTAL NUMBER OF CONTAINERS OR PACKAGES (IN WORDS) 集装箱数或件数合计(大写)		SAY FIFTY FIVE BALES ONLY			

Particulars Furnished by Merchants (托运人提供详细情况)

Container No.(箱号)	Seal No.(封志号)	Pkgs.(件数)	Container No.(箱号)	Seal No.(封志号)	Pkgs.(件数)

		Received (实收)	By Terminal Clerk (场站员签字)
FREIGHT & CHARGES	Prepaid at(预付地点)	Payable at(到付地点)	Place of Issue(签发地点) SHANGHAI
	Total Prepaid(预付总额)	No. of Original B(s)/L (正本提单份数) THREE	Booking(订舱确认) APPROVED BY

Service Type on Receiving ☑-CY, ☐-CFS, ☐-DOOR	Service Type on Delivery ☑-CY, ☐-CFS, ☐-DOOR	Reefer Temperature Required (冷藏温度)	
TYPE OF GOODS (种类)	☑Ordinary ☐Reefer ☐Dangerous ☐Auto. (普通) (冷藏) (危险品) (裸装车辆) ☐Liquid ☐Live Animal ☐Bulk (液体) (活动物) (散装)		危险品	Class: Property: IMDG Code Page: UN NO.

(中华人民共和国放行章 stamp)
(中国上海外轮代理有限公司 OCEAN SHIPPING AGENCY SHANGHAI 签单章 stamp)

海运提单：

1. Shipper Insert Name, Address and Phone	B/L No.
SHANGHAI LIXIN INTERNATIONAL TRADING CO., LTD. 5/F, NO. 2230 WEST ZHONG SHAN ROAD, 200235, SHANGHAI, P. R. CHINA TEL：86-21-64391520　FAX：86-21-64391530	CBHU678551100751

2. Consignee Insert Name, Address and Phone	
TO ORDER OF SHIPPER	中远集装箱运输有限公司 COSCO CONTAINER LINES TLX: 33057 COSCO CN FAX: +86(021) 6545 8984 **ORIGINAL** Port-to-Port or Combined Transport **BILL OF LADING**

3. Notify Party Insert Name, Address and Phone (It is agreed that no responsibility shall attach to the Carrier or his agents for failure to notify)	
PALMAVITO ARTICOLI SPORTIVE S.P.A. VIA G. MAZZINI, 46, 20116 MILANO, ITALY TEL: 39-02-369010　FAX: 39-02-369052	RECEIVED in external apparent good order and condition except as otherwise noted. The total number of packages or unites stuffed in the container, The description of the goods and the weights shown in this Bill of Lading are Furnished by the Merchants, and which the carrier has no reasonable means Of checking and is not a part of this Bill of Lading contract. The carrier has Issued the number of Bills of Lading stated below, all of this tenor and date, One of the original Bills of Lading must be surrendered and endorsed or signed against the delivery of the shipment and whereupon any other original Bills of Lading shall be void. The Merchants agree to be bound by the terms and conditions of this Bill of Lading as if each had personally signed this Bill of Lading. SEE clause 4 on the back of this Bill of Lading (Terms continued on the back hereof, please read carefully). *Applicable Only When Document Used as a Combined Transport Bill of Lading.

4. Combined Transport * Pre-carriage by	5. Combined Transport* Place of Receipt
6. Ocean Vessel Voy. No. **COSCO ANTWERP / 017W**	7. Port of Loading **SHANGHAI, CHINA**
8. Port of Discharge **GENOVA, ITALY**	9. Combined Transport * Place of Delivery

Marks & Nos. Container / Seal No.	No. of Containers or Packages	Description of Goods (If Dangerous Goods, See Clause 20)	Gross Weight Kgs	Measurement
PALMASPORT SC#10LX-PAS075 GENOVA C/NOS.1-55 CBHU4261027/655214	55 BALES	100% COTTON DYED TWILL CREDIT NUMBER: 2010556TLCU0073 FREIGHT PREPAID 1×20'GP FCL CY/CY SHIPPER'S LOAD, COUNT AND SEAL	7425.00 KGS	24.75 CBM SHIPPED ON BOARD SEP. 10, 2010

Description of Contents for Shipper's Use Only (Not part of This B/L Contract)

10. Total Number of containers and/or packages (in words) Subject to Clause 7 Limitation	SAY FIFTY FIVE BALES ONLY				
11. Freight & Charges	Revenue Tons	Rate	Per	Prepaid	Collect
Declared Value Charge					

Ex. Rate:	Prepaid at	Payable at	Place and date of Issue SHANGHAI, CHINA　SEP. 10, 2010
	Total Prepaid	No. of Original B(s)/L THREE(3)	Signed for the Carrier, COSCO CONTAINER LINES CO., LTD. GENERAL MANAGER COSCO CONTAINER LINES CO., LTD. AS CARRIER

LADEN ON BOARD THE VESSEL
DATE **SEP. 10, 2010** BY COSCO CONTAINER LINES CO., LTD.

李新：这份提单表面没有"货损或包装不良"的批注，能看出是"清洁提单"；有船名、航次、提单号、"已装船章"中有装船日期，能看出是"已装船提单"；收货人(Consignee)栏内填写的"TO ORDER OF SHIPPER"的含义是"凭托运人指示"；通知人(Notify Party)栏内填写的是客户，也就是信用证申请人的全称、地址和联系方式；在货物描述(Description of Goods)栏内的提单批注信息中包括信用证号、运费预付(FREIGHT PREPAID)、集装箱箱型箱类($1\times 20'$GP)和流转形态(FCL)。

陈老师：基本功扎实！能再进一步解释一下提单左上角三个当事人之间的关系吗？

李新：当货物即将运抵目的港时，船公司会向Notify Party（也就是客户）发到货通知，但此时货物的物权仍属Shipper（也就是我公司），要等Shipper将提单背书转让给客户后，客户才获得物权，这就是Consignee栏内TO ORDER OF SHIPPER的含义所在，主要是考虑到物权转让的安全性。

陈老师：提单"货物描述"栏内船公司的"SHIPPER'S LOAD, COUNT AND SEAL章"有何含义？

李新：这个图章是和集装箱交接方式CY/CY相匹配的。CY/CY的含义是船公司对所运集装箱的责任期间始于装货港码头CY接收集装箱，止于目的港码头CY交付集装箱，船公司往往会为这一交接方式配一"SHIPPER'S LOAD, COUNT AND SEAL章"，意思是"由托运人装箱、计数及加铅封"，也就是船公司对集装箱内的货物不知情、不承担责任，所以这个图章也叫"不知条款"。

陈老师：解释得很好！知道接下来的活儿吗？

李新：接下来有两件事。第一件事，根据惯例，出口商要在装船后及时向进口商发出装运通知，而且信用证也规定"装船后24小时内向信用证申请人传真装运详情"；第二件事，把全套副本提单通过DHL快递给客户。

陈老师：打住。发装运通知天经地义，快递全套副本提单是怎么回事儿？

李新：信用证中的单据条款第7款要求我们"在装运后24小时内通过DHL向信用证申请人快递一套不可转让的提单"，并且我们还要出具一份"受益人证明"声明此事。陈老师，我这样理解对吗？

陈老师：你对"ONE SET OF N/N SHIPPING DOCUMENTS"的理解有偏差，当然这是新手常遇到的问题。记住，这个条款里的"SHIPPING DOCUMENTS"通常指信用证项下除汇票外的所有单据，只有TRANSPORT DOCUMENTS才是仅指提单。

李新：哦，我知道了。根据这份信用证的要求，我们得快递给客户提单、商业发票、装箱单、保险单、普惠制原产地证明书格式A和品质检验证书等一整套副本单据。

陈老师：倒也不必用副本，只需把这些单据的正本各复印一份，然后在每份复印件上加盖"COPY章"，把这样一套复印件快递过去就算符合要求了。你快去向客户发装运通知和快递单据复印件吧，以便其做好接货准备。

李新：No problem!

（李新回到工位，拟写了一份装运通知，并传真给了客户）

装运通知传真文稿：

上海立信国际贸易有限公司
Shanghai Lixin International Trading Co., Ltd.
5/F, No. 2230 West Zhong Shan Road, 200235, Shanghai, P. R. China

To: Palmavito Articoli Sportive S.P.A.   **From:** Shanghai Lixin International Trading Co., Ltd.
Tel. No.: 39-02-369010   **Tel. No.:** 86-21-64391520
Fax No.: 39-02-369052   **Fax No.:** 86-21-64391530
    Date: Sep. 10, 2010

SHIPPING ADVICE

CREDIT NUMBER: 2010556TLCU0073

We hereby inform you that the goods under the above credit have been shipped on Sep. 10, 2010. The details of shipment are stated below:

Date of Departure:	Sep. 10, 2010
Shipping Marks:	PALMASPORT
	SC#10LX-PAS075
	GENOVA
	C/NOS.1-55
Letter of Credit No.:	2010556TLCU0073
Bill of Lading No.:	CBHU678551100751
Sales Contract No.:	10LX-PAS075
Purchase Order No.:	PAS-PO-CNSHA10043
Number and kind of Packages:	55 Bales
Total Gross Weight:	7425 Kgs
Value of Goods:	USD 80 784.00 CIF
Commodity:	100% Cotton Dyed Twill
Ocean Vessel:	Cosco Antwerp / 017W
Port of Loading:	Shanghai, China
Port of Discharge:	Genova, Italy
ETA:	Oct. 2, 2010

Yours truly,
Shanghai Lixin International Trading Co., Ltd.

李新

Li Xin

（接下来，李新将海运提单、商业发票、装箱单、保险单、普惠制原产地证明书格式 A 和品质检验证书的正本各复印了一份，加盖"COPY 章"后，把这一套复印单据通过 DHL 快递给了客户，之后立刻制作"受益人证明"以证明立信公司已履行信用证规定的寄单义务）

受益人证明：

上海立信国际贸易有限公司
Shanghai Lixin International Trading Co., Ltd.
5/F, No. 2230 West Zhong Shan Road, 200235, Shanghai, P. R. China

BENEFICIARY'S CERTIFICATE

SEP. 10, 2010

TO WHOM IT MAY CONCERN,

CREDIT NUMBER: 2010556TLCU0073
WE HEREBY CERTIFY THAT ONE SET OF N/N SHIPPING DOCUMENTS HAVE BEEN SENT TO THE APPLICANT BY DHL WITHIN 24 HOURS AFTER SHIPMENT.

上海立信国际贸易有限公司
Shanghai Lixin International Trading Co., Ltd.

陈弘毅
(signature)

THINK——理论思考

Think 8-1 出口货物为什么要办理报关手续？

报关是指出口企业在货物进出境时向进出境地海关申报货物内容，按规定缴纳关税并请求海关查验放行的行为。我国《海关法》规定，出口货物必须从设有海关的地方出境，发货人及其代理人必须分别是海关准予注册的、有权经营出口业务和代理出口企业办理报关手续的企业。报关人员必须获得报关员证件。

出口商在外汇管理局取得纸质出口收汇核销单后，登录电子口岸将核销单号码在出境海关备案后，即可报关。报关期限为：应在装货的 24 小时以前向海关申报，海关审核单据、查验货物、办理征税、结关放行。

Think 8-2 出口货物报关要经过哪些流程?

出口货物报关主要经过以下流程:

(1) 报关前准备:进出口货物收发货人接到提货通知或备齐出口货物后,可自行或委托报关公司办理报关业务。若是委托报关的话,应按照有关规定办理委托报关手续,签订报关委托书。

(2) 准备报关单证:进出口货物收发货人根据进出口货物的情况,准备需向海关递交的报关单证,一般包括报关单、货运单证、进出口货物的商业单证(商业发票和装箱单、出口收汇核销单等)、进出口货物的各类管制证件,同时要按照要求完成报关单的预录入工作。

(3) 向海关递交报关单证:按照《海关法》的规定,为了保证货物进出口行为的合法性,提高进出口通关效率,进出口货物收发货人或者他们的代理人在进出口货物时,应当在海关规定的期限内,以纸质报关单或者电子数据报关单方式向海关报告其进出口货物的情况,随附有关单据,申请海关审查并予以放行,并对所申报内容的真实性、准确性承担法律责任。这一环节是报关企业承担报关法律责任的开始,报关企业应对其所申报的内容负责。

(4) 陪同查验:单据递交以后,在海关认为必要的情况下,企业的报关人员要配合海关工作人员对货物进行查验。

(5) 缴纳税费:属于应纳税、应缴费范围的进出口货物,报关人应在海关法律规定的期限内缴纳税费。

(6) 办理放行后的相关手续:进出口货物经海关放行后,报关人可以安排装卸货物。同时为了证明进出口行为的合法性,进出口货物的收发货人可以向海关申请签发有关的《货物进出口证明书》。

Think 8-3 出口公司报关需要交验哪些单证?

出口公司报关需要交验以下单证:
(1) 出口许可证和国家规定的其他批准文件。
(2) 提单、装货单或运单。
(3) 发票一份。
(4) 装箱单一份。散装货物或单一品种且包装内容一致的件装货物可免交。
(5) 减税、免税或免验的证明文件。
(6) 对应实行商品检验、文物鉴定或受其他管制的进出口货物,应交验有关主管部门签发的证件(如商检证、卫生检验证、原产地证、品质证、配额证书等)。
(7) 汇核销单。海关核对报关单与出口收汇核销单,核对无误后盖"验讫章"。

海关在认为必要时,还可调阅买卖合同、产地证明和其他有关单证、账册等。在报关单证齐全有效、填报内容正确无误,并符合政策规定的情况下,海关才接受申报。

Think 8-4 出口货物报关单缮制要点有哪些?

出口货物报关单的填制方法如下:

(1) *预录入编号——由计算机系统对预录入的每票出口报关单自动编制一个标识码。

(2) *海关编号——由计算机系统对接受申报的每票出口报关单自动编制一个标识码。

(3) 出口口岸——货物出境的最后口岸的海关名称及代码。

(4) 备案号——《登记手册》编号或《征免税证明》编号。

(5) 出口日期——装载货物的运输工具办结出境手续的日期。

(6) 申报日期——向海关申报货物出境的日期。

(7) 经营单位——对外签订和执行合同的境内企业或单位(一般是卖方)。注明经营单位的代号,该代号是出口企业办理海关注册登记时,海关设置的编码。

(8) 运输方式——载运货物出境的最后运输方式(如:江海、公路、铁路、航空等)。

(9) 运输工具名称——载运该货物出境的运输工具名称(如:江海填船名及航次;铁路填车次或车厢号;航空填运单号)。

(10) 提运单号——各类货运单据号码。如海运填提单号码,即配舱回单上的D/R编号;铁路填运单号。

(11) 发货单位——货物在境内的生产或销售单位(即国内供货商,也可以填出口商)。

(12) 贸易方式——按海关《贸易方式代码表》中确定的贸易方式简称填写。贸易方式共分为七种:一般贸易(即正常贸易),寄售、代销贸易,对外承包工程,来料加工,免费广告品、免费样品,索赔、换货、补贸和进口货退回。一般贸易的编码为0110。

(13) 征免性质——按海关《征免性质代码表》中确定的征免性质简称填写。

(14) 结汇方式——按海关《结汇方式代码表》确定的结汇方式填写。如:L/C、D/P、D/A、T/T。

(15) 许可证号——货物出口许可证的编号(不需要许可证的,则不用填写)。

(16) 运抵国(地区)——货物最后运抵的国家或地区(一般是进口国)。

(17) 指运港——货物运往国外的目的港。

(18) 境内货源地——货物在境内的产地或原始发货地。

(19) 批准文号——填写除出口许可证外所需的其他批准文件及编号(如无其他批文则不用填写)。在出口退税专用联,此栏要注明出口收汇核销单编号。

(20) 成交方式——海关《成交方式代码表》确定的价格条件编码,如:FOB、CFR、CIF。

(21) 运费——整批货物出口实际支付的运费总额(注明外币种类)。

(22) 保费——出口人实际支付的保险费总额(注明外币种类)。

(23) 杂费——实际支付的国内其他费用(以人民币填写)。

(24) 合同协议号——贸易合同(协议)的编号。

(25) 件数——本次申报出口货物的实际外包装的总件数。

(26) 包装种类——货物外包装的种类(不同种类一一列出)。

(27) 毛重(千克)——申报出口货物的总毛重,用千克表示。

(28) 净重(千克)——申报出口货物的总净重,用千克表示。

(29) 集装箱号——装载货物的集装箱号码(根据配舱回单上的集装箱号码填写)。

(30) 随附单据——随出口货物报关单一并向海关递交的有关单证,一般有合同副本、商业发票和装箱单。特定情况下,还要提供许可证和其他批准文件。

(31) 生产厂家——生产该批出口货物的厂家(如无法确定可填出口商)。

(32) 标记唛码及备注——货物外包装上的标记唛码及其他说明事项。

(33) 项号——这类货物在本报关单中的序号(出口货物将按税则号码归类)。

(34) 商品编号——按海关统计商品编号填写(8位数字)。

(35) 商品名称、规格型号——货物的中英文名称即可。

(36) 数量及单位——海关统计法定计量单位及相应货物的数(重)量。

(37) 最终目的国(地区)——货物的消费、使用或进一步加工制造的国家(地区)。可参照唛头、港口名称填写。运往内陆国的货物除空、邮运外,多要通过其他国家的港口转运,如运往瑞士的货物,经过安特卫普运至日内瓦(GENEVA VIA ANTWERP),则最终目的国为瑞士。

经港澳商人转手的出口货物,不能预知其最后运往国,则最终目的国可填香港或澳门。成交条件为选择港的,以第一选择港所在地为最终目的国。

(38) 单价——货物的单位价格。

(39) 总价——该类货物出口的总价格。

(40) 币制——按海关的《币制代码表》确定的实际对外成交的货币符号填写,如USD、JPY等。

(41) *征免——按海关的《征免方式代码表》确定的税款计征代码填写。

(42) 税费征收情况——税费征收及减免情况。

(43) 报关员——业务员的中文姓名。

(44) 单位地址、邮编、电话——根据实际情况填写。

(45) 申报单位——对本报关内容的真实性直接向海关负责的单位名称,一般应加盖申报单位在海关备案的有效公章(报关专用章)。

(46) 填制日期——填制本报关单的日期。

(47) 海关审单批注及放行日期(签章)一栏——由海关填写。

注:有"*"号者为海关填写项目。不同合同的货物,不能填写在一张报关单上。

Think 8-5 我国的出口报关单有哪些类型?

根据贸易方式、出口企业性质的不同,我国的出口报关单以不同的颜色分为以下几种类型:

(1) 白色,适用于一般贸易。

(2) 粉红色,进料加工贸易专用。

(3) 浅黄色,出口退税专用。

(4) 浅绿色,来料加工装配和补偿贸易专用。

(5) 浅蓝色,外商投资企业专用。

Think 8-6 出口收汇核销单缮制要点有哪些?

出口收汇核销单缮制要点:

(1) 出口单位名称:填对外签订并执行合同的有出口经营权的外贸单位(包括外商投资企业)的全称。委托报关时,填委托单位名称;委托出口并以代理出口单位名义签订出口合同并负责收汇时,填代理出口单位名称;两个或两个以上单位联合出口时,填负责报关的出口单位名称。

(2) 出口币种总价:按应收外汇的原币种填写,为该笔出口货物的应收汇总额。

(3) 收汇方式:按合同要求从信用证、托收、自寄单据(一般仅限于鲜活商品、易腐商品、出境展销商品、出口金额在10万美元及以下的商品、预收货款项下的出口商品,其他商品如采用这种方式收汇,须预先经外汇管理部门批准)三种收汇方式中选填一种,并列明即期或远期收汇,还须列明相应的远期收汇天数;如为分期付款,则须列明每次付款日期和付款金额。

(4) 预计收款日期:应根据合同规定的付款日期或根据合同推算的付款日期填写。

(5) 报关日期:填海关放行日期。

(6) 报关单位备注:① 如委托出口使用代理出口单位的核销单,代理出口单位须在此栏注明委托单位名称,并加盖代理单位公章;② 如两个或两个以上单位联合出口,应由报关单位在此栏加注联合出口单位的名称和各单位的出口金额,并加盖报关单位公章;③ 填写出口货物的发票编号、合同号等核销过程中须附加说明的内容。原出口商品调整或部分退款、部分更换的,还应填写原出口商品核销单的编号等情况。

Think 8-7 出口收汇核销单需要填写的"预计收款日期"如何推算?

即期信用证(或托收)项下的货物,属近洋的,从寄单日起按25天结算;属远洋的,从寄单日起按35天结算。远期信用证(或托收)项下的货物,属近洋的,从汇票规定付款日期起按35天结算,属远洋的,按45天结算。如为分期付款,应列明每次收款日期及金额。寄售项下的最迟收款日期不得超过自报关之日起360天。自寄单据项下的出口货款,须自报关之日起50天内结汇或收账。

Think 8-8 出口货物装运要经过哪些程序?

(一) 散货班轮装船程序

(1) 直接装船方式:也称现装。散货班轮运输中,托运人应将货物送至船边,如果船舶不能靠近码头(如在锚地),托运人还应用驳船将货物驳运至船边,然后进行货物的交接和装船作业。对于特殊货物,如危险货物、鲜活货等,通常采取由托运人直接将货物送至船边、交接装船的形式。

(2) 间接集中装船方式:即所谓的"仓库收货,集中装船"的形式,这是由于散货班轮承运的货物种类多、票数多、包装式样多、挂靠港口多等原因,为防止装货混乱,提高装船效率,减少货损、货差现象。在散货班轮运输中,对于普通货物的交接装船,通常采用由船公司在各装货港指定装船代理人,由装船代理人在各装货港的指定地点(通常为港口码头仓库)接受托运人送来的货物,办理交接手续后,将货物集中整理,并按次序进行装船。外贸业务中较常采用间接集中装船方式。

（二）集装箱班轮装船程序

集装箱班轮运输中,由于船公司基本上以 CY/CY 作为货物的交接方式,所以集装箱货物的装船工作都由船公司负责。船公司或船公司的代理人在承运货物后,根据订舱单或托运单缮制订舱单分送集装箱装卸作业区或集装箱堆场,据以准备空箱的发放和重箱的交接、保管以及装船工作。

（1）发放空箱。通常,集装箱是由船公司无偿借给货主或集装箱货运站使用的。在整箱货的情况下,船公司或其代理人在接受订舱、承运货物后,即签发集装箱发放通知单,连同集装箱设备交接单一并交给托运人或货运代理人,据以到集装箱堆场或内陆站提取空箱。

（2）货物装箱。在整箱货的情况下,由货主自行办理货物出口报关手续,在海关工作人员监督下自行装箱,并缮制装箱单和场站收据。在拼箱货的情况下,由集装箱货运站将分属于不同货主但流向相同的零星货物装箱,拼装为整箱货物。

（3）换取提单。发货人收到经集装箱货运站或集装箱的经营人签署的场站收据后,即可凭场站收据向船公司或其他运输方式的经营人付清运费,换取提单或其他多式联运单证,然后去银行结汇货款。

（4）装船。集装箱进入集装箱装卸作业区的集装箱堆场后,装卸作业区根据待装货箱的流向和装船顺序编制集装箱装船计划或积载计划,在船舶到港前将待装船的集装箱移至集装箱前方堆场,按顺序堆码于指定的箱位,船舶到港后,即可顺次装船。

Think 8-9　在国际货物买卖中,为什么要将装运时间规定在一段期间内,一般如何规定?

能否按时装运,关系到买方能否按时取得货物、卖方能否安全收汇。因此装运时间对于双方来说,均属于合同的重要条款。在国际货物买卖中,很难做到在某一天将货物装运出去。因此装运时间要规定在一段期间内,业务中经常使用以下几种方法:

（1）规定某月装运。
（2）规定跨月装运。
（3）规定在某月底或某日前装运。
（4）规定在收到信用证后若干天内装运。
（5）规定在收到买方预付货款后若干天内装运。

Think 8-10　在确定装运港和目的港时要注意哪些问题?

装运港和目的港不仅关系到卖方在哪里交货和货物风险什么时候转移到买方,还涉及订舱的安排,运费、保险费以至成本核算和确定售价等问题。

业务中,装运港由卖方提出,买方同意后确定。一般选择靠近产地、交通便捷、储运设施完备、费用低廉的港口。在货物分散多处、磋商时确定不了的，可规定两个以上港口。

目的港由买方提出，卖方同意后确定。买方不能确定目的港时，可以规定两个以上目的港（同一航线），运费按较高费率计收，买方开证时即应确定。货物运往无直达船或偏僻港口时，应当允许转运。

Think 8-11 海运提单缮制要点有哪些？

海运提单缮制主要内容有：

（1）B/L No.（提单号码）。提单必须注明承运人及其代理人规定的提单编号，否则无效，提单号码一般可按装船单（下货纸）号码填写。

（2）Shipper（托运人）。指委托运输的人，一般为出口公司，也就是信用证中的受益人或买卖合同的卖方。信用证如要求以第三者为托运人，一般可以接受并须按信用证要求填写。

（3）Consignee（收货人）。该栏的填写与托运单"收货人"一栏的填写完全一致，应严格按照信用证规定填写。实际业务中，信用证通常要求出口商将提单收货人作成"To order"（凭指示）。这种提单须经托运人背书，方可流通转让。

（4）Notify Party（被通知人）。被通知人是货到目的港被船公司通知到货（提货）的人，他通常是货物的进口人或其代理。信用证对被通知人如何填写，一般有明示的规定，须按信用证规定填写"被通知人"的详细名称、地址。若信用证没有此项规定时，通常将开证人作为被通知人，填写开证人的详细名称、地址。

（5）Pre-carriage by，Place of Receipt（前程运输及收货地点）。货物转运时填写。其中，前程运输填写第一程船的船名，如货物不需转运，则空白不填；收货地点填写收货港的名称或地点，如货物不需转运，也空白不填。

（6）Ocean Vessel，Voy. No.，Port of Loading（船名、航次、装货港）。如转运填写第二程船的船名、航次和中转港的名称，不转运填写第一程船的船名、航次和装运港口名称按配舱回单填写。

（7）Port of Discharge，Place of Delivery（卸货港及交货地点）。这些项目均需按实际填写。其中，卸货港填写卸货（目的港）名称；交货地点填写最终目的地名称，如果货物的目的地是目的港，可空白不填。

（8）Marks and Nos.（唛头）。此栏须按信用证填写，如信用证没有规定则应按发票内容填写，如不使用唛头则注明"N/M"字样。

（9）Number and Kind of Packages，Description of goods（件数、包装、货物名称）。包装件数与种类按实际情况填写。货物名称应与托运单一致，与信用证严格相符。货物名称下面空白处注明运费支付情况如运费已付（Freight Prepaid）、运费到付（Freight to Collect）。

（10）Gross Weight、Measurement（毛重和尺码）。毛重一般以千克为单位，保留三位小数；尺码以立方米为单位，保留三位小数，提单上的毛重与尺码要与装箱单（Packing List）上的总毛重与总尺码一致。

(11) Number of Original B/L(正本提单份数)。提单份数须按信用证规定填写(大写英文数字)。如来证无明确规定或仅要求"Full Set"可填写 2 份或 3 份(TWO 或 THREE)。

(12) Place and date of issue（提单签发日及地点）。提单签发日期应为货物交付承运人或货物装船完毕的日期，它不得晚于合同或信用证规定的装运期。提单的签发地点应按装运地点填写。

(13) Signed for the Carrier(签名)。提单必须有船方或其代理人的签字才有效。

Think 8-12　何为"清洁提单"、"不清洁提单"？

根据货物外表状况有无不良批注，提单可分为清洁提单和不清洁提单。

(1) 清洁提单(Clean B/L)，指货物装船时外表状况良好，一般未经添加明显表示货物及/或包装有缺陷的词句或批注的提单。在国际贸易中，银行为了安全起见，在办理议付货款时，都要求提交清洁提单。

(2) 不清洁提单(Unclean B/L)，指承运人对货物的表面状况或其他方面加以批注的提单，如"包装不固"(Insufficiently Packed)，"×箱遭水渍"(… Cartons Wet Stained)，"包装残旧玷污"(Covers Old and Stained)等。

Think 8-13　何为"已装船提单"？

已装船提单(on board B/L or shipped B/L)是指整批货物已全部装入船舱或装在甲板上后由承运人签发的提单。

在 FOB、CIF、CFR 价格条件下，"已装船"是卖方按照合同交货的标志。货物装船后，承运人则开始对提单上所载明的货物承担货物在运输中的损失和损坏的责任。因此，为了确保能在目的地提货，一般在来证中都要求卖方提供已装船提单，以证明货物确已装船。同时，使用已装船提单对买卖双方的责任划分都有利。

Think 8-14　何为"备运提单"？"备运提单"能否用于交单结汇？

备运提单(Received for Shipment B/L)是指承运人在收到托运货物等待装船期间，向托运人签发的提单。随着集装箱运输的发展，这种提单日益增多。因为集装箱承运人必须在内陆场站收货，而收货时显然不能签发已装船提单。对于非集装箱货物，买方一般不愿接受备运提单，这是因为备运提单没有明确肯定的装运日期，并且往往不注明装运船只的名称，将来货物能否装出以及能否凭单提到货物均无确切保障。另外在跟单信用证的支付方式下，银行一般也不予接受。

Think 8-15　"备运提单"如何转换为"已装船提单"？

"备运提单"转换为"已装船提单"的方式有两种：① 在提单的空白处加"已装船"(shipped on board 或 on board)批注或加盖类似内容的戳记，然后加注装船日期和签字。② 在备运提单下端印有专供填写装船条款的栏目，即"已装船标注"(laden on board the vessel)，装船后承运人在此栏处加注装船日并由签字人签字。

此外，如果在提单的船名前有"预期船"(intended vessel)字样或类似有关词语，则必须加注"装船批注"，把实际装货的船名、装货港口、卸货港口等注明，即使和预期的船名和装卸港口相比并无变动，也必须重复列出。

Think 8-16 什么情况下提单需要做背书？如何背书？

提单必须按信用证要求做背书(endorsement)。"记名收货人"的提单无须背书，但是"凭指示"和"记名指示"的提单要根据信用证做背书。其中，"To order"与"To the order of shipper"均由托运人进行背书，由银行指示如"To our order"、"To order of ×××Bank"的提单，出口商不进行背书，由指定的银行背书。

背书方式主要有记名背书、不记名背书和指示背书等三种方式：

（1）记名背书。指信用证明确规定背书给被背书人（受让人），如"made out to order and endorsed to ×××Bank"，则出口商（背书人）在提单背面要写明被背书人的名称并签名的背书形式。

（2）不记名背书，又称空白背书。如信用证要求"made out to order and endorsed in blank"，背书人在提单背面由自己签名，但不记载任何被背书人的背书形式。

（3）指示背书。背书人在提单背面写明"To the order of ×××"，同时由背书人签名的背书形式。经过指示背书的指示提单还可以进行背书，但背书必须连续。

Think 8-17 装运通知拟写有哪些要点？

装运通知也称装船通知(shipping advice)，是受益人完成订舱或装船后发给申请人的通知文件。

装运通知不限格式，只要内容符合信用证要求即可。在缮制装运通知时，要注意以下几点：

（1）抬头人(to)：填写抬头人时应按信用证的具体要求。抬头人可以是承保该笔货物的保险公司（与买方预约保险单的保险公司）、信用证申请人，或者是信用证规定的其他抬头人。

（2）相关单据的编号：主要包括信用证号码和开证银行名称，发票号码、日期。

（3）装船情况：包括装运港名称、目的港名称、信用证号码和开证银行名称。

（4）货物内容：应与发票、提单等单据的内容一致；特别注意发票金额，它是计算投保金额和保险费的基础。

（5）签署：应由单据的出具人或负责人签字。

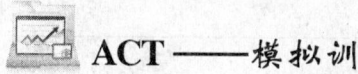

ACT——模拟训练

Act 8-1 出口商缮制报关单据

2010年12月20日，钱晓俊收到出入境检验检疫局签章的一般原产地证明书。12月23

日,钱晓俊备齐报关文件,向上海吴淞海关申报货物出口。

请以钱晓俊的身份,缮制出口货物报关单(批准文号:025418724、20′集装箱号:TTNU5744120、40′集装箱号:GESU2039606、40′集装箱皮重:3780千克)。

出口货物报关单:

中华人民共和国海关出口货物报关单			
预录入编号:2202201009273 72764			海关编号:2202201009 27372764
出口口岸 吴淞海关	备案号	出口日期	申报日期
经营单位 上海海纳进出口有限公司 3102516112	运输方式	运输工具名称	提运单号
发货单位 上海海纳进出口有限公司 3102516112	贸易方式	征免性质	结汇方式
许可证号	运抵国(地区)	指运港	境内货源地
批准文号	成交方式	运费 保费	杂费
合同协议号	件数	包装种类 毛重(千克)	净重(千克)
集装箱号	随附单据		生产厂家
标记唛码及备注			

项号	商品编号	商品名称、规格型号	数量及单位	最终目的国(地区)	单价	总价	币制	征免

税费征收情况		
录入员 录入单位	兹声明以上申报无讹并承担法律责任	海关审单批注及放行日期(签章)
		审单 审价
报关员 3113641802810741 报关员 龚西华	申报单位(签章)	征税 统计
单位地址 上海市华山路12号永安大厦905室		查验 放行
邮编 200040 电话 021-54105623	填制日期	

Act 8-2 出口商缮制装运通知

12月25日,货物顺利通关并装船后,钱晓俊即向客户发出装运通知传真。

请以钱晓俊的身份,缮制装运通知(预计抵达目的港时间ETA:2011年1月18日)。

装运通知传真文稿：

上海海纳进出口有限公司
Shanghai Haina Import & Export Company Limited
Rm. 905 Yong An Mansion, No. 12 Huashan Rd., 200040, Shanghai, P. R. China

To: Gulfland Dainecess Inc. From: Shanghai Haina Import & Export Company Limited
Tel. No.: 1-713-2283700 Tel. No.: 86-21-54105623
Fax No.: 1-713-2282332 Fax No.: 86-21-54742511
Date: _____

SHIPPING ADVICE

Yours truly,
Shanghai Haina Import & Export Company Limited

钱晚俊

Damon Chan

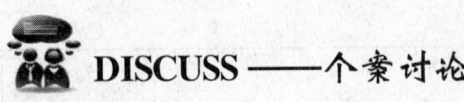

Discuss 8

在本实训 ACT 环节中,12 月 25 日,当货物装船后,中外运集装箱运输有限公司签发海运提单。根据之前实训的 ACT 和 DISCUSS 环节中已缮制完成的单据,船公司该如何缮制提单?

海运提单:

Shipper			B/L No.		
			SINOTRANS		
Consignee or order			中外运集装箱运输有限公司 SINOTRANS CONTAINER LINES CO., LTD		
			BILL OF LADING		
Notify address			SHIPPED on board in apparent good order and condition (unless otherwise indicated) the goods or packages specified herein and to be discharged at the mentioned port of discharge or as near thereto as the vessel may safely get and be always afloat. The weight, measure, marks and numbers, quality, contents and value, being particulars furnished by the Shipper, are not checked by the Carrier on loading. The Shipper, Consignee and the Holder of this Bill of Lading hereby expressly accept and agree to all printed, written or stamped provisions, exceptions and conditions of this Bill of Lading, including those on the back hereof. IN WITNESS whereof the number of original Bills of Lading stated below have been signed, one of which being accomplished the other(s) to be void.		
Pre-carriage by	Port of loading				
Vessel	Port of transshipment				
Port of discharge	Final destination				
Container. seal No. or marks and Nos.	Number and kind of package	Description of goods	Gross weight (kgs.)		Measurement (m³)
Freight and charges			REGARDING TRANSHIPMENT INFORMATION PLEASE CONTACT		
Ex. rate	Prepaid at	Freight payable at	Place and date of issue		
	Total prepaid	Number of original Bs/L	Signed for or on behalf of the Carrier SINOTRANS CONTAINER LINES CO., LTD **AS CARRIER**		

情景模拟实训九

履行合同五——交单结汇

 LOOK ——情景示范

（李新备齐信用证、信用证修改书及已制作完成的全套单据,向王经理请教）

李新：王经理,我已经做好信用证单据条款中要求的所有单据,请过目。

王经理：（边浏览全套单据边问）清楚接下来要做什么吗?

李新：这份信用证需要提交即期汇票,做完汇票后审核全套单据,再往后就得准备向银行交单结汇了。

王经理：思路清楚! 关于制作汇票,你向财务结算部的吴经理多请教吧。

李新：知道了,谢谢王经理!

（李新来到财务结算部,找到了吴经理）

吴经理：小李,我问你,汇票有什么作用啊?

李新：吴经理,我得先请教您一下,这份信用证的兑付方式为 Available with any bank in China by negotiation,也就是说信用证受益人可以选择中国的任何一家银行进行交单议付,我们公司一般选择哪家银行作为议付行呢?

吴经理：问得好。因为中国银行上海分行是这份信用证的通知银行,同时也是我们公司的开户银行,双方多年来合作愉快,所以这笔业务也不例外,我们将仍旧向中行上海分行交单议付。

李新：哦,现在我试着说说看汇票的作用吧。当我们公司向中国银行上海分行办理议付时,需要出具汇票,连同其他的所有结汇单据一起提交,中行上海分行审核全套单据是否"单证一致,单单一致",若通过审核,就将向我们公司垫付货款,汇票的主要作用是议付银行(也就是中行上海分行)向开证银行(也就是 BANCA INTESA SANPAOLO S. P. A. 银行)索回货款的依据。

吴经理：说得到位。从严格意义上来说,信用证业务里的 documents 并不包括汇票,但在实际业务中,通常将议付信用证项下的汇票作为结汇单据的一部分。我再问你,结汇是什么意思?

李新：我们国家实行外汇管制,所有出口商的出口外汇收入将由我国银行按照当时的"现汇买入价"兑换为人民币才能入账。所以,顾名思义,"结汇"就是外汇流转到我国银行那儿就被终结了。至于到银行办理交单结汇时所需要的单据,就被统称为"结汇单据"。在我们这笔业务中,办理结汇的银行就是议付行中行上海分行。

吴经理：好,掌握得不错。切记在办理交单结汇之前把所有单据好好审核一遍啊!

汇票第一联：

BILL OF EXCHANGE

凭 不可撤销信用证
Drawn Irrevocable L/C
Under **BANCA INTESA SANPAOLO S.P.A., MILANO, ITALY**   No. **2010556TLCU0073**

日期
Date **AUG. 4, 2010**   支取 Payable With interest @ **** % **** 按 **** 息 **** 付款

号码   汇票金额   上海
No. **LX-PAS10075**   Exchange for **USD 80784.00**   Shanghai **SEP. 15, 2010**

见票   日后（本汇票之副本未付）付交
at *************** sight of this **FIRST** of Exchange (Second of Exchange
Being unpaid）Pay to the order of_____**BANK OF CHINA, SHANGHAI BRANCH**_____

金额
the sum of **SAY U. S. DOLLARS EIGHTY THOUSAND SEVEN HUNDRED AND EIGHTY FOUR ONLY**

此致
To: **BANCA INTESA SANPAOLO S.P.A.,**   **SHANGHAI LIXIN INTERNATIONAL**
    MILANO, ITALY   **TRADING CO., LTD.**
                                            陈弘毅
                                            (signature)

汇票第二联：

BILL OF EXCHANGE

凭 不可撤销信用证
Drawn Irrevocable L/C
Under **BANCA INTESA SANPAOLO S.P.A., MILANO, ITALY**   No. **2010556TLCU0073**

日期
Date **AUG. 4, 2010**   支取 Payable With interest @ **** % **** 按 **** 息 **** 付款

号码   汇票金额   上海
No. **LX-PAS10075**   Exchange for **USD 80784.00**   Shanghai **SEP. 15, 2010**

见票   日后（本汇票之副本未付）付交
at *************** sight of this **SECOND** of Exchange (First of Exchange
Being unpaid）Pay to the order of_____**BANK OF CHINA, SHANGHAI BRANCH**_____

金额
the sum of **SAY U. S. DOLLARS EIGHTY THOUSAND SEVEN HUNDRED AND EIGHTY FOUR ONLY**

此致
To: **BANCA INTESA SANPAOLO S.P.A.,**   **SHANGHAI LIXIN INTERNATIONAL**
    MILANO, ITALY   **TRADING CO., LTD.**
                                            陈弘毅
                                            (signature)

信用证交单委托书：

中国银行 出口信用证交单委托书

致： 中国银行 __上海市__ 分行

兹随附下列银行正本信用证（修改书）及所属出口单据，请贵行根据国际商会跟单信用证统一惯例（UCP600）予以审核并办理寄单索汇：

开证行： BANCA INTESA SANPAOLO S.P.A., MILANO, ITALY	信用证号： 2010556TLCU0073
	通知编号： BP51039971
发票号码： LX-PAS10075	发票金额： USD80784.00

单据名称	汇票	商业发票	提单	副本提单	保险单	装箱单	重量单	原产地证明	普惠制原产地证明	商检证书	受益人证明	船公司证明	装船通知副本	装船通知	寄单证明
份数	2	3	3	3	2	3		1		1	1		1		

注：框内填写"✓"以示选择

付款指示： 核销单编号：__017336422__

请将收汇款以 ☐ 原币或者，☑ 人民币划入我司下列账户：

开户行： __中国银行上海分行__   账号：__061157-12442410979361__

特别指示：
1. 邮寄方式： ☑ 快邮   ☐ 普邮   ☐ 指定快邮
2. 本次提交的正本信用证含 __1__ 份正本修改书。

公司联系人姓名： __李新__
电话：__64391520__ 传真：__64391530__   2010 年 9 月 15 日

（公司签章：SHANGHAI LIXIN INTERNATIONAL TRADE CO., LTD）

以下栏目由我行填写

银行签收人：	签收日期

改单/退单记录：

注：本委托书一式三份，一份于交单时银行签收后退回公司，一份结汇时作回单退公司，一份交由银行留底

汇票第一联：

BILL OF EXCHANGE

凭   不可撤销信用证
Drawn   Irrevocable   L/C
Under **BANCA INTESA SANPAOLO S.P.A., MILANO, ITALY**   No. **2010556TLCU0073**

日期
Date **AUG. 4, 2010** 支取 Payable With interest @ ****%**** 按 **** 息 **** 付款

号码   汇票金额   上海
No. **LX-PAS10075** Exchange for **USD 80784.00** Shanghai **SEP. 15, 2010**

见票   日后(本汇票之副本未付)付交
at ************** sight of this **FIRST** of Exchange (Second of Exchange
Being unpaid) Pay to the order of **BANK OF CHINA, SHANGHAI BRANCH**

金额
the sum of **SAY U. S. DOLLARS EIGHTY THOUSAND SEVEN HUNDRED AND EIGHTY FOUR ONLY**

此致
To: **BANCA INTESA SANPAOLO S.P.A.,**   SHANGHAI LIXIN INTERNATIONAL
       MILANO, ITALY   TRADING CO., LTD.

陈弘毅
(signature)

汇票第二联：

BILL OF EXCHANGE

凭   不可撤销信用证
Drawn   Irrevocable   L/C
Under **BANCA INTESA SANPAOLO S.P.A., MILANO, ITALY**   No. **2010556TLCU0073**

日期
Date **AUG. 4, 2010** 支取 Payable With interest @ ****%**** 按 **** 息 **** 付款

号码   汇票金额   上海
No. **LX-PAS10075** Exchange for **USD 80784.00** Shanghai **SEP. 15, 2010**

见票   日后(本汇票之副本未付)付交
at ************** sight of this **SECOND** of Exchange (First of Exchange
Being unpaid) Pay to the order of **BANK OF CHINA, SHANGHAI BRANCH**

金额
the sum of **SAY U. S. DOLLARS EIGHTY THOUSAND SEVEN HUNDRED AND EIGHTY FOUR ONLY**

此致
To: **BANCA INTESA SANPAOLO S.P.A.,**   SHANGHAI LIXIN INTERNATIONAL
       MILANO, ITALY   TRADING CO., LTD.

陈弘毅
(signature)

商业发票：

SHANGHAI LIXIN INTERNATIONAL TRADING CO., LTD.
5/F, NO. 2230 WEST ZHONG SHAN ROAD, 200235, SHANGHAI, P. R. CHINA
TEL: 86-21-64391520 FAX: 86-21-64391530

COMMERCIAL INVOICE

TO: PALMAVITO ARTICOLI SPORTIVE S.P.A.
VIA G. MAZZINI, 46, 20116 MILANO, ITALY
TEL: 39-02-369010 FAX: 39-02-369052

INVOICE NO.: LX-PAS10075
INVOICE DATE: AUG. 25, 2010
S/C NO.: 10LX-PAS075
L/C NO.: 2010556TLCU0073

FROM: SHANGHAI, CHINA   **TO:** GENOVA, ITALY

MARKS & NOS.	DESCRIPTION OF GOODS	QUANTITY	UNIT PRICE	AMOUNT
PALMASPORT SC#10LX-PAS075 GENOVA C/NOS.1-55	100% COTTON DYED TWILL "MILKY WAY" ANTIBACTERIAL FINISHED DYED TWILL ART. NO. KJ2001	26400 METERS	CIFC5% GENOVA USD 3.06/METER TOTAL:	USD 80784.00 USD 80784.00

AS PER SALES CONTRACT NO. 10LX-PAS075 DATED JUL. 21, 2010

TERMS OF DELIVERY: CIFC GENOVA INCLUDING 5 PERCENT COMMISSION

ORIGIN OF THE GOODS: P. R. CHINA

TOTAL AMOUNT IN WORDS: SAY U. S. DOLLARS EIGHTY THOUSAND SEVEN HUNDRED AND EIGHTY FOUR ONLY

TOTAL G.W. / TOTAL N.W.: 7425.00 KGS / 7150.00 KGS
TOTAL PACKAGES: 55 BALES

SHANGHAI LIXIN INTERNATIONAL TRADING CO., LTD.

陈弘毅

(signature)

装箱单：

SHANGHAI LIXIN INTERNATIONAL TRADING CO., LTD.
5/F, NO. 2230 WEST ZHONG SHAN ROAD, 200235, SHANGHAI, P. R. CHINA
TEL：86-21-64391520 FAX：86-21-64391530

PACKING LIST

TO: PALMAVITO ARTICOLI SPORTIVE S.P.A.
VIA G. MAZZINI, 46, 20116 MILANO, ITALY
TEL: 39-02-369010 FAX: 39-02-369052

INVOICE NO: LX-PAS10075
INVOICE DATE: AUG. 25, 2010
S/C NO: 10LX-PAS075
L/C NO: 2010556TLCU0073

FROM: SHANGHAI, CHINA **TO:** GENOVA, ITALY

MARKS & NOS.	DESCRIPTION OF GOODS	PACKAGE	QUANTITY	G.W. (KGS)	N.W. (KGS)	MEAS. (CBM)

PALMASPORT   100% COTTON DYED TWILL
SC#10LX-PAS075
GENOVA
C/NOS.1-55   ART. NO. KJ2001   55 BALES   26400 METERS   @135.00/7425.00   @130.00/7150.00   @0.45/24.75

PACKING: 120 METERS IN ONE PIECE,
          4 PIECES IN ONE BALE,
          TOTAL 55 BALES.

TOTAL: 55 BALES   26400 METERS   7425.00 KGS   7150.00 KGS   24.75 CBM

AS PER SALES CONTRACT NO. 10LX-PAS075 DATED JUL. 21, 2010

TERMS OF DELIVERY: CIFC GENOVA INCLUDING 5 PERCENT COMMISSION

TOTAL PACKAGES IN WORDS: SAY FIFTY FIVE BALES ONLY

SHANGHAI LIXIN INTERNATIONAL TRADING CO., LTD.

陈弘毅

(signature)

海运提单：

1. Shipper Insert Name, Address and Phone SHANGHAI LIXIN INTERNATIONAL TRADING CO., LTD. 5/F, NO. 2230 WEST ZHONG SHAN ROAD, 200235, SHANGHAI, P. R. CHINA TEL：86-21-64391520　FAX：86-21-64391530	B/L No. CBHU678551100751
2. Consignee Insert Name, Address and Phone TO ORDER OF SHIPPER	中远集装箱运输有限公司 COSCO CONTAINER LINES TLX: 33057 COSCO CN FAX: +86(021) 6545 8984 **ORIGINAL** Port-to-Port or Combined Transport
3. Notify Party Insert Name, Address and Phone (It is agreed that no responsibility shall attach to the Carrier or his agents for failure to notify) PALMAVITO ARTICOLI SPORTIVE S.P.A. VIA G. MAZZINI, 46, 20116 MILANO, ITALY TEL: 39-02-369010　FAX: 39-02-369052	**BILL OF LADING** RECEIVED in external apparent good order and condition except as otherwise noted. The total number of packages or unites stuffed in the container, The description of the goods and the weights shown in this Bill of Lading are Furnished by the Merchants, and which the carrier has no reasonable means Of checking and is not a part of this Bill of Lading contract. The carrier has

4. Combined Transport * Pre - carriage by	5. Combined Transport* Place of Receipt
6. Ocean Vessel Voy. No. **COSCO ANTWERP / 017W**	7. Port of Loading **SHANGHAI, CHINA**
8. Port of Discharge **GENOVA, ITALY**	9. Combined Transport * Place of Delivery

Issued the number of Bills of Lading stated below, all of this tenor and date, One of the original Bills of Lading must be surrendered and endorsed or signed against the delivery of the shipment and whereupon any other original Bills of Lading shall be void. The Merchants agree to be bound by the terms and conditions of this Bill of Lading as if each had personally signed this Bill of Lading.
SEE clause 4 on the back of this Bill of Lading (Terms continued on the back hereof, please read carefully).
*Applicable Only When Document Used as a Combined Transport Bill of Lading.

Marks & Nos. Container / Seal No.	No. of Containers or Packages	Description of Goods (If Dangerous Goods, See Clause 20)	Gross Weight Kgs	Measurement
PALMASPORT SC#10LX-PAS075 GENOVA C/NOS.1-55 CBHU4261027/655214	55BALES	100% COTTON DYED TWILL CREDIT NUMBER: 2010556TLCU0073 FREIGHT PREPAID 1×20′GP FCL CY/CY SHIPPER'S LOAD, COUNT AND SEAL	7425.00 KGS	24.75 CBM

SHIPPED ON BOARD
SEP. 10, 2010

Description of Contents for Shipper's Use Only (Not part of This B/L Contract)

10. Total Number of containers and/or packages (in words) Subject to Clause 7 Limitation	SAY FIFTY FIVE BALES ONLY				
11. Freight & Charges	Revenue Tons	Rate	Per	Prepaid	Collect
Declared Value Charge					

Ex. Rate:	Prepaid at	Payable at	Place and date of issue SHANGHAI, CHINA　SEP. 10, 2010
	Total Prepaid	No. of Original B(s)/L **THREE(3)**	Signed for the Carrier, COSCO CONTAINER LINES CO., LTD. GENERAL MANAGER COSCO CONTAINER LINES CO., LTD. AS CARRIER

LADEN ON BOARD THE VESSEL
DATE **SEP. 10, 2010** BY　COSCO CONTAINER LINES CO., LTD.

货物运输保险单:

PICC
中国人保财险

货物运输保险单
CARGO TRANSPORTATION INSURANCE POLICY

总公司设于北京　Head Office Beijing　　一九四九年创立　Established in 1949

发票号(INVOICE NO.) LX-PAS10075	保单号次 POLICY NO. PYIE201014258770335917
合同号(CONTRACT NO.) 10LX-PAS075	
信用证号(L/C NO.) 2010556TLCU0073	

被保险人：
INSURED: SHANGHAI LIXIN INTERNATIONAL TRADING CO., LTD.

中国人民财产保险股份有限公司(以下简称公司)根据被保险人的要求，由被保险人向本公司缴付约定的保险费，按照本保险单承保险别和背面所载条款与下列特款承保下述货物运输保险，特立本保险单。
THIS POLICY OF INSURANCE WITNESSES THAT PICC PROPERTY AND CASUALTY COMPANY LIMITED (HEREINAFTER CALLED "THE COMPANY") AT THE REQUEST OF THE INSURED AND IN CONSIDERATION OF THE AGREED PREMIUM PAID TO THE COMPANY BY THE INSURED, UNDERTAKES TO INSURE THE UNDERMENTIONED GOODS IN TRANSPORTATION SUBJECT TO THE CONDITIONS OF THIS POLICY AS PER THE CLAUSES PRINTED OVERLEAF AND OTHER SPECIAL CLAUSES ATTACHED HEREON.

标 记 MARKS & NOS	包装及数量 QUANTITY	保险货物项目 DESCRIPTION OF GOODS	保险金额 AMOUNT INSURED
AS PER INVOICE NO. LX-PAS10075	55 BALES	100% COTTON DYED TWILL	USD88863.00
		CREDIT NUMBER: 2010556TLCU0073	

总保险金额
TOTAL AMOUNT INSURED: **SAY U.S. DOLLARS EIGHTY EIGHT THOUSAND EIGHT HUNDRED AND SIXTY THREE ONLY**

保费：
PERMIUM: **AS ARRANGED**　　启运日期 DATE OF COMMENCEMENT: **AS PER B/L**　　装载运输工具：PER CONVEYANCE: **COSCO ANTWERP/ 017W**

自
FROM: **SHANGHAI, CHINA**　　经 VIA　　　　至 TO: **GENOVA, ITALY**

承保险别：
CONDITIONS:

COVERING INSTITUTE CARGO CLAUSES (C)

所保货物，如发生保险单项下可能引起索赔的损失或损坏,应立即通知本公司下述代理人查勘。如有索赔,应向本公司提交保单正本(本保险单共有 **贰** 份正本)及有关文件。如一份正本已用于索赔，其余正本自动失效。
IN THE EVENT OF LOSS OR DAMAGE WITCH MAY RESULT IN A CLAIM UNDER THIS POLICY, IMMEDIATE NOTICE MUST BE GIVEN TO THE COMPANY'S AGENT AS MENTIONED HEREUNDER. CLAIMS, IF ANY, ONE OF THE ORIGINAL POLICY WHICH HAS BEEN ISSUED IN **2** ORIGINAL(S) TOGETHER WITH THE RELEVANT DOCUMENTS SHALL BE SURRENDERED TO THE COMPANY. IF ONE OF THE ORIGINAL POLICY HAS BEEN ACCOMPLISHED. THE OTHERS TO BE VOID.

中国人民财产保险股份有限公司 上海市分公司
PICC Property and Casualty Company Limited,
Shanghai Branch

赔款偿付地点
CLAIM PAYABLE AT/IN **GENOVA IN USD**

出单日期
ISSUING DATE **SEP. 2, 2010**

钟退思
GENERAL MANAGER

普惠制原产地证明书格式 A：

	ORIGINAL	
1. Goods consigned from (Exporter's business name, address, country) SHANGHAI LIXIN INTERNATIONAL TRADING CO., LTD. 5/F, NO. 2230 WEST ZHONG SHAN ROAD, 200235, SHANGHAI, P. R. CHINA TEL：86-21-64391520　FAX：86-21-64391530	Reference No.　G10/248101/L640 **GENERALIZED SYSTEM OF PREFERENCES CERTIFICATE OF ORIGIN** (Combined declaration and certificate) **FORM A** Issued in THE PEOPLE'S REPUBLIC OF CHINA (country)	
2. Goods consigned to (Consignee's name, address, country) PALMAVITO ARTICOLI SPORTIVE S.P.A. VIA G. MAZZINI, 46, 20116 MILANO, ITALY TEL: 39-02-369010　FAX: 39-02-369052	See Notes overleaf	
3. Means of transport and route (as far as known) FROM SHANGHAI, CHINA TO GENOVA, ITALY BY SEA	4. For official use	

5. Item number	6. Marks and numbers of packages	7. Number and kind of packages; description of goods	8. Origin criterion (see Notes overleaf)	9. Gross weight or other quantity	10. Number and date of invoices
01	PALMASPORT SC#10LX-PAS075 GENOVA C/NOS.1-55	55(FIFTY FIVE) BALES OF 100% COTTON DYED TWILL ************************************* CREDIT NUMBER: 2010556TLCU0073	"P"	26400 METERS	LX-PAS10075 AUG. 25, 2010

| 11. Certification
It is hereby certified, on the basis of control carried out, that the declaration by the exporter is correct.

[stamp: 中华人民共和国 上海 FORM A 出入境检验检疫局]

SHANGHAI, CHINA　SEP. 4, 2010　宋子铮
Place and date, signature and stamp of certifying authority | 12. Declaration by the exporter
The undersigned hereby declares that the above details and statements are correct, that all the goods were

produced in
　　　　CHINA
　　　　(country)
and that they comply with the origin requirements specified for those goods in the Generalized System of Preferences for goods exported to
　　　　ITALY
　　　　(importing country)
[stamp: SHANGHAI LIXIN INTERNATIONAL TRADING CO., LTD.]
SHANGHAI, CHINA　SEP. 3, 2010　李新
Place and date, signature and stamp of authorized signatory |

品质检验证书：

中华人民共和国出入境检验检疫
ENTRY-EXIT INSPECTION AND QUARANTINE OF THE PEOPLE'S REPUBLIC OF CHINA

第 1 页共 1 页 Page 1 of 1

编号 No.: 042552078010624

QUALITY INSPECTION CERTIFICATE

发货人 Consignor	SHANGHAI LIXIN INTERNATIONAL TRADING CO., LTD.	
收货人 Consignee	PALMAVITO ARTICOLI SPORTIVE S.P.A.	
品名 Description of Goods	100% COTTON DYED TWILL	标记及号码 Mark & No.
报检数量/重量 Quantity/Weight Declared	-26 400-METERS / -7 425-KGS	PALMASPORT SC#10LX-PAS075
包装种类及数量 Number and Type of Packages	-55-BALES	GENOVA C/NOS.1-55
运输工具 Means of Conveyance	COSCO ANTWERP / 017W	

检验结果：
RESULTS OF INSPECTION:

At the request of consignor, our inspectors attended at the warehouse of the consignment on 2010/8/29. In accordance with FZ61002-91 and the relevant state stipulations GB2541 and GB5523, 2 bales were taken and opened at random for visual inspection, from which representative samples were drawn and inspected according to the stipulation mentioned above. The results are as follows:

Appearance: Pass
Specifications: Pass
Quantity: -26 400-METERS, -55-BALES
Safety: Pass
Hygienics: Pass

印章 Official Stamp

签证地点 Place of Issue **SHANGHAI**　　签证日期 Date of Issue **AUG. 30, 2010**

授权签字人 Authorized Officer **XIA SIYU**　　签名 Signature *夏斯语*

我们已尽所知和最大能力实施上述检验，不能因我们签发本证书而免除卖方或其他方面根据合同和法律所担的产品责任和其他责任。
All inspections are carried out conscientiously to the best of our knowledge and ability. This certificate does not in any respect absolve the seller and other related parties from his contractual and legal obligations especially when product quality is concerned.

装运通知传真文稿复印件：

上海立信国际贸易有限公司
Shanghai Lixin International Trading Co., Ltd.
5/F, No. 2230 West Zhong Shan Road, 200235, Shanghai, P. R. China

To: Palmavito Articoli Sportive S.P.A.   **From:** Shanghai Lixin International Trading Co., Ltd.
Tel. No.: 39-02-369010   **Tel. No.:** 86-21-64391520
Fax No.: 39-02-369052   **Fax No.:** 86-21-64391530
   Date: Sep. 10, 2010

SHIPPING ADVICE

CREDIT NUMBER: 2010556TLCU0073

We hereby inform you that the goods under the above credit have been shipped on Sep. 10, 2010. The details of shipment are stated below:

Date of Departure:	Sep. 10, 2010
Shipping Marks:	PALMASPORT
	SC#10LX-PAS075
	GENOVA
	C/NOS.1-55
Letter of Credit No.:	2010556TLCU0073
Bill of Lading No.:	CBHU678551100751
Sales Contract No.:	10LX-PAS075
Purchase Order No.:	PAS-PO-CNSHA10043
Number and kind of Packages:	55 Bales
Total Gross Weight:	7425 Kgs
Value of Goods:	USD 80 784.00 CIF
Commodity:	100% Cotton Dyed Twill
Ocean Vessel:	Cosco Antwerp / 017W
Port of Loading:	Shanghai, China
Port of Discharge:	Genova, Italy
ETA:	Oct. 2, 2010

Yours truly,
Shanghai Lixin International Trading Co., Ltd.

李新
Li Xin

受益人证明:

上海立信国际贸易有限公司
Shanghai Lixin International Trading Co., Ltd.
5/F, No. 2230 West Zhong Shan Road, 200235, Shanghai, P. R. China

BENEFICIARY'S CERTIFICATE

SEP. 10, 2010

TO WHOM IT MAY CONCERN,

<u>CREDIT NUMBER: 2010556TLCU0073</u>
WE HEREBY CERTIFY THAT ONE SET OF N/N SHIPPING DOCUMENTS HAVE BEEN SENT TO THE APPLICANT BY DHL WITHIN 24 HOURS AFTER SHIPMENT.

上海立信国际贸易有限公司
Shanghai Lixin International Trading Co., Ltd.

陈弘毅
(signature)

李新:一定!

吴经理:你去制作即期汇票吧,出票日期就打5天后的9月15日,我们争取在那天向银行交单结汇。

李新:谢谢吴经理的指点!

[李新回到工位,开始制作汇票……

20分钟后,李新将制作完成的汇票正本一式两联(见第188页)呈送吴经理审核]

吴经理:我问你,为什么出两联汇票啊?

李新:根据业务惯例,正本汇票出一式两联,其中任何一联被使用后,另一联自动失效,这叫"付一不付二"或"付二不付一"。

吴经理:很好!汇票没什么问题了。下一步又要考验你了,说说看你准备怎样审单吧。

李新:我准备采用"纵横审单法"。具体来说,先将各结汇单据按照信用证及其修改书规定的单据种类、份数、日期、内容要求进行纵向审核,以确保"单证一致";接下来再以商业发票作为中心,对各单据之间进行横向审核,以确保"单单一致"。总之,尽一切可能,保证单据质量的绝对可靠,以便顺利办理结汇手续。

吴经理:有思路就好!你去审单吧。

李新:遵命!

（李新回到工位，根据信用证及信用证修改书，开始认真细致地审核全套单据……）

〔经过忙碌的5天，在王经理完成对全套单据的复核后，李新填制"出口信用证交单委托书"（见第189页），带齐全套单据（见190~198页），跟随财务结算部的钱老师至中国银行上海分行办理交单结汇……〕

THINK——理论思考

Think 9-1 交单结汇环节的主要工作是什么？如何理解其在出口贸易中的重要性？

"交单结汇"是指出口商在将货物装运出口后，应立即按照信用证的规定，正确缮制各种单据（包括在装运前已经准备好的单据和凭证），并在信用证规定的有效交单期限之内将各种单据和必要的凭证送交指定的银行办理要求付款、承兑或议付手续，并向银行进行结汇。外贸出口的目的是为了换取外汇，实现收入，所以"交单结汇"是出口合同履行程序的一个非常重要的环节。

Think 9-2 信用证项下的交单日期如何掌握？

信用证项下的交单期要求既不能超过信用证的有效期，又不能超过运输单据签发日期后21天，议付银行在收到单据后应立即按照信用证规定进行审核，并在收到单据次日起不超过5个银行工作日将审核结果通知受益人。

Think 9-3 交单结汇要注意的原则有哪些？

（1）单据的种类和份数以及单据本身的项目与信用证的规定相符，单单之间相互印证，做到单证一致，单单一致。

（2）交单时间必须在信用证规定的交单期和有效期之内。

（3）单据内容正确，包括所用文字与信用证一致，按信用证要求和国际惯例填写，力求简明。

（4）单据缮写或打印的字迹要清楚，单据表面要清洁。

Think 9-4 交单结汇需要哪些单据？

信用证要求的单据种类很多，通常根据这些单据的作用和性质的不同，可以分为主要单据和辅助单据两种。主要单据包括汇票、商业发票、提单、保险单等；辅助单据包括商检证书、出口许可证、产地证、装箱单和重量单等。按单据签发人的不同，可以分为出口商签发的单据如汇票、发票、装箱单、重量单等，有关机构或团体签发的单据如提单、保险单、商检证书、出口许可证等。

Think 9-5 缮制出口结汇单据有哪些基本要求？

在信用证业务中，开证行只有在审核单据与信用证表面完全相符后，才承担付款的责任。开证行如发现出口商所提交的单据与信用证有任何不符,均有可能出现拒付货款的情况。因此,结汇单据的缮制是否正确完备与安全迅速收汇有着十分重要的关系。对于结汇单据,一般都要本着"正确、完整、及时、简明、整洁"的原则来制作和审核。

(1) 正确:制作的单据只有正确,才能够保证及时收汇。单据应做到两个一致,即:单据与信用证保持一致、所提交的单据与单据之间也要保持严格一致。此外,单据与货物也应一致。这样,单据才能真实地代表货物,以免发生错装错运事故。

(2) 完整:必须按照信用证的规定提供各项单据,不能短少或缺项。单据的份数和单据本身的项目,如产地证明书上的原产国别、签章;其他单据上的货物名称、数量;海运提单和汇票的背书签字或人名章、公司章等内容和形式,也必须完整无缺。

(3) 及时:应在信用证的有效期内,及时将单据送交议付银行,以便银行早日寄出单据,按时收汇。此外,在货物出运之前,应尽可能将有关结汇单据送交银行预先审核,使银行有较充裕的时间来检查单证、单单之间有无差错或问题。如发现一般差错,可以提前改正,如有重大问题,也可及早由进出口企业与国外买方联系修改信用证,避免在货物出运后不能收汇。

(4) 简明:单据的内容,应按信用证要求和国际惯例填写,力求简明,切勿加列不必要的内容,以免弄巧成拙。

(5) 整洁:单据的布局要美观、大方。缮写或打印的字迹要清楚。单据表面要清洁,对更改地方要加盖校对图章。有些单据,如提单、汇票以及其他一些单据的主要项目,如金额、件数、重量等,一般不宜更改。

Think 9-6　信用证项下主要出口结汇单据的缮制要求有哪些?

信用证项下主要出口结汇单据的缮制要求如下:

1) 汇票:必须列明出票条件(Drawn Clauses),在信用证收付方式下,须说明是根据哪家银行在何日开立的哪一份信用证出具的;应按信用证的规定填写付款人;议付汇票的受款人通常应为议付行;汇票一般开具一式两份,两份具有同等效力,任何一份付讫,另一份自动失效。信用证汇票基本上是跟单汇票,信用证对随付的单据会提出具体要求。

2) 提单:提单是代表货物所有权的凭证,因而也是卖方提供的各项单据中最重要的一种。提单的各项内容如提单的种类、收货人、货物的名称和件数、目的港、有关运费的记载、提单的份数等一定要与信用证相符。

信用证通常要求提供"全套清洁已装船作成凭指示和空白背书的提单"。对此要求应注意:

(1) 全套,是指由承运人签发的正本提单份数,包括仅有一份的正本提单,通常是一式两份或三份。

(2) 清洁,即提单上不能有"货物受损"、"包装不良"等批注。

(3) 已装船,即提单上应注明船名和装船日期,并有承运人或船长签名。

(4) 凭指示,是指提单上的收货人一栏中填有"凭指示"、"凭××指示"字样。

(5) 空白背书,是指背书人(出口商)仅在提单背面签字,并不注明被背书人。

3) 保险单和保险凭证:保险单(大保单)一般要求被保险人的名称,被保险货物的名称、数量或重量、唛头、运输工具的种类和名称,承保险别,起讫地点,保险期限和保险金额与信用证条款一致。

保险凭证（小保单）与保险单有同等的效力。但如果信用证要求提交"Insurance Policy"，则出口商不能使用保险凭证。我国保险公司大都签发大保单。

在信用证没有特别规定的前提下，信用证受益人为被保险人，并加空白背书以转让保险权益。

4) 商业发票：简称发票，它是出口企业开立的凭此向买方收款的发货价目清单，是供买卖双方凭此发货、收货、记账、收付货款和报关纳税的依据。发票并无统一格式，但其内容大致相同。主要包括：发票编号、开立日期、有关出口合同号码、信用证号码、收货人名称地址、运输标志以及商品的名称、规格、数量、包装方法、单价、总值和装运地、目的地等。发票内容必须符合买卖合同规定，在采用信用证付款方式时，则应与信用证的规定严格相符，绝不能有丝毫差异。商业发票可以只标明出单人名称而不加签署。如需签字，来证中应明确规定。

5) 装箱单和重量单：装箱单（Packing List）也称包装单，它和重量单（Weight Memo）是商业发票的补充单据。装箱单主要用于工业品，对每件包装内的货物名称、规格、花色等逐一进行详细说明，以便进口地的海关检验和进口商核对。重量单多用于以重量计价的初级产品，载明每件商品的重量，有的还分别列明每件商品毛重、净重，其作用与装箱单相同。

6) 检验证书：我国的检验证书一般由中国出入境检验检疫局出具，如信用证无特别规定，也可区分不同情况，由进出口公司或生产企业出具，但证书的名称及所列项目或检验结果，应与信用证规定相同。须注意的是检验证书的有效期，一般货物为60天，新鲜果蔬类为2～3个星期，出口货物务必在有效期内出运，如超过期限，应重新报验。

7) 产地证明书：普通产地证用以证明货物的生产国别，进口国海关凭以核定应征收的税率。在我国，普通产地证可由出口商自行签发，或由进出口商品检验局签发，或由中国国际贸易促进委员会签发。在实际业务中，应根据买卖合同或信用证的规定，提交相应的产地证。

Think 9-7　信用证项下各种出口结汇单据的审核要点有哪些？

信用证项下各种出口结汇单据的审核要点如下：

(1) 综合审核。检查规定的单证是否齐全包括所需单证的份数；检查所提供的文件名称和类型是否符合要求；有些单证是否按规定进行了认证；单证之间的货物描述、数量、金额、重量、体积、运输标志等是否一致；单证出具或提交的日期是否符合要求。

(2) 分类审核。严格对汇票、商业发票、保险单据、运输单据、装箱单、重量单、产地证书、商检证书等进行审核。需要注意的是，均须先与信用证的条款进行核对，再与其他有关单据核对，求得"单证一致、单单一致"。

(3) 常见差错。汇票大、小写金额打错；汇票的付款人名称、地址打错；发票的抬头人打错；有关单据如汇票、发票、保险单等的币制名称不一致或不符合信用证的规定；发票上的货物描述不符合信用证的规定；多装或短装；有关单据的类型不符合信用证要求；单单之间商品名称、数量、件数、唛头、毛净重等不一致；应提交的单据提交不全或份数不足；未按信用证要求对有关单据如发票、产地证等进行认证；漏签字或盖章；汇票、运输提单、保险单据上未按要求进行背书;逾期装运;逾期交单。

Think 9-8　如何处理单证不符的情况?

当单据出现不符点时,首先要争取时间及时修改更换单证,使其与信用证相符。如果来不及,视具体情况,选择如下办法处理:

(1) 表提:单据出现不符点时,受益人向议付行书面提出不符点并出具保函,担保日后遭到拒付时,一切后果由受益人承担,这种做法也称"担保结汇"。适用于不符点并不严重或虽然是实质性不符,但事先已经买方确认可以接受的情形。

(2) 电提:即出现单证不符时,议付行先给国外开证行去电,列明不符点,待开证行同意后再将单据寄出。如买方同意,开证行授权议付,出口地银行立即寄单收汇;如不同意,卖方要及时处理运输中的货物。

(3) 跟单托收:议付行不同意表提担保结汇或电提征询开证行意见的做法,这时,卖方只能采用托收方式收款。

此外,出现不符点时,出口商无论如何都要头脑冷静,认真仔细分析市场动向,密切关注货物的下落,弄清拒付原因及拒付理由,同时与进口商取得联系,积极寻求解决办法,如说服对方接受单据,付款赎单;或适当降价;或寻求当地其他买主。在进口商缴纳定金的条件下,也可以考虑把货运回。如果不是我方的失误,而是由于开证行水平问题,对信用证理解有误,则我方应当与议付行一道,向开证行阐明立场观点,说明缘由,并催促对方尽快支付货款,否则逾期收款的利息由开证行承担。语气坚定有力而不缺少委婉之词,以达到解决问题的目的。

Think 9-9　信用证业务中常见的有哪几种结汇方式?

结汇是指出口商将所收取的外汇按照银行牌价卖给国家外汇银行。在信用证结算方式下,我国银行提供以下三种结汇方式。

(1) 收妥结汇:又称收妥付款,是指信用证议付行收到出口企业的出口单据后,经审查无误,将单据寄交国外付款行索取货款的结汇做法。在这种方式下,议付行都是在收到付款行的货款后,即从国外付款行收到该行账户的贷记通知书(Credit Note),才按当日外汇牌价,按照出口企业的指示,将货款折成人民币拨入出口企业的账户。

(2) 押汇:又称买单结汇,即指议付行在审单无误情况下,按信用证条款贴现受益人的汇票或者以一定的折扣买入信用证下的货运单据,从票面金额中扣除从议付日到估计收到票款之日的利息,将余款按议付日外汇牌价折成人民币,拨给出口企业。议付行向受益人垫付资金、买入跟单汇票后,即成为汇票持有人,可凭票向付款行索取票款。银行之所以做出口押汇,是为了给出口企业提供资金融通的便利,这有利于加速出口企业的资金周转。

(3) 定期结汇:指议付行根据向国外付款行索偿所需时间,预先确定一个固定的结汇期限,并与出口企业约定,该期限到期后,无论是否已经收到国外付款行的货款,都将主动将票款金额折成人民币拨交出口企业。

Think 9-10　押汇和收妥结汇做法有什么区别？

押汇指议付银行议付时垫付货款，但要扣除垫付日至收款日的利息，然后向开证行寄单索偿。收妥结汇是议付行不垫付货款，先将单据寄住开证行，待开证审核单证相符给议付行付款后，再将货款按当日外汇买入价折成人民币划入出口人账户。

Think 9-11　什么情况下银行拒绝办理押汇？

有下列情况之一或两种以上情况存在的，我国议付行不作押汇：① 信用证有允许电汇索偿条款的；② 开证行资信较差的；③ 开证行所在国外汇短缺的；④ 付款行或偿付行所在地政治局势紧张的；⑤ 使用货币疲软的或不可兑换的；⑥ 单证不符的；⑦ 受益人经济拮据的。

Think 9-12　出口商是否可以轻易采用担保结汇？

担保结汇是在单据出现不符合信用证条款情况下的变通结汇方式。当有不符合单据时，议付银行应出口商要求，有出口商向银行开出"担保书"，承担开证行/开证人提出异议时所发生的一切损失和风险，议付行凭以议付或接受单据，同时向开证行寄单，寄单时列明单证中存在的不符点。如开证行/开证人拒付，则议付行凭"担保书"向出口商追回票款。如开证行/开证人同意付款，则"担保书"不再有效。

担保结汇有很大风险，除非出口商与开证人关系很好，而且是在取得书面同意下才可办理。

ACT——模拟训练

Act 9　出口商缮制汇票

2010 年 12 月 28 日，钱晓俊根据信用证及其修改书，缮制并审核所有结汇单据。在经理完成对全套结汇单据的复核后，2011 年 1 月 5 日，钱晓俊向中国银行上海分行交单结汇。

请以钱晓俊的身份，缮制汇票。（见第 204 页）

DISCUSS——个案讨论

Discuss 9

在本实训 ACT 环节中，2011 年 1 月 4 日，根据信用证对单据的要求，钱晓俊提请中外运集装箱运输有限公司出具一份"船公司证明"，以便向银行交单结汇时一并提交。根据之前实训的 ACT 和 DISCUSS 环节中已缮制完成的单据，船公司该如何缮制"船公司证明"？（见第 204 页）

汇票:

```
                        BILL OF EXCHANGE

凭                                  不可撤销信用证
Drawn                               Irrevocable   L/C
Under_____ No._____
日期
Date_____ 支取 Payable With interest @ **** % **** 按 **** 息 **** 付款
号码           汇票金额                        上海
No._____ Exchange for _____ Shanghai_____
                    见票              日后(本汇票之副本未付)付交
                    at_____ sight of this FIRST of Exchange (Second of Exchange
Being unpaid) Pay to the order of_____
金额
the sum of _____


此致
To:                          SHANGHAI HAINA IMPORT & EXPORT
                             COMPANY LIMITED
                                   周致君
_____          _____
                                   (signature)
```

船公司证明:

中外运集装箱运输有限公司
SINOTRANS CONTAINER LINES CO., LTD

CERTIFICATE

DATE:_____

中外运集装箱运输有限公司
SINOTRANS CONTAINER LINES CO., LTD

情景模拟实训十

收汇核销与退税

 LOOK——情景示范

[在办理交单结汇后的两周内,李新陆续收到洋山海关加盖验讫章的"出口货物报关单收汇核销联"、"出口货物报关单出口退税专用"和"出口收汇核销单"(见第206~208页),中国银行上海分行开具的"涉外收入申报单"(又称"银行水单")]

(李新向王经理请教)

李新: 王经理,这些是洋山海关和中国银行上海分行反馈给我们的单据。

王经理:(边细看这些单据边说)小李,顺利结汇标志着我们这笔交易圆满结束啦!但从整个出口业务流程来看,还剩最后两步。

李新: 您指的最后两步就是核销和退税吧?

王经理: 正是!不过在办理核销退税手续前,你先给客户发一封E-mail,对整笔交易做一下回顾并对今后合作进行一下展望。

李新: 知道了,谢谢王经理!

[李新回到工位,拟写了一封业务善后函E-mail(见第208页)发给了客户]

(第二天,李新向王经理请教)

李新: 王经理,关于我手上这笔已经结汇的业务,您看我可以去办理核销退税了吗?

王经理: 我倒想先听你解释一下"出口收汇核销"和"出口退税"。

李新: 出口收汇核销,就是出口商在货物报关出口后,向外汇管理局报送银行出具的收汇证明和出口货物报关单等文件,从而完成相应的核对程序。完成出口收汇核销后,出口商就可以向国税局申请办理出口退税手续了,国税局根据出口商品对应的退税率,退还出口商之前在国内生产和流通环节缴纳的增值税和消费税等流转税,退税款是出口商盈利的重要组成部分。

王经理: 很好!你跟着财务结算部的钱老师去办理核销退税吧。

李新: 明白了!

(李新跟随财务结算部的钱老师向国家外汇管理局上海市分局提交"涉外收入申报单"、"出口货物报关单收汇核销联"和"出口收汇核销单",办理出口收汇核销手续。外管局受理核销后,分别在"涉外收入申报单"和"出口收汇核销单"上加盖"已核销章",并返还给钱老师。他们又向上海市国家税务局提交"增值税发票抵扣联"、"商业发票"、"出口货物报关单

经海关加盖验讫章的出口货物报关单(收汇核销联):

中华人民共和国海关出口货物报关单

收汇核销联

预录入编号:224820100493215380　　　海关编号:224820100493215380

出口口岸 洋山海关（港区）	备案号	出口日期	申报日期 2010-09-08
经营单位 上海立信国际贸易有限公司 3103070520	运输方式 江海运输	运输工具名称 COSCO ANTWERP/017W	提运单号 CBHU678551100751
发货单位 上海立信国际贸易有限公司 3103070520	贸易方式 一般贸易	征免性质 一般征税	结汇方式 信用证
许可证号	运抵国（地区） 意大利	指运港 热那亚	境内货源地 闵行其他
批准文号 017336422	成交方式 CIF	运费 502/1800.0000/3	保费 502/133.2945/3	杂费 000//
合同协议号 10LX-PAS075	件数 55	包装种类 BALES	毛重（千克） 7425	净重（千克） 7150
集装箱号 CBHU4261027 / 20 / 2275	随附单据 出境货物通关单:310834042802273		生产厂家

标记唛码及备注
PALMASPORT
SC#10LX-PAS075
GENOVA
C/NOS.1-55

项号	商品编号	商品名称、规格型号	数量及单位	最终目的国(地区)	单价	总价	币制	征免
1	52083300 00	全棉染色布 100% COTTON DYED TWILL KJ2001	26400.000 米 7425.000 千克	意大利	3.0600	80784.00	USD	照章

税费征收情况

录入员　录入单位	兹声明以上申报无讹并承担法律责任	海关审单批注及放行日期(签章)
报关员 3192714518236750 报关员 张闻信 单位地址 上海市中山西路2230号5楼 邮编 200235 电话 021-64391520	申报单位（签章） 报关专用章 填制日期 2010-09-08	审单 征税 统计 放行

经海关加盖验讫章的出口货物报关单(出口退税专用联):

中华人民共和国海关出口货物报关单

出口退税专用

预录入编号: 224820100493215380 海关编号: 224820100493215380

出口口岸 洋山海关（港区）	备案号	出口日期	申报日期 2010-09-08
经营单位 上海立信国际贸易有限公司 3103070520	运输方式 江海运输	运输工具名称 COSCO ANTWERP/017W	提运单号 CBHU678551100751
发货单位 上海立信国际贸易有限公司 3103070520	贸易方式 一般贸易	征免性质 一般征税	结汇方式 信用证
许可证号	运抵国（地区） 意大利	指运港 热那亚	境内货源地 闵行其他
批准文号 017336422	成交方式 CIF	运费 502/1800.0000/3	保费 502/133.2945/3	杂费 000//
合同协议号 10LX-PAS075	件数 55	包装种类 BALES	毛重（千克） 7425	净重（千克） 7150
集装箱号 CBHU4261027/20/2275	随附单据 出境货物通关单：310834042802273		生产厂家

标记唛码及备注
PALMASPORT
SC#10LX-PAS075
GENOVA
C/NOS.1-55

项号	商品编号	商品名称、规格型号	数量及单位	最终目的国(地区)	单价	总价	币制	征免
1	5208330000	全棉染色布 100% COTTON DYED TWILL KJ2001	26400.000 米 7425.000 千克	意大利	3.0600	80784.00	USD	照章

税费征收情况

兹声明以上申报无讹并承担法律责任

录入员	录入单位		海关审单批注及放行日期(签章)
报关员 3192714518236750 报关员 张闻信		申报单位（签章） 报关专用章	审单 征税 验讫章
单位地址 上海市中山西路2230号5楼			
邮编 200235 电话 021-64391520		填制日期 2010-09-08	查验 放行

经海关加盖验讫章的出口收汇核销单：

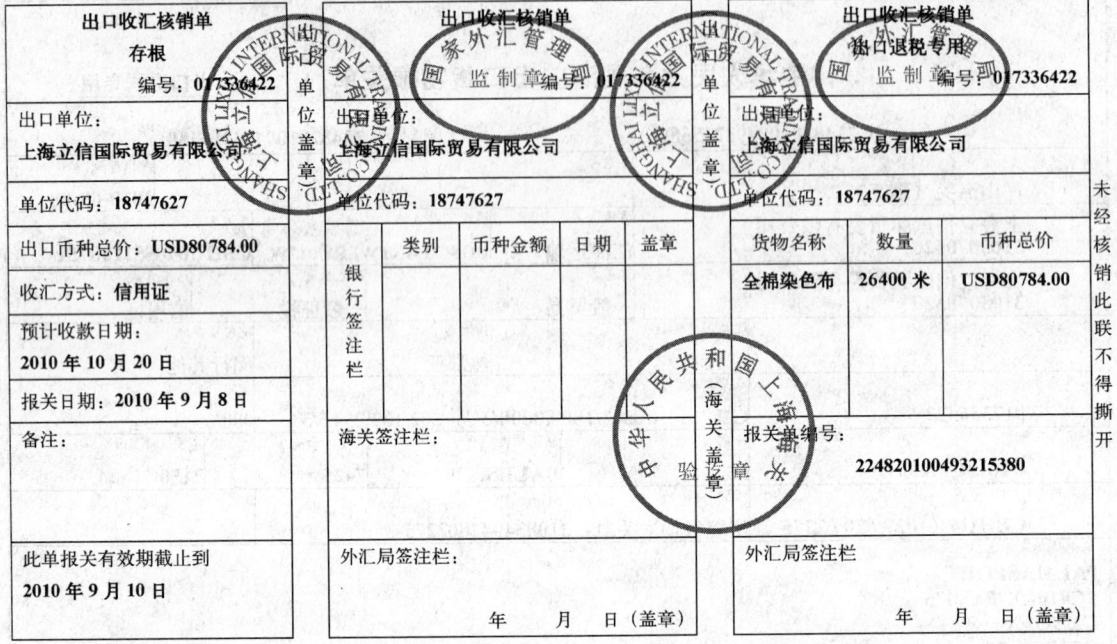

出口商业务善后函：

发件人：	Li_xin@lixin.com.cn
收件人：	f.taldelli@palmavito.com
日　期：	2010-09-28
主　题：	A More Prospective Future

Dear Mr. Taldelli,

We are pleased to receive the proceeds under L/C No. 2010556TLCU0073 against S/C No. 10LX-PAS075.

We appreciate your cooperation during the past months and are pleased to see the initial transaction going through smoothly.

We are sure that you will find the consignment to your entire satisfaction and looking forward to your repeat orders.

We trust that through our joint efforts, we will have a more prospective future.

Yours truly,
Shanghai Lixin International Trading Co., Ltd.
Li Xin

出口退税专用"和外管局加盖已核销章的"出口收汇核销单出口退税专用",办理出口退税手续,国税局审核无误后,将出口货物的退税款项拨付给了立信公司)

(王经理找到李新)

王经理: 小李,你已经成功完成了一整笔出口业务,各部门对你的反映都不错。熟悉业务流程的各个环节是一名合格外销员的基本功,我准备让你再锻炼几个月,到年底实习期结束后给你定岗。

李新: 谢谢王经理,您和公司里的各位老师们给了我很大的支持与帮助!能从事自己喜欢的行业是我的幸运,能进入立信公司更是我的幸事!

王经理: 的确,如果没有我们这些老业务员们引领着你,你的成长可能不会如此之快,当然如果没有你个人的努力跟进,那一切也只是空谈。我真替你感到高兴,继续加油,只要坚持不懈,你的前途会越加光明!

李新: 自己的路要靠自己走,我一定再接再厉!

THINK ——理论思考

Think 10-1 出口收汇核销制度的目的是什么?出口企业进行出口收汇核销经过哪些流程?

出口收汇核销是国家加强出口收汇管理,确保国家外汇收入,防止外汇流失,指定外汇管理部门对出口企业贸易下的外汇收入情况进行监督检查的一种制度。出口企业进行出口收汇核销主要经过以下流程:

(1)出口商向海关制卡中心申办中国电子口岸IC卡。

(2)出口商网上申请出口收汇核销单(简称核销单)的份数。

(3)出口商提供下列资料到外汇管理局申领纸质出口收汇核销单:① 核销员证;② IC卡;③ 出口合同复印件(首次申领时提供)。

(4)将核销单编号上网向出口报关地海关备案。

(5)填写纸质核销单,加盖公司印章,出口报关。

(6)海关进行纸质核销单与电子底账一致性的核查。货物出口后,海关在出口收汇核销单上签注盖章,并随同报关单(出口退税专用联)返还给出口商。

(7)出口商交银行结汇,银行把数据通过计算机网络发给外汇管理局;同时出口商把海关返还的核销单和报关单在电子口岸交单。

(8)银行收汇签注返还给出口商。

(9)出口商备齐已出口收汇的下列单证到外汇局办理核销:① 出口收汇核销单;② 报关单(出口收汇核销联);③ 银行结(收)汇水单;④ 一般贸易出口收汇核销档案信息登记表。

Think 10-2 我国的出口收汇核销需要提供的材料有哪些?

出口商收到收汇水单后,连同出口报关单(退税专用)向外管局核销外汇。核销时需要以下单据：收汇水单、出口收汇核销单、出口报关单及出口发票。

办理一般贸易全额收汇核销应提供以下材料：

(1) 企业出口收汇核销手册。

(2) 加盖海关"验讫章"的核销单正本及退税联。

(3) 加盖海关"验讫章"的出口货物报关单正本。

(4) 商业发票正本。

外商投资企业应提供由税务部门统一制定的出口发票，加盖企业公章或发票专用章；其他出口企业提供的出口发票须加盖企业发票专用章。

(5) 银行出具的出口收汇核销专用联。

Think 10-3　出口收汇核销单有哪些内容？如何填制？

出口收汇核销单的主要内容和填制方法：

(1) 单位名称：填对外签订并执行合同的有出口经营权的外贸单位（包括外商投资企业）的全称。委托报关时，填委托单位名称；委托出口并以代理出口单位名义签订出口合同并负责收汇时，填代理出口单位名称；两个或两个以上单位联合出口时，填负责报关的出口单位名称。

(2) 出口币种总价：按应收外汇的原币种填写，为该笔出口货物的应收汇总额。

(3) 收汇方式：按合同要求从信用证、托收、自寄单据（一般仅限于鲜活商品、易腐商品、出境展销商品、出口金额在10万美元及以下的商品、预收货款项下的出口商品。其他商品如采用这种方式收汇须预先经外汇管理部门批准）三种收汇方式中选填一种，并列明即期或远期收汇，还须列明相应的远期收汇天数；如为分期付款，则须列明每次付款日期和付款金额。

(4) 预计收款日期：应根据合同规定的付款日期或根据合同推算的付款日期填写。即期信用证（或托收）项下的货物，属近洋的，从寄单日起按25天结算；属远洋的，从寄单日起按35天结算。远期信用证（或托收）项下的货物，属近洋的，从汇票规定付款日期起按35天结算；属远洋的按45天结算。如为分期付款，应列明每次收款日期及金额。寄售项下的最迟收款日期不得超过自报关之日起360天。自寄单据项下的出口货款，须自报关之日起50天内结汇或收账。

(5) 报关日期：填海关放行日期。

(6) 报关单位备注：① 如委托出口使用代理出口单位的核销单时，代理出口单位须在此栏注明委托单位名称，并加盖代理单位公章；② 如两个或两个以上单位联合出口时，应由报关单位在此栏加注联合出口单位名址和各单位的出口金额，并加盖报关单位公章；③ 填写出口货物的发票编号、合同号等核销过程中须附加说明的内容。原出口商品调整或部分退款、部分更换的，还应填写原出口商品核销单的编号等情况。

Think 10-4　出口退税政策的目的是什么？

出口退税是指对出口产品退还其在国内生产和流通环节实际缴纳的产品税、增值税、营业税和特别消费税的一种制度，它主要通过退还出口产品的国内已纳税款来平衡国内产品的税收负担，使本国产品以不含税成本进入国际市场，与国外产品在同等条件下进行竞争，从而增强竞争能力,扩大产品出口。

Think 10-5　出口退税要经过哪些程序?

出口退税的一般程序如下:

(1) 出口商准备出口收汇核销单的出口退税专用联和报关单的出口退税专用联,以及在国税局网上作过认证的增值税发票。

(2) 出口商对有关单证资料进行处理:① 审核单证;② 审核账务;③ 整理单证;④ 录入数据;⑤ 处理数据,制作软盘。

(3) 出口商将申报软盘报送税务局进行预审(现在也可在网上预审)。

(4) 出口商根据预审反馈的情况,进行数据稽核和修改。

(5) 出口商向所在地市国家税务局退税管理分局正式申请退税。

(6) 在电子信息和资料齐全正确的情况下,一般在正式申请之日起1个月内出口商可收到退税款。

Think 10-6　申请出口退税需要哪些凭证?

出口单位申请出口退税,应向国家税务机关提交"三单两票":
(1) 结汇水单(银行出具的)。
(2) 出口收汇核销单(出口退税专用联)。
(3) 出口货物报关单。
(4) 出口销售发票。
(5) 出口购货发票。

Think 10-7　业务善后函的作用以及撰写要点有哪些?

拟写善后函是出口商在业务善后阶段的重要工作,对于确定双方间(出口商与进口商之间,出口商与供应商之间)长期的业务关系是非常有帮助的。根据面临的情况和对象不同,不同的善后函撰写要点是不同的。

1. 开证行接受单据时给进口商的善后函

由于此时整笔交易进展得非常顺利,写法上就显得相对比较随意。出口商可以回顾该笔交易中值得肯定的地方,诸如感谢对方所做的努力,对交易增进了双方的了解而表示高兴等等。也可展望未来,如希望能继续扩大合作,收到更多的订单,建立长期业务往来关系,或借此推荐新产品等。

2. 遭到开证行拒付时给进口商的善后函

虽然这种善后函会因单证不符的内容不同而写法各异,但总的说来,由于出口商处于极为不利的地位,语气应当诚恳、委婉,并且具有说服力,以赢得买方的谅解。要尽量解释清楚单证不符的原因,对由此造成的不便表示歉意,并回顾双方以往的愉快合作等。更重要的是,出口商应当强调单证不符点的细微和交易的实质,并不影响商品的品质,不会对进口商的实际利益造成损害。当然,有时做一些适当的让步,比如减价,也是必要的和明智的。

3. 给供应商的善后函

当一笔交易结束时,除了给进口商拟写善后函之外,一般还要去函给供应商。如果该笔业务进展顺利,通常告知供应商货款已汇出,注意查收并感谢对方的合作。如果当进口商收到货后,提出一些和供应商有关的建议和意见,通常也应该将此反映给供应商,以便在将来的合作中改进。

ACT——模拟训练

Act 10 出口商撰写业务善后函

2011年1月20日,钱晓俊收到中国银行上海分行开具的涉外收入申报单,获知开证银行CHASE MANHATTAN BANK, HOUSTON, U.S.A.已付款,此笔交易顺利结汇。钱晓俊向客户发出业务善后函E-mail并随附2011年第一季度最新商品目录,圆满结束本笔交易。1月22日,钱晓俊顺利办结核销退税手续。

请以钱晓俊的身份,撰写该业务善后E-mail。

出口商业务善后函:

发件人:	damonchan@hainaco.com.cn
收件人:	ray.sinclair@gulfday.com
日　期:	2011-01-20
主　题:	Nice Cooperation

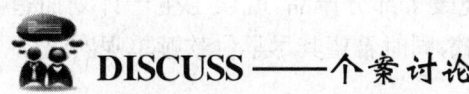

DISCUSS ——个案讨论

Discuss 10

2011年5月，立信国贸公司向英国Roefster International Corp.公司出口一批纺织品。5月底，李新向中国银行上海分行交单结汇。6月初，李新收到中行上海分行转自开证银行STANDARD CHARTERED BANK, LONDON, U.K.的"拒付通知书"如下：

拒付通知书：

拒 付 通 知 书
Notification of Dishonor

DATE: JUN. 4, 2011

To: 致： SHANGHAI LIXIN INTERNATIONAL TRADING CO., LTD. 5/F, NO. 2230 WEST ZHONG SHAN ROAD, 200235, SHANGHAI, P. R. CHINA TEL：021-64391520　FAX：021-64391530		WHEN CORRESPONDING PLEASE QUOTE OUR REFERENCE NO. BKCNSHA1130158	
Issuing Bank 开证行 STANDARD CHARTERED BANK, LONDON, U.K.			**Transmitted to us through**
L/C No. 信用证号 AD07221EA91253	**Dated** 开证日期 APRIL 17, 2011		**Amount** 金额 USD 164187.60

Dear Sirs, 敬启者，
We hereby advise you that we have received from the a/m bank a(n) Notification of Dishonor reads:
兹通知贵司，我行收自上述银行的拒付通知如下：
WE FIND THE DOCUMENTS UNDER CAPTIONED L/C CONTAINING FOLLOWING DISCREPANCIES:
*THE ON BOARD DATE IN THE B/L IS FOUR DAYS LATER THAN THE LATEST SHIPMENT DATE SPECIFIED IN THE L/C.

Please contact the Buyer and we hold your documents at your disposal.
请联络买方，我行保留单据以听候贵司处置。

Yours faithfully,
For **BANK OF CHINA SHANGHAI BRANCH**
高志笃
Gao Zhidu (Mr.)

经查,此次装船延误是由于工厂仓库遭到火灾,烧毁了部分产品,耽误了生产计划而造成的。针对以上情况,李新该如何向英国客户去函致歉,同时希望其尽早付款赎单呢?

出口商业务善后函:

发件人:	li_xin@lixin.com.cn
收件人:	h.wolfe@roefstercorp.com
日　　期:	2011 - 06 - 05
主　　题:	Concerning the Dishonor of L/C No. AD07221EA91253

Dear Ms. Wolfe,

参 考 答 案

情景模拟实训一　交易前准备

Act 1-1

询价索样传真文稿：

上海海纳进出口有限公司
Shanghai Haina Import & Export Company Limited
Rm. 905 Yong An Mansion, No. 12 Huashan Rd., Shanghai, P. R. China
Tel: 0086-21-54105623　Fax: 0086-21-54742511　E-mail: sales@hainaco.com

致：采薇杯业有限公司
刘总：
　　您好！
　　经我司孙志远先生的介绍，得知贵司专业生产真空保温杯系列产品，我们很感兴趣，愿与贵司建立长期业务关系。
　　我司准备参加下个月在上海举办的国际日用品展销会，届时将有众多国外日用品专营客户光顾。我们希望贵司能够提供一些产品目录及样品并请附上含税价格单，同时注明包装方式、交货时间、交货地点、付款方式及最低起订数量等详细的产品信息。
　　盼复！
　　顺颂商祺！

钱晓俊
2010年9月15日

Act 1-2

出口商建交函：

发件人：	damonchan@hainaco.com.cn
收件人：	ray.sinclair@gulfday.com
日　期：	2010-10-12
主　题：	Establishment of Business Relations

Dear Mr. Sinclair,

We have obtained your name and address from the Commercial Counselor of your Embassy at Shanghai International Commodity Expo and write you for the establishment of business relations.

We specialize in the exportation of high quality stainless steel vacuum products which have enjoyed great popularity in world markets such as sport type vacuum flask, travel type vacuum flask, vacuum coffee pot, vacuum food jug, etc.

We will forward you our latest catalog for your reference in a few days and hope that you would contact us if any item is of interest to you.

For our business and financial standing, we may refer you to our bankers:
BANK OF CHINA SHANGHAI BRANCH
NO. 34 EAST ZHONG SHAN ROAD, SHANGHAI, P. R. CHINA

In addition, would you please let us have your bank reference?

We are looking forward to your favorable reply.

Yours truly,
Shanghai Haina Import & Export Company Limited
Damon Chan (Mr.)

Act 1-3

进口商询盘函：

From:	ray.sinclair@gulfday.com
To:	damonchan@hainaco.com.cn
Date:	2010-10-22
Re:	Inquiry

Dear Mr. Chan,

We are pleased to receive your E-mail of your catalog on Oct. 12.

We are one of the largest importers of daily necessities in southwest of United States and wish to expand our present range with more excellent commodities. We believe there is a promising market here for moderately priced and excellent quality products.

After studying commodities on your catalog, we are particularly interested in the following items: Sport type vacuum flask (Art No. CWS3-50) and Travel type vacuum flask (Art No. CWT2-100). Please quote us on FOB LOADING PORT, CFR AND CIF HOUSTON (effected by FCL). It would be helpful if you could supply relevant samples, please advise us the cost of the samples including postal charges so that we could remit to you.

Our bank information is as follows:
CHASE MANHATTAN BANK
147 PETITE STATON AVENUE, HOUSTON, TX 40132, U.S.A.

We hope to hear from you soon.

Yours sincerely,
Raymond Sinclair
Gulfland Dainecess Inc.

Discuss 1-1

资信调查函：

发件人：	li_xin@lixin.com.cn
收件人：	enterprise@anzbank.com
日　期：	2011-03-10
主　题：	Credit Inquiry

Dear Sir or Madam,

We have received an initial business letter from Glamour International Company Limited in Melbourne, who has given us your name as bank reference. Before we get down to business with them we should be obliged if you could let us have your opinion on their reputation and their financial standing.

Any information you may give us will, of course, be treated as strictly confidential. We assure you that we shall be pleased at any time to render you a sound service.

Yours faithfully,
Shanghai Lixin International Trading Co., Ltd.
Li Xin (Mr.)

出口商询盘函：

发件人：	li_xin@lixin.com.cn
收件人：	k.sheldon@claco.com
日　期：	2011-03-15
主　题：	Inquiry for Innovative Textile

Dear Mr. Sheldon,

Thank you for your E-mail of March 10 showing your interest in our product of textiles.

As you know, we mainly specialize in the exportation and development of textile products. Recently, we developed an innovative kind of textile with special antibacterial finished material both bleached and dyed. A number of international manufacturers have placed large orders for our new product. As you asked, we are happy to attach our latest illustrated catalogue which includes the above-mentioned new product. Also, we are separately sending you samples of textile both bleached and dyed per 10 M and feel confident that when you have examined them you will agree the new product is promising.

We will give you reasonable quotation and discount if quantity is available. The earliest date of shipment is the end of March and the payment is to be made by L/C at sight according to our practice. For our business and financial standing, we may refer you to our bankers:
BANK OF CHINA SHANGHAI BRANCH
NO. 34 EAST ZHONG SHAN ROAD, SHANGHAI, P. R. CHINA

We look forward to your specific offer and hope to have the opportunity to work together with you in the future.

Yours sincerely,
Shanghai Lixin International Trading Co., Ltd.
Li Xin

Attachment: Latest Illustrated Catalogue

Discuss 1-2 （略）

情景模拟实训二 交易磋商一——报价核算与发盘

Act 2-1

出口实际成本核算：

出口实际成本核算
1. CWS3-50 的实际成本 退税收入 $=\dfrac{采购成本}{1+增值税率}\times$ 退税率 $=\dfrac{12.6}{1+17\%}\times 11\% = 1.18$ 元/个 实际成本 = 采购成本 - 退税收入 = 12.6 - 1.18 = 11.42 元/个 2. CWT2-100 的实际成本 退税收入 $=\dfrac{19.2}{1+17\%}\times 11\% = 1.81$ 元/个 实际成本 = 19.2 - 1.81 = 17.39 元/个

Act 2-2

出口报价基础数量计算：

报价基础数量计算
1. 计算 20 尺集装箱装入 CWS3-50 的数量 CWS3-50 积载因数 = 体积÷毛重 = 0.0619÷0.0294 = 2.11 立方米/吨 20 尺箱最少可装 25 立方米，因为积载系数大于 1，属于轻货，故按体积法计算。 可装外包装数量 = 集装箱体积÷单位外包装体积 = 25÷0.0619 = 403.88 箱，即 403 箱 货物数量 = 403×40 = 16120 个 2. 计算 20 尺集装箱装入 CWT2-100 的数量 CWT2-100 积载因数 = 0.0773÷0.0273 = 2.83 立方米/吨，按体积法计算。 可装外包装数量 = 25÷0.0773 = 323.42 箱，即 323 箱 货物数量 = 323×20 = 6460 个

Act 2-3

表 2-7 费用核算表

	项 目	CWS3-50	CWT2-100
费 用	包干费	1250/16120 = 0.0775 元/个	1250/6460 = 0.1935 元/个
	业务费用	美元报价×5%	美元报价×5%
	垫款利息	12.6×3/12×6% = 0.189 元/个	19.2×3/12×6% = 0.288 元/个
	保险费	美元报价×(1+10%)×0.15%	美元报价×(1+10%)×0.15%
	银行手续费	美元报价×0.35%	美元报价×0.35%
	出口运费	2300/16120 = 0.1427 美元/个	2300/6460 = 0.3560 美元/个

Act 2-4

出口报价核算：

出口报价核算

(1) CWS3-50 的报价核算：

实际成本：11.42 元/个，换算成美元 = 11.42/6.8 = 1.68 美元/个

人民币费用：包干费 0.0775 + 垫款利息 0.189 = 0.2665 元/个，换算成美元
= 0.2665/6.8 = 0.0392 美元/个

美元费用：业务费用 报价×5% + 保险费 报价×(1+10%)×0.15% + 银行手续费
报价×0.35% + 出口运费 0.1427

利润：报价×10%

报价 = 实际成本 + 人民币费用 + 美元费用 + 利润

FOB 报价 = 1.68 + 0.0392 + 报价×5% + 报价×10% + 报价×0.35%

FOB 报价 = 2.03 美元/个

CFR 报价 = 1.68 + 0.0392 + 报价×5% + 报价×10% + 报价×0.35% + 0.1427

CFR 报价 = 2.20 美元/个

CIF 报价 = 1.68 + 0.0392 + 报价×5% + 报价×10% + 报价×(1+10%)×0.15% +
报价×0.35% + 0.1427

CIF 报价 = 2.21 美元/个

(2) CWT2-100 的报价核算：

实际成本：17.39 元/个，换算成美元 = 17.39/6.8 = 2.56 美元/个

人民币费用：包干费 0.1935 + 垫款利息 0.288 = 0.4815 元/米，换算成美元 =
0.4815/6.8 = 0.0708 美元/个

美元费用：业务费用 报价×5% + 保险费 报价×(1+10%)×0.15% + 银行手续费
报价×0.35% + 出口运费 0.3560

利润：报价×10%

报价 = 实际成本 + 人民币费用 + 美元费用 + 利润

FOB 报价 = 2.56 + 0.0708 + 报价×5% + 报价×10% + 报价×0.35%

FOB 报价 = 3.11 美元/个

CFR 报价 = 2.56 + 0.0708 + 报价×5% + 报价×10% + 报价×0.35% + 0.356

CFR 报价 = 3.53 美元/个

CIF 报价 = 2.56 + 0.0708 + 报价×5% + 报价×10% + 报价×(1+10%)×0.15% +
报价×0.35% + 0.356

CIF 报价 = 3.54 美元/个

报价汇总

	CWS3-50(美元/个)	CWT2-100(美元/个)
FOB Shanghai	2.03	3.11
CFR Houston	2.20	3.53
CIF Houston	2.21	3.54

Act 2-5

出口商发盘函：

发件人：	damonchan@hainaco.com.cn
收件人：	ray.sinclair@gulfday.com
日　期：	2010-10-25
主　题：	Offer

Dear Mr. Sinclair,

We are in receipt of your inquiry dated Oct 22 2010 and hear you are interested in our Sport type vacuum flask (Art No. CWS3-50) and Travel type vacuum flask (Art No. CWT2-100). As requested, we have sent you the samples of vacuum flasks which are free of charge. We hope it will reach you in due course and will help you in making your selection.

In order to start a concrete transaction between us we take pleasure in making you a special offer as follows:

Sport type vacuum flask (Art No. CWS3-50)
Packing: 40 pcs/carton, 403 cartons (16120pcs)/20'FCL
USD2.03/pc FOB SHANGHAI
USD2.20/pc CFR HOUSTON
USD2.21/pc CIF HOUSTON

Travel type vacuum flask (Art No. CWT2-100)
Packing: 20 pcs/carton, 323 cartons (6460pcs)/20'FCL
USD3.11/pc FOB SHANGHAI
USD3.53/pc CFR HOUSTON
USD3.54/pc CIF HOUSTON

Shipment: to be effected within 45 days after receipt of the relevant L/C
Payment: by sight L/C
Insurance: for 110% of invoice value covering F.P.A. risk

This offer is firm subject to your immediate reply which should reach us not later than the end of this month. You may rest assured that our goods are in excellent quality and at right price. There is little likelihood of the goods remaining unsold once this particular offer has lapsed.

Looking forward to your favorable reply.

Yours truly,
Shanghai Haina Import & Export Company Limited
Damon Chan

参考答案

Discuss 2-1

出口报价核算：

出口报价核算

1. 单位运费计算
   (1) 在表 2-9 中，查得纺织品面料的等级为 10 级；从本实训 LOOK 环节中的积载因数计算可知，该货物的计费标准为 M。
   (2) 在表 2-10 中，查得 10 级货和计算标准 M 相对应的运价为 84 美元/运费吨。
   (3) 12000/120＝100 匹　100/4＝25 包　25×1.5×0.5×0.6＝11.25 运费吨
   总运费＝11.25×84＝945 美元　单位运费＝945/12000＝0.079 美元

2. KJ1001 的报价核算（美元的汇率为 6.8 人民币元/1 美元）
   实际成本：2.29 美元
   人民币费用：包干费 0.5＋垫款利息 0.3＝0.8 元/米，换算成美元＝0.8/6.8＝0.118 美元
   美元费用：业务费用报价×2%＋银行费用报价×0.35%＋出口运费 0.079＋保险费
   　　　　　报价×(1＋10%)×0.15%＋佣金报价×3%
   利润：报价×10%
   报价＝实际成本＋人民币费用＋美元费用＋利润
   FOBC3%报价＝2.29＋0.118＋报价×2%＋报价×0.35%＋报价×3%＋报价×10%
   FOBC3%报价＝2.84 美元/米
   CFRC3%报价＝2.29＋0.118＋报价×2%＋报价×0.35%＋0.079＋报价×3%＋
   　　　　　　报价×10%
   CFRC3%报价＝2.94 美元/米
   CIFC3%报价＝2.29＋0.118＋报价×2%＋报价×0.35%＋0.079＋报价×
   　　　　　　(1＋10%)×0.15%＋报价×3%＋报价×10%
   CIFC3%报价＝2.95 美元/米

3. KJ2001 的报价核算
   实际成本：2.54 美元
   人民币费用：包干费 0.5＋垫款利息 0.33＝0.83 元/米，换算成美元＝
   　　　　　　0.83/6.8＝0.122 美元
   美元费用：业务费用报价×2%＋银行费用报价×0.35%＋出口运费 0.079＋保险费
   　　　　　报价×(1＋10%)×0.15%＋佣金报价×3%
   利润：报价×10%
   报价＝实际成本＋人民币费用＋美元费用＋利润
   FOBC3%报价＝2.54＋0.122＋报价×2%＋报价×0.35%＋报价×3%＋报价×10%
   FOBC3%报价＝3.14 美元/米
   CFRC3%报价＝2.54＋0.122＋报价×2%＋报价×0.35%＋0.079＋报价×3%＋
   　　　　　　报价×10%
   CFRC3%报价＝3.24 美元/米
   CIFC3%报价＝2.54＋0.122＋报价×2%＋报价×0.35%＋0.079＋报价×
   　　　　　　(1＋10%)×0.15%＋报价×3%＋报价×10%
   CIFC3%报价＝3.25 美元/米

(续上)

<table>
<tr><th colspan="3">报 价 汇 总</th></tr>
<tr><td></td><td>KJ1001（美元/米）</td><td>KJ2001（美元/米）</td></tr>
<tr><td>FOB Shanghai</td><td>2.84</td><td>3.14</td></tr>
<tr><td>CFR Genova</td><td>2.94</td><td>3.24</td></tr>
<tr><td>CIF Genova</td><td>2.95</td><td>3.25</td></tr>
</table>

Discuss 2 - 2

出口商发盘函：

发件人：	li_xin@lixin.com.cn
收件人：	k.eisenbach@ulschelke.com.de
日　期：	2011 - 03 - 18
主　题：	Offer for All Cotton Bed-sheets

Dear Mrs. Eisenbach,

We are very pleased to receive your inquiry of Mar. 16, 2011.

Attached are our latest catalog and price list, which can give the details you asked for. Also by separate post we are forwarding you our full range of samples. When you have had an opportunity to examine them, we feel confident that you will agree that the goods are excellent in quality and reasonable in price.

We usually offer a discount of 5% on purchases in quality of not less than 8000 of individual items. For your information, we do business on the basis of sight L/C.

All cotton products are becoming popular because they are warm and light. You will not be surprised to learn that we are finding it difficult to meet the demand after studying our prices. If you place your order not later than the end of this month, we would guarantee delivery within 30 days from receipt of the L/C.

Looking forward to receiving your order.

Yours sincerely,
Shanghai Lixin International Trading Co., Ltd.
Li Xin

Attachment: Latest Catalog
　　　　　　Price List

情景模拟实训三 交易磋商二——还盘与盈亏测算

Act 3-1

表 3-1 CWT2-100 还价利润率核算表(20′集装箱)

核算项目(总价)	20′集装箱
销售收入	还价后单价=3.54×(1-6%)=3.3276 美元 销售收入=3.3276×6460×6.8=146174.8128 元
实际成本	19.2×6460×(1+17%-11%)/(1+17%)=112370.8718 元
包干费	1250 元
业务费用	3.3276×6460×5‰×6.8=7308.7406 元
垫款利息	19.2×6460×3/12×6%=1860.4800 元
保险费	3.3276×6460×(1+10%)×0.15%×6.8=241.1884 元
银行手续费	3.3276×6460×0.35%×6.8=511.6118 元
出口运费	2300×6.8=15640.0000 元
利润额	146174.8128-112370.8718-1250-7308.7406-1860.48-241.1884- 511.6118-15640=6991.9202 元
利润率	6991.9202/146174.8128=4.78%

表 3-2 CWT2-100 还价利润率核算表(40′集装箱)

核算项目(总价)	40′集装箱
销售收入	基础数量=55÷0.0773=711.51 箱,即 711 箱(40′内容积约为 55 立方米) 货物数量=711×20=14220 个 还价后单价=3.54×(1-6%)=3.3276 美元 销售收入=3.3276×14220×6.8=321765.6096 元
实际成本	19.2×14220×(1+17%-11%)/(1+17%)=247355.0769 元
包干费	2200 元
业务费用	3.3276×14220×5‰×6.8=16088.2805 元
垫款利息	19.2×14220×3/12×6%=4095.3600 元
保险费	3.3276×14220×(1+10%)×0.15%×6.8=530.9133 元
银行手续费	3.3276×14220×0.35%×6.8=1126.1796 元
出口运费	4500×6.8=30600.0000 元
利润额	321765.6096-247355.0769-2200-16088.2805-4095.36-530.9133- 1126.1796-30600=19769.7993 元
利润率	19769.7993/321765.6096= 6.14%

Act 3-2

出口商还盘函：

发件人：	damonchan@hainaco.com.cn
收件人：	ray.sinclair@gulfday.com
日　期：	2010-10-31
主　题：	Reply for Counter Offer

Dear Mr. Sinclair,

We have received your E-mail of Oct. 30, 2010.

For your information, we have received a crowd of inquiries from buyers in other directions and they expect to close business at something near our level. However, in view of you are new friend in our business line and if your quantity is larger such as 1×40′ (FCL), we will accept your proposal of 6% discount of Art No. CWT2-100 and give you the special offer as follow:

Art No. CWT2-100 14220 PCS (1×40′ FCL) USD 3.33 PER PC CIF HOUSTON

As you know, the good quality is more important than the low price. We believe you will accept the price and place an order as soon as possible. This offer is valid only for 5 days.

In addition, the price term of Art. No. CWS3-50 on CIF basis remains unchanged.

Looking forward to receiving your trial order.

Yours truly,
Shanghai Haina Import & Export Company Limited
Damon Chan

Discuss 3-1

还价成本核算：

还价成本核算

(1) 还价后 KJ2001 的单位销售收入：

单位销售收入＝(3.06－0.50)×6.8＝17.41 元

(2) 还价后 KJ2001 的各项费用：

费用项目	单　　　价
国内运输费	2000÷26400＝0.076 元
港区港杂费	600÷26400＝0.023 元
商检费	350÷26400＝0.013 元
报关费	150÷26400＝0.006 元
垫款利息	采购成本×4.98％×4/12
业务费用	(3.06－0.50)×2％×6.8＝0.35 元
出口运费	1800÷26400×6.8＝0.46 元
保险费	(3.06－0.50)×(1＋10％)×0.15％×6.8＝0.03 元
佣金	(3.06－0.50)×5％×6.8＝0.87 元

单位费用总额＝0.076＋0.023＋0.013＋0.006＋采购成本×4.98％×4/12＋
　　　　　　0.35＋0.46＋0.03＋0.87＝
　　　　　　1.828＋采购成本×4.98％×4/12

(3) 还价后 KJ2001 的单位利润：

单位利润＝(3.06－0.50)×10％×6.8＝1.74 元

(4) 还价后 KJ2001 的单位采购成本：

单位采购成本＝单位销售收入－单位费用总额－单位利润＝
　　　　　　17.41－1.828－采购成本×4.98％×
　　　　　　4/12－1.74＝13.62 元

Discuss 3-2

出口商还盘函:

发件人:	li_xin@lixin.com.cn
收件人:	fcy@aumedical.com
日 期:	2011-03-19
主 题:	Counter Offer for Non-Woven Fabrics

Dear Mr. Fung,

Thank you for E-mail but we are sorry to hear that you think our last offer is not good enough.

In fact, as the continual appreciation of CNY has caused the sharp rise in our export cost, the prices we offered are exceptionally low.

However, after careful consideration and discussion with our manager, we finally agree to allow you a 2% discount on our original offer in order to support you to promote our non-woven fabrics into your market.

As to the payment, it is the usual practice of our company to accept sight L/C for the first transaction. Please kindly understand and cooperate.

We hope our above support will help you to place your initial order soon.

Yours truly,
Shanghai Lixin International Trading Co., Ltd.
Li Xin

情景模拟实训四 交易磋商三——成交谈判与合同签订

Act 4-1

合同核算表

上海海纳进出品有限公司
Shanghai Haina Import & Export Company Limited
合同核算表

填表日期：2010年11月5日　　　填表人：钱晓俊　　　编号：HNHTE10160

核算时，成本、费用及利润项目一律保留2位小数。

进口商		成交术语	装运港	目的港
GULFLAND DAINECESS INC.		CIF	SHANGHAI	HOUSTON
包干费(CNY)		出口海运费(USD)		
1250/20′FCL	2200/20′FCL	2300/20′FCL	4500/40′FCL	
增值税率	出口退税率	银行手续费	银行年利率	资金周转周期(月)
17%	11%	成交价格0.35%	6%	3
保险加成率	保险费率	业务费用	佣金率	汇率(USD1=CNY)
10%	0.15%	成交价格5%	/	6.80
分货号成交信息				

包装	货号	计价单位	采购成本CNY	成交价格USD	成交数量
	CWS3-50	PC	12.60	2.21	16120PCS IN 1×20′FCL
	包装方式	毛重KGS	净重KGS	长CM	宽CM	高CM
	40PCS/CTN 403CTNS/20′	29.40	21.80	61	39	26
	货号	计价单位	采购成本CNY	成交价格USD	成交数量
	CWT2-100	PC	19.20	3.33	14220PCS IN 1×40′FCL
	包装方式	毛重KGS	净重KGS	长CM	宽CM	高CM
	20PCS/CTN 711CTNS/20′	27.30	20.70	65	41	29

成交利润核算		
核算项目	计算过程	计算结果
收入(CNY)		
销售收入总额	(2.21×16120+3.33×14220)×6.8	564249.04
支出(CNY)		
实际成本总额	[12.60−12.60/(1+17%)×11%]×16120+ [19.20−19.20/(1+17%)×11%]×14220	431371.08
包干费总额	1250+2200	3450.00
银行手续费总额	(2.21×16120+3.33×14220)×0.35%×6.8	1974.87
垫款利息总额	(12.60×16120+19.20×14220)×6%×3/12	7142.04
业务费用总额	(2.21×16120+3.33×14220)×5%×6.8	28212.45
出口海运费总额	(2300+4500)×6.8	46240.00
保险费总额	(2.21×16120+3.33×14220)×(1+10%)×0.15%×6.8	931.01
支出总额	431371.08+3450+1974.87+7142.04+28212.45+ 46240+931.01	519321.45
利润(CNY)		
利润总额	564249.04−519321.45	44927.59
销售利润率	44927.59÷564249.04	7.96%

Act 4-2

销售确认书

销售确认书
SALES CONFIRMATION

卖方 SELLER:	SHANGHAI HAINA IMPORT & EXPORT COMPANY LIMITED RM. 905 YONG AN MANSION, NO. 12 HUASHAN RD., SHANGHAI, P. R. CHINA TEL: 0086-21-54105623 FAX: 0086-21-54742511 E-MAIL：SALES@HAINACO.COM	编号 NO.:	SCHN-GD10174
		日期 DATE:	NOV. 6, 2010
		地点 PLACE:	SHANGHAI, CHINA
买方 BUYER:	GULFLAND DAINECESS INC. 404 BRENNIN ST., SUITE 255, HOUSTON, TX 75013, UNITED STATES		

买卖双方同意就以下条款达成交易：
This confirmation is made by and agreed between the BUYER and SELLER, in accordance with the terms and conditions stipulated below:

1. 商品号 Art No.	2. 品名及规格 Commodity & Specification	3. 数量 Quantity	4. 单价及价格条款 Unit Price & Trade Terms	5. 金额 Amount
CWS3-50	SPORT TYPE VACUUM FLASK	16120PCS	CIF HOUSTON USD2.21 / PC	USD35625.20
CWT2-100	TRAVEL TYPE VACUUM FLASK AS PER SAMPLES DISPATCHED BY THE SELLER ON OCT. 25, 2010	14220PCS	USD3.33 / PC	USD47352.60
			TOTAL:	USD82977.80

6. 总值（大写） Total Amount in Words	SAY U. S. DOLLARS EIGHTY TWO THOUSAND NINE HUNDRED AND SEVENTY SEVEN AND CENTS EIGHTY ONLY
允许 With ***	溢短装，由卖方决定 More or less of shipment allowed at the sellers' option
7. 包装 Packing	CWS3-50: PACKED IN CARTONS OF 40 PCS EACH, TOTAL 403 CARTONS, LOADED IN 1×20′ FCL CWT2-100: PACKED IN CARTONS OF 20 PCS EACH, TOTAL 711 CARTONS, LOADED IN 1×40′ FCL
8. 唛头 Shipping Marks	GULFDAINE S/CNO.SCHN-GD10174 HOUSTON C/NOS.1-UP
9. 装运期及运输方式 Time of Shipment & means of Transportation	EFFECTED NOT LATER THAN THE END OF DECEMBER 2010 BY SEA WITHOUT PARTIAL SHIPMENTS AND WITHOUT TRANSSHIPMENT
10. 装运港及目的地 Port of Loading & Destination	FROM SHANGHAI, CHINA TO HOUSTON, TX, US
11. 保险 Insurance	FOR 110% OF INVOICE VALUE COVERING F.P.A. RISK AS PER OMCC PICC DATED 1/1/1981
12. 付款方式 Terms of Payment	THE BUYER SHOULD OPEN THROUGH A BANK ACCEPTABLE TO THE SELLER AN IRREVOCABLE LETTER OF CREDIT PAYABLE AT SIGHT TO REACH THE SELLER BY THE END OF NOVEMBER 2010 AND VALID FOR NEGOTIATION IN CHINA UNTIL 15TH DAY AFTER THE DATE OF SHIPMENT

（续上）

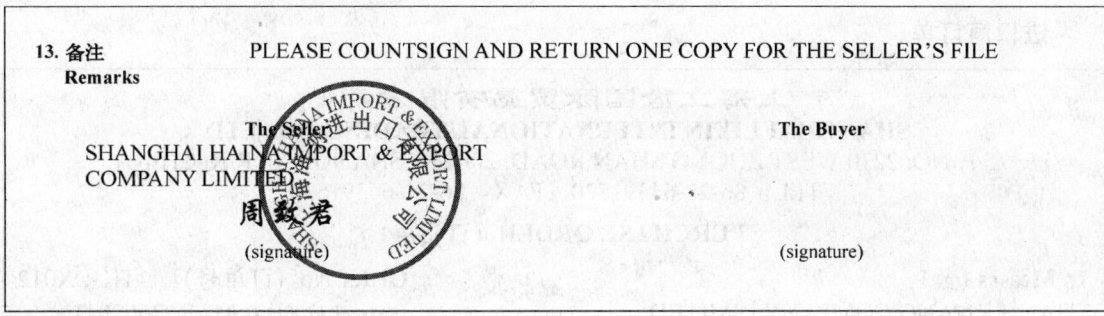

Act 4-3

出口商签约函：

发件人：	damonchan@hainaco.com.cn
收件人：	ray.sinclair@gulfday.com
日　期：	2010-11-06
主　题：	Sales Confirmation

Dear Mr. Sinclair,

Thank you for your Order No. GD-PO-CNSHA129 and we are pleased to commence the initial cooperation with you.

We will do our best to execute your order. In order to ensure the shipment in time, please instruct your banker to open the relevant letter of credit without delay.

We have sent you today the relevant Sales Confirmation No. SCHN-GD10174 in duplicate by TNT. Please kindly countersign them and return one copy for our file.

We appreciate your kind attention to all the above and look forward to your L/C.

Yours truly,
Shanghai Haina Import & Export Company Limited
Damon Chan

Discuss 4 - 1

进口商订单：

上海立信国际贸易有限公司
SHANGHAI LIXIN INTERNATIONAL TRADING CO., LTD.
5/F, NO. 2230 WEST ZHONG SHAN ROAD, 200235, SHANGHAI, P. R. CHINA
TEL：86-21-64391520　　FAX：86-21-64391530

PURCHASE ORDER（订货单）

To Messrs（致）：
THANH KUANG COMPANY LIMITED
59 NGUYEN TAT THANH, DISTRICT 7,
HO CHI MINH CITY, VIETNAM

Order No.（订单号）：11TK-LX012
Date（日期）：MAR. 26, 2011

We hereby place the order for the following goods with you on the terms and conditions set forth hereunder:

Description （品名及规格）	Quantity （数量）	Unit Price （单价）	Amount （金额）
COTTON SPANDEX FABRIC SPECIFICATION: SINGLE JERSEY KNITTED 95% COTTON, 5% SPANDEX WEIGHT: 138 GSM WIDTH: 155 CM	50000 KGS	FOB HO CHI MINH CITY INCOTERMS 2010 USD6.30 / KG	USD315000.00

Total Amount（合计金额）： USD315000.00

Packing（包装）：	120 METERS WINDED IN ONE ROLL SHIPPING MARKS ARE AT THE SELLER'S OPTION LOADED IN THREE 40 FEET CONTAINERS FCL
Payment（付款）：	IRREVOCABLE L/C PAYABLE AT 60 DAYS AFTER SIGHT ISSUED BEFORE APR. 20, 2011
Shipment（装运）：	NOT LATER THAN MAY 20, 2011 BY SEA
Port of loading（装运港）：	HO CHI MINH CITY, VIETNAM
Port of destination（目的港）：	SHANGHAI, CHINA
Partial shipments（分批装运）：	NOT ALLOWED
Transshipment（转运）：	ALLOWED
Insurance（保险）：	EFFECTED BY BUYER

Accepted and confirmed by（双方签章确认）：

　　　　Seller（卖方）　　　　　　　　　　　　　　　Buyer（买方）
　　　　　　　　　　　　　　　　　SHANGHAI LIXIN INTERNATIONAL TRADING CO., LTD.

Discuss 4-2

销售确认书：

<table>
<tr><td colspan="5" align="center">SALES CONFIRMATION</td></tr>
<tr><td>SELLER:</td><td colspan="2">THANH KUANG COMPANY LIMITED
59 NGUYEN TAT THANH, DISTRICT 7, HO CHI MINH CITY, VIETNAM</td><td>NO.:
DATE:</td><td>TK-CN-SC32
MAR. 28, 2011</td></tr>
<tr><td>BUYER:</td><td colspan="2">SHANGHAI LIXIN INTERNATIONAL TRADING CO., LTD.
5/F, NO. 2230 WEST ZHONG SHAN ROAD, 200235, SHANGHAI, P. R. CHINA
TEL：86-21-64391520　FAX：86-21-64391530</td><td>PLACE:</td><td>HO CHI MINH CITY, VIETNAM</td></tr>
<tr><td colspan="5">This confirmation is made by and agreed between the BUYER and SELLER, in accordance with the terms and conditions stipulated below:</td></tr>
<tr><td colspan="2">1. Commodity & Specification</td><td>2. Quantity</td><td>3. Unit Price & Trade Terms</td><td>4. Amount</td></tr>
<tr><td colspan="2">COTTON SPANDEX FABRIC
SPECIFICATION:
SINGLE JERSEY KNITTED
95% COTTON, 5% SPANDEX
WEIGHT: 138 GSM
WIDTH: 155 CM</td><td>50000 KGS</td><td>FOB HO CHI MINH CITY
INCOTERMS 2010
USD6.30 / KG</td><td>USD315000.00</td></tr>
<tr><td colspan="2" align="right">Total:</td><td>50000 KGS</td><td></td><td>USD315000.00</td></tr>
<tr><td colspan="5">With　5%　More or less of quantity and amount allowed at the sellers' option</td></tr>
<tr><td colspan="2">5. Total Value in Words</td><td colspan="3">SAY U. S. DOLLARS THREE HUNDRED AND FIFTEEN THOUSAND ONLY</td></tr>
<tr><td colspan="2">6. Packing</td><td colspan="3">120 METERS WINDED IN ONE ROLL；
LOADED IN THREE 40 FEET CONTAINERS FCL</td></tr>
<tr><td colspan="2">7. Shipping Marks</td><td colspan="3">LXCNSHA
P/O.11TK-LX012
SHANGHAI
ROLL NOS.1-UP</td></tr>
<tr><td colspan="2">8. Time of Shipment & Means of Transportation</td><td colspan="3">NOT LATER THAN MAY 20, 2011 BY SEA
WITH PARTIAL SHIPMENTS NOT ALLOWED AND
TRANSSHIPMENT ALLOWED</td></tr>
<tr><td colspan="2">9. Port of Loading & Destination</td><td colspan="3">FROM HO CHI MINH CITY, VIETNAM TO SHANGHAI, CHINA</td></tr>
<tr><td colspan="2">10. Insurance</td><td colspan="3">EFFECTED BY BUYER</td></tr>
<tr><td colspan="2">11. Terms of Payment</td><td colspan="3">THE BUYER SHOULD OPEN AN IRREVOCABLE L/C PAYABLE AT 60 DAYS AFTER SIGHT TO REACH THE SELLER NOT LATER THAN APR. 22, 2011 AND VALID FOR NEGOTIATION IN VIETNAM UNTIL 15TH DAY AFTER THE DATE OF SHIPMENT</td></tr>
<tr><td colspan="2">12. Remarks</td><td colspan="3">PLEASE COUNTSIGN AND RETURN ONE COPY FOR THE SELLER'S FILE</td></tr>
<tr><td colspan="2" align="center">The Seller
THANH KUANG COMPANY LIMITED
Nguyen Yuan Quynh
NGUYEN YUAN QUYNH
(signature)</td><td colspan="3" align="center">The Buyer

(signature)</td></tr>
</table>

情景模拟实训五 履行合同一——落实信用证

Act 5-1

信用证审核意见：

1. 信用证条款	42C　30 DAYS AFTER BILL OF LADING DATE
存在问题	汇票付款期限与销售确认书规定 PAYABLE AT SIGHT 不符
修改意见	改为即期，即 AT SIGHT
2. 信用证条款	44B　SAN ANTONIO, TX, US
存在问题	目的港与销售确认书规定 HOUSTON, TX, US 不符
修改意见	改为 HOUSTON, TX, US
3. 信用证条款	31D　EXPIRY DATE 110105
存在问题	到期日与销售确认书规定 UNTIL 15TH DAY AFTER THE DATE OF SHIPMENT 不符，现最迟装运日期为 101231，则到期日应为 110115
修改意见	改为 110115
4. 信用证条款	45A　SALES CONFIRMATION NO. SCHN-GD10147
存在问题	销售确认书号与销售确认书规定 SCHN-GD10174 不符
修改意见	改为 SCHN-GD10147
5. 信用证条款	45A　PRICE TERM：CIF SAN ANTONIO
存在问题	价格术语与销售确认书规定 CIF HOUSTON 不符
修改意见	改为 CIF HOUSTON
6. 信用证条款	45A　SHIPPING MARKS：GULFDAINE 　　　　　　　　S/CNO. SCHN-GD10147 　　　　　　　　SAN ANTONIO 　　　　　　　　C/NOS. 1-UP
存在问题	运输标志与销售确认书规定不符，具体为 GULFDAINE 　　　　　　　　　　　　S/CNO. SCHN-GD10174 　　　　　　　　　　　　HOUSTON 　　　　　　　　　　　　C/NOS. 1-UP
修改意见	改为 GULFDAINE 　　　S/CNO. SCHN-GD10174 　　　HOUSTON 　　　C/NOS. 1-UP

(续上)

7. 信用证条款	46A　3 COMPLETE SET OF ORIGINAL CLEAN ON BOARD STRAIGHT OCEAN BILLS OF LADING … MARKED "FREIGHT TO COLLECT".	
存在问题	运费条款与价格术语 CIF HOUSTON 不匹配	
修改意见	改为"FREIGHT PREPAID"	
8. 信用证条款	46A　5 INSURANCE POLICY … SHOWING THE INSURANCE COVERAGE AS: ALL RISKS AND WAR RISKS	
存在问题	保险险别与销售确认书规定 F.P.A. RISK 不符,将引致额外保险费	
修改意见	留待客户进一步确认	
9. 信用证条款	47B　7 THE ISSUING BANK IS OBLIGED TO PAYMENT ONLY AFTER GOODS ARE SHIPPED TO THE PORT OF DESTINATION.	
存在问题	此条款为延迟开证行付款的"软条款"	
修改意见	删去此条款	
10. 信用证条款	71B　ALL BANKING CHARGES INCLUDING ADVISING, NEGOTIATION AND REIMBURSEMENT ARE FOR THE ACCOUNT OF BENEFICIARY.	
存在问题	按贸易惯例,由受益人承担发生在开证国以外的银行费用	
修改意见	改为 ALL BANKING CHARGES OUTSIDE U.S.A. ARE FOR THE ACCOUNT OF BENEFICIARY.	
11. 信用证条款	48　DOCUMENTS TO BE PRESENTED WITHIN 5 DAYS AFTER THE DATE OF SHIPMENT …	
存在问题	交单期与销售确认书规定 UNTIL 15TH DAY AFTER THE DATE OF SHIPMENT 不符	
修改意见	改为 WITHIN 15 DAYS AFTER THE DATE OF SHIPMENT	

Act 5-2

出口商改证函：

发件人：	damonchan@hainaco.com.cn
收件人：	ray.sinclair@gulfday.com
日　期：	2010-11-20
主　题：	Amendment of L/C

Dear Mr. Sinclair,

Thank you for your L/C No. CHASEMBKLC72075359 issued by CHASE MANHATTAN BANK, HOUSTON, U.S.A. dated Nov. 19, 2010.

However, we have found the following discrepancies after checking with our S/C No. SCHN-GD10174:

1) 31D Date and place of expiry
   The date of expiry should be extended to 110115 as contracted to be 15 days after shipment.
2) 42C Draft at
   The draft should be paid at sight as contracted, instead of at 30 days after bill of lading date.
3) 44B For transportation to
   The port of destination should be Houston, TX, US as contracted, instead of San Antonio, TX, US.
4) 45A Descript. of goods
   The Sales Confirmation No. should be SCHN-GD10174 as contracted, instead of SCHN-GD10147.
   The price term should be CIF Houston as contracted, instead of CIF San Antonio.
   The shipping marks should be GULFDAINE/S/CNO. SCHN-GD10174/HOUSTON/C/NOS. 1-UP as contracted, instead of GULFDAINE/S/CNO. SCHN-GD10147/SAN ANTONIO/C/NOS. 1-UP.
5) 46A Documents required
   3 It is the wording "Freight Prepaid" which should be marked onto the bills of lading according to the price term, instead of the wording "Freight to Collect".
   5 We have noticed that you changed the insurance coverage to All Risks and War Risks instead of F.P.A. Risk as contracted. This will incur the additional premium, which is to be borne by you. Please confirm the change.
6) 47B Additional cond
   6 Please delete the clause "The issuing bank is obliged to payment only after goods are shipped to the port of destination" on the basis of mutual benefit.
7) 71B Details of charges
   According to the usual practices, the charges outside the country of applicant are borne by the beneficiary. Please amend to "All banking charges outside U.S.A. are for the account of beneficiary".
8) 48 Presentation period
   The period of presentation should be "within 15 days after the date of shipment" as contracted, instead of "within 5 days after the date of shipment".

Please let us have the L/C Amendment soon so that we can effect shipment within the contracted time.

Yours truly,
Shanghai Haina Import & Export Company Limited
Damon Chan

Discuss 5

信用证开证申请书：

IRREVOCABLE DOCUMENTARY CREDIT APPLICATION

To: BANK OF CHINA SHANGHAI BRANCH	Issued by SWIFT Date: 2011-04-01
Applicant (Full name and address) SHANGHAI LIXIN INTERNATIONAL TRADING CO., LTD. 5/F, NO. 2230 WEST ZHONG SHAN ROAD, 200235, SHANGHAI, P. R. CHINA TEL：86-21-64391520 FAX：86-21-64391530	Credit No. Date and place of expiry JUN. 5, 2011 IN VIETNAM
Beneficiary (Full name and address) THANH KUANG COMPANY LIMITED 59 NGUYEN TAT THANH, DISTRICT 7, HO CHI MINH CITY, VIETNAM	Amount (both in figures and words) USD 315000.00 SAY U. S. DOLLARS THREE HUNDRED AND FIFTEEN THOUSAND ONLY
Partial shipments ☐allowed ☑not allowed	Transshipment ☑allowed ☐not allowed	Credit available with **ANY BANK IN VIETNAM** By
Loading on board/dispatch/taking in charge at/from HO CHI MINH CITY, VIETNAM not later than MAY 20, 2011 For transportation to: SHANGHAI, CHINA	☐sight payment ☐acceptance ☑negotiation ☐deferred payment at against the documents detailed herein ☑and beneficiary's draft(s) for __100__ % of invoice value at __60 DAYS AFTER__ sight
☑FOB ☐CFR ☐CIF ☐or other terms	drawn on __BANK OF CHINA SHANGHAI BRANCH__ Price term: **FOB HO CHI MINH CITY INCOTERMS2010**

Documents required: (marked with ☑)
1. ☑ Signed commercial invoice in __4__ copies indicating L/C No. and Contract No. __TK-CN-SC32__
2. ☑ Full set of clean on board Bills of Lading made out to **ORDER OF ISSUING BANK** and blank endorsed, marked "freight ☐ to collect / ☑ prepaid ☐ showing freight amount" notifying __APPLICANT__ .
3. ☐ Airway bills/cargo receipt/copy of railway bills issued by _____ showing "freight ☐ to collect / ☐ prepaid ☐ indicating freight amount" and consigned to _____
4. ☑ Insurance Policy/Certificate in __2__ copies for __110__ % of the invoice value showing claims payable at destination in currency of the draft, blank endorsed, covering **ALL RISKS AND THEFT, PILFERAGE AND NON-DELIVERY RISK**.
5. ☑ Packing List/Weight Memo in __4__ copies indicating quantity, gross and net weights of each package.
6. ☐ Certificate of Quantity/Weight in _____ copies issued by _____.
7. ☑ Certificate of Quality in __2__ copies issued by ☐ manufacturer/ ☑ public recognized surveyor __SOCIETE GENERALE DE SURVEILLANCE S.A.__ .
8. ☑ Certificate of Origin in __2__ copies issued by __COMPETENT AUTHORITY__ .
9. ☑ Beneficiary's certified copy of fax / telex dispatched to the applicant within __24__ hours after shipment advising L/C No., name of vessel, date of shipment, name, quantity, weight and value of goods.

Other documents, if any

Description of goods:
COTTON SPANDEX FABRIC
SPECIFICATION: SINGLE JERSEY KNITTED; 95% COTTON, 5% SPANDEX
WEIGHT: 138 GSM; WIDTH: 155 CM
PRICE: USD6.30 / KG
QUANTITY: 50 000 KGS

Additional instructions:
1. ☑ All banking charges outside the opening bank are for beneficiary's account.
2. ☑ Documents must be presented within __15__ days after date of issuance of the transport documents but within the validity of this credit.
3. ☐ Third party as shipper is not acceptable, Short Form/Blank back B/L is not acceptable.
4. ☑ Both quantity and credit amount __5__ % more or less are allowed.
5. ☑ All documents must be sent to issuing bank by courier/speed post in one lot.
   ☐ Other terms, if any

Account No.: _____ with BANK OF CHINA SHANGHAI BRANCH _____ (name of bank)
Transacted by: **SHANGHAI LIXIN INTERNATIONAL TRADING CO., LTD.**
Telephone No.: __64391520__

(Applicant: name, signature of authorized person)

情景模拟实训六　履行合同二——托运订舱和报检

Act 6 - 1

海运出口订舱委托书：

上海海纳进出口有限公司
SHANGHAI HAINA IMPORT & EXPORT COMPANY LIMITED
RM. 905 YONG AN MANSION, NO. 12 HUASHAN RD., SHANGHAI, P. R. CHINA
TEL: 0086-21-54105623　　FAX: 0086-21-54742511　　E-MAIL：SALES@HAINACO.COM

海运出口订舱委托书

发货人：Shipper:	SHANGHAI HAINA IMPORT & EXPORT COMPANY LIMITED RM. 905 YONG AN MANSION, NO. 12 HUASHAN RD., SHANGHAI, P. R. CHINA TEL: 0086-21-54105623 FAX: 0086-21-54742511		编号	BNHN-GD10203		
			日期	2010/12/10		
收货人：Consignee:	GULFLAND DAINECESS INC. 404 BRENNIN ST., SUITE 255, HOUSTON, TX 75013, UNITED STATES		合同号	SCHN-GD10174		
通知人：Notify Party:	SAME AS CONSIGNEE		信用证号	CHASEMBKLC72075359		
			贸易国别	UNITED STATES		
运费支付方式	FREIGHT PREPAID	是否要求代报关	☐ 是　☑ 否		提单份数	3正6副
起运港	SHANGHAI, CHINA	目的港	HOUSTON, TX, US	可否转运	ALLOWED	可否分批	NOT ALLOWED
标记唛码	总件数及包装名称	货物描述		总毛重	总体积	成交条件
AS PER INVOICE NO. INVHN-GD10174	1114 CARTONS	VACUUM FLASK		31258.50 KGS	79.9060 CBM	CIF
装箱方式	☑ FCL ☐ LCL	门点装箱地点	宝山区杨行镇杨鑫路836号甲			
箱型箱量	1×20'GP 1×40'GP	电话	36121494	联系人	韩音德	
货物备妥日期	2010/12/15	特种集装箱要求		☐ 冷藏货	☐ 危险品	
备注	1. 请配 SINOTRANS 2010/12/25 2. 提单须标注 FREIGHT PREPAID 3. 提单须标注所载集装箱数量，集装箱号及封志号 4. 提单须标注开证银行名称 CHASE MANHATTAN BANK, HOUSTON, U.S.A. 5. 提单须标注信用证号 CHASEMBKLC72075359 6. 提单须标注销售合同号 SCHN-GD10174					

商业发票：

SHANGHAI HAINA IMPORT & EXPORT COMPANY LIMITED
RM. 905 YONG AN MANSION, NO. 12 HUASHAN RD., SHANGHAI, P. R. CHINA
TEL: 0086-21-54105623　　FAX: 0086-21-54742511　　E-MAIL：SALES@HAINACO.COM

COMMERCIAL INVOICE

TO: GULFLAND DAINECESS INC. 404 BRENNIN ST., SUITE 255, HOUSTON, TX 75013, UNITED STATES	INVOICE NO: INVHN-GD10174 INVOICE DATE: DEC. 10, 2010 S/C NO: SCHN-GD10174 L/C NO: CHASEMBKLC72075359 L/C ISSUED BY: CHASE MANHATTAN BANK, HOUSTON, U.S.A.
FROM: SHANGHAI, CHINA	TO: HOUSTON, TX, US

MARKS & NOS.	DESCRIPTION OF GOODS	QUANTITY	UNIT PRICE	AMOUNT
	VACUUM FLASK			
GULFDAINE S/CNO.SCHN-GD10174 HOUSTON C/NOS.1-1114	SPORT TYPE VACUUM FLASK ART. NO. CWS3-50	16120PCS	CIF HOUSTON USD2.21 / PC	USD35625.20
	TRAVEL TYPE VACUUM FLASK ART. NO. CWT2-100	14220PCS	USD3.33 / PC	USD47352.60
			TOTAL:	USD82977.80

AS PER SALES CONFIRMATION NO. SCHN-GD10174 DATED NOV. 6, 2010

WE HEREBY STATE THAT THE ABOVE-MENTIONED COMMODITIES ARE IN ACCORDANCE WITH APPLICANT'S ORDER NO. GD-PO-CNSHA129.

　　　　FOB VALUE:　　　　USD 76040.89
　　　　FREIGHT:　　　　　USD 6800.00
　　　　INSURANCE CHARGES:　USD 136.91

TOTAL AMOUNT IN WORDS:　SAY U. S. DOLLARS EIGHTY TWO THOUSAND NINE HUNDRED AND SEVENTY SEVEN AND CENTS EIGHTY ONLY

TOTAL G.W. / TOTAL N.W.:　31258.50 KGS / 23503.10 KGS
TOTAL PACKAGES:　1114 CARTONS

SHANGHAI HAINA IMPORT & EXPORT COMPANY LIMITED

周致君
(signature)

装箱单：

SHANGHAI HAINA IMPORT & EXPORT COMPANY LIMITED
RM. 905 YONG AN MANSION, NO. 12 HUASHAN RD., SHANGHAI, P. R. CHINA
TEL: 0086-21-54105623   FAX: 0086-21-54742511   E-MAIL: SALES@HAINACO.COM

PACKING LIST

TO: GULFLAND DAINECESS INC.
404 BRENNIN ST., SUITE 255,
HOUSTON, TX 75013, UNITED STATES

INVOICE NO: INVHN-GD10174
INVOICE DATE: DEC. 10, 2010
S/C NO: SCHN-GD10174
L/C NO: CHASEMBKLC72075359
L/C ISSUED BY: CHASE MANHATTAN BANK, HOUSTON, U.S.A.

FROM: SHANGHAI, CHINA   **TO:** HOUSTON, TX, US

MARKS & NOS.	DESCRIPTION OF GOODS	PACKAGE	QUANTITY	G.W. (KGS)	N.W. (KGS)	MEAS. (CBM)
	VACUUM FLASK					
GULFDAINE S/CNO.SCHN-GD10174	ART. NO. CWS3-50	403CARTONS	16120PCS	@29.40/11848.20	@21.80/8785.40	@0.0619/24.9457
HOUSTON C/NOS.1-1114	ART. NO. CWT2-100	711CARTONS	14220PCS	@27.30/19410.30	@20.70/14717.70	@0.0773/54.9603

PACKING: CWS3-50: IN CARTONS OF 40 PCS EACH, TOTAL 403 CARTONS, LOADED IN 1×20′ FCL
CWT2-100: IN CARTONS OF 20 PCS EACH, TOTAL 711 CARTONS, LOADED IN 1×40′ FCL

TOTAL: 1114CARTONS   30340PCS   31258.50 KGS   23503.10 KGS   79.9060 CBM

AS PER SALES CONFIRMATION NO. SCHN-GD10174 DATED NOV. 6, 2010

TOTAL PACKAGES IN WORDS: SAY ONE THOUSAND ONE HUNDRED AND FOURTEEN CARTONS ONLY

SHANGHAI HAINA IMPORT & EXPORT COMPANY LIMITED

周致君

(signature)

Act 6-2

出境货物报检单：

中华人民共和国出入境检验检疫
出境货物报检单

报检单位（加盖公章）：	上海海纳进出口有限公司		*编　号	
报检单位登记号：3100022150	联系人：徐可彤	电话：54107535	报检日期：2010年12月13日	

发货人	（中文）	上海海纳进出口有限公司
	（外文）	SHANGHAI HAINA IMPORT & EXPORT COMPANY LIMITED
收货人	（中文）	***
	（外文）	GULFLAND DAINECESS INC.

货物名称(中/外文)	H.S.编码	产地	数/重量	货物总值	包装种类及数量
真空保温瓶	96170090.00	浙江省永康市	30340个	82977.80美元	1114纸箱

运输工具名称号码	船舶 SINOTRANS SEATTLE / 045E	贸易方式	一般贸易	货物存放地点	***
合同号	SCHN-GD10174	信用证号	CHASEMBKLC72075359	用途	***
发货日期	***	输往国家(地区)	美国	许可证/审批号	***
启运地	上海口岸	到达口岸	休斯敦	生产单位注册号	***
集装箱规格、数量及号码	1个海运20尺普通箱，1个海运40尺普通箱				

合同、信用证订立的检验检疫条款或特殊要求	标记及号码	随附单据（划"✓"或补填）	
	参见发票 INVHN-GD10174	□合同 □信用证 ✓发票 ✓换证凭单 ✓装箱单 □厂检单	□包装性能结果单 □许可/审批文件 □ □ □ □

需要证单名称（划"✓"或补填）			*检验检疫费
□品质证书　　正　副	□植物检疫证书　　正　副		总金额（人民币元）
□重量证书　　正　副	□熏蒸/消毒证书　　正　副		
□数量证书　　正　副	□出境货物换证凭单　正　副		计费人
□兽医卫生证书　正　副	✓出境货物通关单　1正2副		
□健康证书　　正　副	□		收费人
□卫生证书　　正　副	□		
□动物卫生证书　正　副	□		

报检人郑重声明： 1. 本人被授权报检。 2. 上列填写内容正确属实，货物无伪造或冒用他人的厂名、标志、认证标志，并承担货物质量责任。 签名：徐可彤	领　取　证　单
	日期
	签名

注：有"*"号栏由出入境检验检疫机关填写　　　◆国家出入境检验检疫局制
[1-2 (2000.1.1)]

Discuss 6-1

集装箱货物托运单第九联——配舱回单(1)：

Shipper (发货人)	D/R No. (编号)	众联
SHANGHAI HAINA IMPORT & EXPORT COMPANY LIMITED RM. 905 YONG AN MANSION, NO. 12 HUASHAN RD., SHANGHAI, P. R. CHINA TEL: 0086-21-54105623　FAX: 0086-21-54742511	SNLU3743520522	第九联

Consignee (收货人)	
GULFLAND DAINECESS INC. 404 BRENNIN ST., SUITE 255, HOUSTON, TX 75013, UNITED STATES	配舱回单（1）

Notify Party (通知人)
SAME AS CONSIGNEE

Pre-carriage by (前程运输)	Place of Receipt (收货地点)	
Ocean Vessel(船名) Voy. No.(航次) SINOTRANS SEATTLE　045E	Port of Loading (装货港) SHANGHAI, CHINA	
Port of Discharge (卸货港) HOUSTON, TX, US	Place of Delivery (交货地点)	Final Destination for the Merchant's Reference(目的地)

Container No. (集装箱号)	Seal No.(封志号) Mark & Nos. (标志与号码)	No. of contai- ners or p'kgs. (箱数或件数)	Kind of Packages; Description of Goods (包装种类与货名)	Gross Weight 毛重(千克)	Measurement 呎码(立方米)
	GULFDAINE S/CNO.SCHN-GD10174 HOUSTON C/NOS.1-1114	1114 CARTONS	VACUUM FLASK FREIGHT PREPAID	31258.50 KGS	79.9060 CBM

TOTAL NUMBER OF CONTAINERS OR PACKAGES (IN WORDS) 集装箱数或件数合计(大写)	SAY ONE THOUSAND ONE HUNDRED AND FOURTEEN CARTONS ONLY

FREIGHT & CHARGES (运费与附加费)	Revenue Tons (运费吨)	Rate (运费率)	Per (每)	Prepaid (运费预付)	Collect (到付)

Ex. Rate: (兑换率)	Prepaid at(预付地点)	Payable at(到付地点)	Place of Issue(签发地点) SHANGHAI
	Total Prepaid(预付总额)	No. of Original B(s)/L (正本提单份数) THREE	Booking(订舱确认) APPROVED BY

Service Type on Receiving ☑-CY, ☐-CFS, ☐-DOOR	Service Type on Delivery ☑-CY, ☐-CFS, ☐-DOOR	Reefer Temperature Required (冷藏温度)	°F	°C

TYPE OF GOODS (种类)	☑Ordinary ☐Reefer ☐Dangerous ☐Auto. (普通)　(冷藏)　(危险品)　(裸装车辆) ☐Liquid ☐Live Animal ☐Bulk (液体)　(活动物)　(散装)	危险品	Class: Property: IMDG Code Page: UN NO.

可否转船：YES	可否分批：NO
装　　期：DEC. 31, 2010	效　　期：JAN. 15, 2011
金　　额：USD 82977.80	
制单日期：DEC. 11, 2010	

Discuss 6-2

出境货物通关单：

中华人民共和国出入境检验检疫
出境货物通关单

编号：310233480059197

1. 发货人 上海海纳进出口有限公司 ***		5. 标记及唛码 GULFDAINE S/CNO.SCHN-GD10174 HOUSTON C/NOS.1-1114
2. 收货人 ***		
3. 合同／信用证号 SCHN-GD10174/CHASEMBKLC7207535	4. 输往国家或地区 美国	
6. 运输工具名称及号码 船舶 SINOTRANS SEATTLE / 045E	7. 发货日期 ***	8. 集装箱规格及数量 1个海运20尺普通箱 1个海运40尺普通箱
9. 货物名称及规格 真空保温瓶 *** （以下空白）	10. H.S.编码 96170090.00 *** （以下空白）	11. 申报总值 *82977.80 美元 *** （以下空白）	12. 数／重量、包装数量及种类 *30340 个 *1114 纸箱 *** （以下空白）

13. 证明

上述货物业经检验检疫，请海关予以放行。

本通关单有效期至　二〇一一年　一月　五日

签字：陈怀德　　　　　　　日期：2010年12月15日

14. 备注
***

情景模拟实训七 履行合同三——投保与原产地认证

Act 7-1

货物运输保险投保单：

PICC 中国人民财产保险股份有限公司 上海市分公司
PICC Property and Casualty Company Limited, Shanghai Branch

地址：中国上海市中山南路 700 号
ADD: No. 700 Zhongshan Road(S) Shanghai, China
邮编(Post Code)：200010
电话(TEL)：021-63773000
传真(FAX)：021-63764678

货物运输保险投保单
APPLICATION FORM FOR CARGO TRANSPORTATION INSURANCE

被保险人：
INSURED: SHANGHAI HAINA IMPORT & EXPORT COMPANY LIMITED

发票号(INVOICE NO.)　　INVHN-GD10174
合同号(CONTRACT NO.)　 SCHN-GD10174
信用证号(L/C NO.)　　　CHASEMBKLC72075359
发票金额(INVOICE AMOUNT)　USD 82977.80　　投保加成(PLUS)　10%

兹有下列物品向中国人民财产保险股份有限公司 上海分 公司投保。(INSURANCE IS REQUIRED ON THE FOLLOWING COMMODITIES:)

标记 MARKS & NOS.	包装及数量 QUANTITY	保险货物项目 DESCRIPTION OF GOODS	保险金额 AMOUNT INSURED
AS PER INVOICE NO. INVHN-GD10174	1114 CARTONS	VACUUM FLASK	USD91276.00

启运日期：
DATE OF COMMENCEMENT: DEC. 25, 2010
装载运输工具： SINOTRANS
PER CONVEYANCE: SEATTLE 045E

自 FROM　SHANGHAI, CHINA　经 VIA　至 TO　HOUSTON, TX, US

提单号：
B/L NO.: SNLU3743520522
赔款偿付地点：
CLAIM PAYMENT AT: HOUSTON

投保险别：(PLEASE INDICATE THE CONDITIONS &/OR SPECIAL COVERAGES)
COVERING F.P.A. RISK AS PER OCEAN MARINE CARGO CLAUSES OF P.I.C.C. DATED 1/1/1981

备注：(REMARKS)　1) 须两份正本保单
　　　　　　　　 2) 保单须注明开证银行名称　CHASE MANHATTAN BANK, HOUSTON, U.S.A.
　　　　　　　　　 信用证号码　CHASEMBKLC72075359
　　　　　　　　　 销售确认书号码 SCHN-GD10174

请如实告知下列情况：(如"是"在[ ]中打"×") IF ANY, PLEASE MARK "×":
1. 货物种类 普通[×]　散装[ ]　冷藏[ ]　液体[ ]　活动物[ ]　机器/汽车[ ]　危险品等级[ ]
   GOODS ORDINARY BULK REEFER LIQUID LIVE ANIMAL MACHINE/AUTO DANGEROUS CLASS
2. 集装箱种类 普通[×]　开顶[ ]　框架[ ]　平板[ ]　冷藏[ ]
   CONTAINER ORDINARY OPEN FRAME FLAT REFRIGERATOR
3. 转运工具 海轮[ ]　飞机[ ]　驳船[ ]　火车[ ]　汽车[ ]
   BY TRANSIT SHIP PLANE BARGE TRAIN TRUCK
4. 船舶资料　船籍[ ]　　　　　　　船龄[ ]
   PARTICULAR OF SHIP REGISTRY AGE

备注：被保险人确认本保险合同条款和内容已经完全了解
THE ASSURED CONFIRMS HEREWITH THE TERMS AND
CONDITIONS OF THESE INSURANCE CONTRACT FULLY
UNDERSTOOD.

投保人(签名盖章) APPLICANT'S SIGNATURE
钱晓俊

投保日期：(DATE)　DEC. 17, 2010
电话：(TEL) 021-54105623
地址：(ADD) RM. 905 YONG AN MANSION, NO. 12 HUASHAN RD., SHANGHAI, P.R. CHINA

本公司自用(FOR OFFICE USE ONLY)
经办人 Made By _____
核保人 Checked By _____
NO.: PICC 0817554

Act 7-2
一般原产地证明书申请书：

中国贸促会上海市分会
中国国际商会上海商会
一般原产地证明书/加工装配证明书
申 请 书

申请单位注册号：	072150	证书号：	D03/182041/L916	全部国产填上 P	"P"
申请人郑重声明：		发票号：	INVHN-GD10174	含进口成分填上 W	

本人被授权代表本企业办理和签署本申请书。

本申请书及一般原产地证明书/加工装配证明书所列内容正确无误，如发现弄虚作假，冒充证书所列货物，擅改证书、愿按《中华人民共和国出口货物原产地规则》有关规定接受惩处并承担法律责任，现将有关情况申报如下：

商品名称	真空保温瓶	H.S.编码（八位数）	9617.0090
商品生产、制造、加工单位、地点		浙江永康采薇杯业有限公司	
含进口成分产品主要制造加工工序		***	
商品 FOB 总值（以美元计）	76040.89 美元	最终目的地国/地区	美国
拟出运日期	2010 年 12 月 25 日	转口国（地区）	***
包装数量或毛重或其他数量		1114 纸箱	

贸易方式和企业性质	
贸易方式	企业性质
一般贸易	国内合资

现提交中国出口货物商业发票一份、一般原产地证明书/加工装配证明书一正三副，以及其他附件 *** 份，请予审核签证。

申请单位盖章：

申领人（签名）钱晓俊
电话：021-54105623
日期：2010 年 12 月 19 日

如有补发、重发或更改 C.O.证书，请填写背面申请单。

一般原产地证明书：

ORIGINAL	
1.Exporter SHANGHAI HAINA IMPORT & EXPORT COMPANY LIMITED RM. 905 YONG AN MANSION, NO. 12 HUASHAN RD., SHANGHAI, P. R. CHINA TEL: 0086-21-54105623　　FAX: 0086-21-54742511	Certificate No.　D03/182041/L916 CERTIFICATE OF ORIGIN OF THE PEOPLE'S REPUBLIC OF CHINA
2.Consignee GULFLAND DAINECESS INC. 404 BRENNIN ST., SUITE 255, HOUSTON, TX 75013, UNITED STATES	
3.Means of transport and route FROM SHANGHAI, CHINA TO HOUSTON, TX, US BY SEA	5.For certifying authority use only
4.Country / region of destination UNITED STATES OF AMERICA	

6.Marks and numbers	7.Number and kind of packages; description of goods	8.H.S.Code	9.Quantity	10.Number and date of Invoices
GULFDAINE S/CNO.SCHN-GD10174 HOUSTON C/NOS.1-1114	1114 (ONE THOUSAND ONE HUNDRED AND FOURTEEN) CARTONS OF VACUUM FLASK ** WE HEREBY STATE THAT THE GOODS ARE OF CHINESE ORIGIN. CREDIT ISSUED BY: CHASE MANHATTAN BANK, HOUSTON, U.S.A CREDIT NUMBER: CHASEMBKLC72075359 S/C NUMBER: SCHN-GD10174	96170090.00	30340 PIECES	INVHN-GD10174 DEC. 10, 2010

| 11.Declaration by the exporter
　The undersigned hereby declares that the above details and statements are correct, that all the goods were produced in China and that they comply with the Rules of Origin of the People's Republic of China.

[SEAL: SHANGHAI HAINA IMPORT & EXPORT LIMITED] 钱晓俊

SHANGHAI　DEC. 19, 2010

Place and date, signature and stamp of authorized signatory | 12.Certification
　It is hereby certified that the declaration by the exporter is correct.

Place and date, signature and stamp of certifying authority |

Discuss 7

货物运输保险单：

PICC 中国人保财险		货物运输保险单 CARGO TRANSPORTATION INSURANCE POLICY 总公司设于北京 一九四九年创立 Head Office Beijing Established in 1949	

发票号(INVOICE NO.)   INVHN-GD10174
合同号(CONTRACT NO.)   SCHN-GD10174   保单号次 POLICY NO. PYIE2010168912170768 23
信用证号(L/C NO.)   CHASEMBKLC72075359
被保险人：
INSURED: SHANGHAI HAINA IMPORT & EXPORT COMPANY LIMITED

中国人民财产保险股份有限公司(以下简称公司)根据被保险人的要求，由被保险人向本公司缴付约定的保险费，按照本保险单承保险别和背面所载条款与下列特款承保下述货物运输保险，特立本保险单。

THIS POLICY OF INSURANCE WITNESSES THAT PICC PROPERTY AND CASUALTY COMPANY LIMITED (HEREINAFTER CALLED "THE COMPANY") AT THE REQUEST OF THE INSURED AND IN CONSIDERATION OF THE AGREED PREMIUM PAID TO THE COMPANY BY THE INSURED, UNDERTAKES TO INSURE THE UNDERMENTIONED GOODS IN TRANSPORTATION SUBJECT TO THE CONDITIONS OF THIS POLICY AS PER THE CLAUSES PRINTED OVERLEAF AND OTHER SPECIAL CLAUSES ATTACHED HEREON.

标 记 MARKS & NOS	包装及数量 QUANTITY	保险货物项目 DESCRIPTION OF GOODS	保险金额 AMOUNT INSURED
AS PER INVOICE NO. INVHN-GD10174	1114 CARTONS	VACUUM FLASK	USD91276.00
	CREDIT ISSUED BY:	CHASE MANHATTAN BANK, HOUSTON, U.S.A.	
	CREDIT NUMBER:	CHASEMBKLC72075359	
	S/C NUMBER:	SCHN-GD10174	

总保险金额   SAY U.S. DOLLARS NINETY ONE THOUSAND TWO HUNDRED AND SEVENTY
TOTAL AMOUNT INSURED: SIX ONLY

保费   启运日期   装载运输工具： SINOTRANS SEATTLE
PERMIUM: AS ARRANGED   DATE OF COMMENCEMENT: AS PER B/L PER CONVEYANCE: 045E

自   经
FROM: SHANGHAI, CHINA   VIA _____   TO   HOUSTON, TX, US

承保险别：
CONDITIONS:

COVERING F.P.A. RISK AS PER OCEAN MARINE CARGO CLAUSES OF P. I. C. C. DATED 1/1/1981

所保货物，如发生保险单项下可能引起索赔的损失或损坏，应立即通知本公司下述代理人查勘。如有索赔，应向本公司提交保单正本(本保险单共有 **贰** 份正本)及有关文件。如一份正本已用于索赔，其余正本自动失效。

IN THE EVENT OF LOSS OR DAMAGE WITCH MAY RESULT IN A CLAIM UNDER THIS POLICY, IMMEDIATE NOTICE MUST BE GIVEN TO THE COMPANY'S AGENT AS MENTIONED HEREUNDER. CLAIMS, IF ANY, ONE OF THE ORIGINAL POLICY WHICH HAS BEEN ISSUED IN **2** ORIGINAL(S) TOGETHER WITH THE RELEVANT DOCUMENTS SHALL BE SURRENDERED TO THE COMPANY. IF ONE OF THE ORIGINAL POLICY HAS BEEN ACCOMPLISHED. THE OTHERS TO BE VOID.

中国人民财产保险股份有限公司 上海市分公司
PICC Property and Casualty Company Limited,
Shanghai Branch

赔款偿付地点
CLAIM PAYABLE AT/IN **HOUSTON IN USD**

出单日期
ISSUING DATE DEC. 18, 2010   GENERAL MANAGER

情景模拟实训八 履行合同四——报关与装运

Act 8-1

出口货物报关单：

中华人民共和国海关出口货物报关单

预录入编号：220220100927372764　　　海关编号：220220100927372764

出口口岸 吴淞海关		备案号		出口日期	申报日期 2010-12-23
经营单位 上海海纳进出口有限公司 3102516112		运输方式 江海运输	运输工具名称 SINOTRANS SEATTLE/045E		提运单号 SNLU3743520522
发货单位 上海海纳进出口有限公司 3102516112		贸易方式 一般贸易		征免性质 一般征税	结汇方式 信用证
许可证号		运抵国（地区） 美国	指运港 休斯敦		境内货源地 宝山
批准文号 025418724		成交方式 CIF	运费 502/6800.0000/3	保费 502/136.9140/3	杂费 000//
合同协议号 SCHN-GD10174		件数 1114	包装种类 纸箱	毛重（千克） 31258.50	净重（千克） 23503.10
集装箱号 TTNU5744120 / 20 / 2275		随附单据 出境货物通关单：310233480059197			生产厂家
标记唛码及备注 GULFDAINE　　GESU2039606 / 40 / 3780 S/CNO.SCHN-GD10174 HOUSTON C/NOS.1-1114					

项号	商品编号	商品名称、规格型号	数量及单位	最终目的国(地区)	单价	总价	币制	征免
1	96170090 00	真空保温瓶 VACUUM FLASK	16120.000 个	美国	2.2100	35625.20	USD	照章
2	96170090 00	真空保温瓶 VACUUM FLASK	14220.000 个	美国	3.3300	47352.60	USD	照章

税费征收情况

录入员	录入单位	兹声明以上申报无讹并承担法律责任	海关审单批注及放行日期(签章)	
			审单	审价
报关员 3113641802810741　报关员 龚西华			征税	统计
单位地址 上海市华山路12号永安大厦905室 邮编 200040　电话 021-54105623		填制日期 2010-12-23	查验	放行

Act 8 – 2

装运通知传真文稿：

上海海纳进出口有限公司
Shanghai Haina Import & Export Company Limited
Rm. 905 Yong An Mansion, No. 12 Huashan Rd., 200040, Shanghai, P. R. China

To: Gulfland Dainecess Inc. **From:** Shanghai Haina Import & Export Company Limited
Tel. No.: 1-713-2283700 **Tel. No.:** 86-21-54105623
Fax No.: 1-713-2282332 **Fax No.:** 86-21-54742511
  Date: Dec. 25, 2010

SHIPPING ADVICE

CREDIT NUMBER: CHASEMBKLC72075359

We hereby inform you that the goods under the above credit have been shipped on Dec. 25, 2010. The details of shipment are stated below:

Date of Departure:	Dec. 25, 2010
Shipping Marks:	GULFDAINE
	S/CNO.SCHN-GD10174
	HOUSTON
	C/NOS.1-1114
Letter of Credit No.:	CHASEMBKLC72075359
L/C Issued by:	Chase Manhattan Bank, Houston, U.S.A.
Bill of Lading No.:	SNLU3743520522
Sales Contract No.:	SCHN-GD10174
Purchase Order No.:	GD-PO-CNSHA129
Number and kind of Packages:	1114 Cartons
Total Gross Weight:	31258.50 Kgs
Value of Goods:	USD 82 977.80 CIF
Commodity:	Vacuum Flask
Ocean Vessel:	SINOTRANS SEATTLE / 045E
Port of Loading:	Shanghai, China
Port of Discharge:	Houston, TX, US
ETA:	Jan. 18, 2011

Yours truly,
Shanghai Haina Import & Export Company Limited

钱晓俊
Damon Chan

Discuss 8

海运提单：

Shipper SHANGHAI HAINA IMPORT & EXPORT COMPANY LIMITED RM. 905 YONG AN MANSION, NO. 12 HUASHAN RD., SHANGHAI, P. R. CHINA TEL: 0086-21-54105623　　FAX: 0086-21-54742511	B/L No.　SNLU3743520522 **SINOTRANS** 中外运集装箱运输有限公司 SINOTRANS CONTAINER LINES CO., LTD BILL OF LADING
Consignee or order GULFLAND DAINECESS INC. 404 BRENNIN ST., SUITE 255, HOUSTON, TX 75013, UNITED STATES TEL: 1-713-2283700　　FAX: 1-713-2282332	
Notify address SAME AS CONSIGNEE	SHIPPED on board in apparent good order and condition (unless otherwise indicated) the goods or packages specified herein and to be discharged at the mentioned port of discharge or as near thereto as the vessel may safely get and be always afloat. 　　The weight, measure, marks and numbers, quality, contents and value, being particulars furnished by the Shipper, are not checked by the Carrier on loading. 　　The Shipper, Consignee and the Holder of this Bill of Lading hereby expressly accept and agree to all printed, written or stamped provisions, exceptions and conditions of this Bill of Lading, including those on the back hereof. 　　IN WITNESS whereof the number of original Bills of Lading stated below have been signed, one of which being accomplished the other(s) to be void.

Pre-carriage by	Port of loading SHANGHAI, CHINA
Vessel SINOTRANS SEATTLE / 045E	Port of transshipment
Port of discharge HOUSTON, TX, US	Final destination

Container. seal No. or marks and Nos.	Number and kind of package	Description of goods	Gross weight (kgs.)	Measurement (m³)
GULFDAINE S/CNO.SCHN-GD10174 HOUSTON C/NOS.1-1114 TTNU5744120 / 740368 GESU2039606 / 557371	1114 CARTONS L/C NO.: CHASEMBKLC72075359 ISSUED BY: CHASE MANHATTAN BANK, HOUSTON, U.S.A. S/C NO.: SCHN-GD10174	VACUUM FLASK FREIGHT PREPAID 1×20′GP 1×40′GP CY/CY	31258.50 KGS	79.9060 CBM

Freight and charges	REGARDING TRANSHIPMENT INFORMATION PLEASE CONTACT
Ex. rate	Prepaid at	Freight payable at	Place and date of issue SHANGHAI, CHINA　DEC. 25, 2010
	Total prepaid	Number of original Bs/L THREE(3)	Signed for or on behalf of the Carrier SINOTRANS CONTAINER LINES CO., LTD AS CARRIER

情景模拟实训九 履行合同五——交单结汇

Act 9

汇票：

```
                          BILL OF EXCHANGE
凭                                 不可撤销信用证
Drawn                              Irrevocable   L/C
Under  CHASE MANHATTAN BANK, HOUSTON, U.S.A.   No.  CHASEMBKLC72075359
日期
Date      NOV. 19, 2010      支取 Payable With interest @ **** % **** 按 **** 息 **** 付款
号码                汇票金额                           上海
No.  INVHN-GD10174   Exchange for   USD 82977.80   Shanghai   JAN. 5, 2011
                见票              日后（本汇票之副本未付）付交
                at *************** sight of this FIRST of Exchange (Second of Exchange
Being unpaid)  Pay to the order of        BANK OF CHINA, SHANGHAI BRANCH
金额
the sum of  SAY U. S. DOLLARS EIGHTY TWO THOUSAND NINE HUNDRED AND SEVENTY
SEVEN AND CENTS EIGHTY ONLY
此致
To:   CHASE MANHATTAN BANK,            SHANGHAI HAINA IMPORT & EXPORT
      HOUSTON, U.S.A.                  COMPANY LIMITED
                                                周致君
                                              (signature)
```

Discuss 9

船公司证明：

SINOTRANS 中外运集装箱运输有限公司
SINOTRANS CONTAINER LINES CO., LTD

CERTIFICATE

DATE: JAN. 4, 2011

TO WHOM IT MAY CONCERN,

CREDIT NUMBER: CHASEMBKLC72075359
ISSUED BY: CHASE MANHATTAN BANK, HOUSTON, U.S.A.
S/C NUMBER: SCHN-GD10174
B/L NUMBER: SNLU3743520522
OCEAN VESSEL: SINOTRANS SEATTLE / 045E

WE HEREBY CERTIFY THAT THE CARRYING VESSEL BELONGS TO CONFERENCE LINE AND IS NOT MORE THAN TWENTY YEARS OLD.

中外运集装箱运输有限公司
SINOTRANS CONTAINER LINES CO., LTD

情景模拟实训十　收汇核销与退税

Act 10

出口商业务善后函：

发件人：	damonchan@hainaco.com.cn
收件人：	ray.sinclair@gulfday.com
日　期：	2011-01-20
主　题：	Nice Cooperation

Dear Mr. Sinclair,

We are glad to receive the proceeds under L/C No. CHASEMBKLC72075359 against S/C No. SCHN-GD10147.

We are already old friends and this smooth first transaction will be the basis of the further development of our business relationship.

We trust that the goods will arrive at Houston safe and sound and give you great satisfaction.

Attached is our latest catalog for the first quarter of 2011, in which you may come across quite a few new items. If you have any further requirement, please let us know.

We look forward to the pleasure of doing further business with you in the near future.

Yours truly,
Shanghai Haina Import & Export Company Limited
Damon Chan

Attachment: Latest Catalog for 2011 First Quarter

Discuss 10

出口商业务善后函：

发件人：	li_xin@lixin.com.cn
收件人：	h.wolfe@roefstercorp.com
日　期：	2011-06-05
主　题：	Concerning the Dishonor of L/C No. AD07221EA91253

Dear Ms. Wolfe,

We are extremely regret when we are notified that the issuing bank dishonor payment against L/C No. AD07221EA91253.

We feel deeply sorry that we were unable to deliver your order in time. But we would like to explain that it was caused by an unforeseen fire accident in our warehouse, which damaged a large part of finished products. Although after that we operated production line at its full capacity and gave priority to old clients like you, we could only arrange shipment four days later than that was contracted.

However, we are pleased that the goods will arrive at your end on June 11 and assume they are just in time for the sales season. We sincerely hope the four-day delay will not bring too much difficulty to you in meeting the requests of your customers.

Therefore, considering our long standing relations as well as for our mutual interests, would you please effect the payment through your bank?

We are very appreciated for your kind understanding.

Yours truly,
Shanghai Lixin International Trading Co., Ltd.
Li Xin

附录

出口贸易英语口语——示范对话

Sample Dialogue 1　Company Introduction

A: What line of business are you in?

你们是从事什么行业的?

B: We're one of the leading manufactures of household electric appliances and electronics in China and we also engage in real estate, pharmacy, advertising, logistics, telecommunications etc.

我公司是中国主要的家用电器、电子生产商之一,另外我们也做房地产、药品、广告、物流、电信等。

A: Then what are your main products?

你们的主要产品是什么?

B: We produce a wide variety of household electric and electronic appliances, such as refrigerators, freezers, washing machines, air-conditioners, TV sets, microwave ovens, mobile phones, computers and so on.

我公司生产各种家用电器、电子产品,像冰箱、冷柜、洗衣机、空调、电视机、微波炉、手机、电脑等等。

A: How about their sales figures?

他们的销售情况如何?

B: Well, their sales figures vary from product to product. But each year we sell 15 million sets of all of them combined in the domestic market only and our products have been exported to more than 170 countries and regions in the world. Our sales amount last year totaled CNY 50 billion. In China, we now have a 35% market share.

随产品不同而不同。但是我们每年仅在国内市场就销售各种家电 1500 万台,并且我们的产品已销往全世界 170 多个国家和地区。我们去年的销售额总计人民币 500 亿元。在中国的市场占有率为 35%。

A: Very impressive. When was your company founded?

真了不起。贵公司什么时候创立的?

B: In 1986. We were once appraised as the fastest-growing enterprise by *Fortune*, exceeding Philips.

1986年。但《财富》杂志曾经将我公司评为发展最快的企业,超过了飞利浦。

A: Were you?

是吗?

B: Yes.

是的。

A: Impressive. Then how many employees do you have now?

真棒。那你们现有员工多少?

B: About 35000 in all so far.

目前为止总共约35000人。

A: I understand that you're now developing to multinational company, aren't you?

我知道你们正在向跨国公司发展,是吗?

B: That's right. We now have 84 distributors and 42000 sales outlets across the world. And we have set up 16 manufacturing plants in some overseas areas, including the North America, South America and East Europe. Our aim is to create a world-famous brand and be one of the world's top 500 companies.

是的。我们在全世界现有84家经销商,42000个销售点。并且我们在包括北美、南美和东欧在内的海外地区建立起了16家工厂。我们的目标是创立世界名牌,进入世界500强。

A: Really? Now I'm eager to visit your company. Where's your company located?

真的吗?我热切地希望参观一下你们公司。你们公司在哪儿?

B: In Suzhou, Jiangsu Province. I'd be pleased to arrange for you to visit our company.

江苏苏州。我将很愿意安排您到我公司参观。

Sample Dialogue 2 Introduction to Products

A: Hello, Mr. Fang.

方先生,你好。

B: Hello, Mr. Hayes. Glad to meet you again.

你好,海耶斯先生,很高兴再次见到你。

A: I'm very interested in your products, and would like to know more about them.

我对你们的产品很感兴趣,想多了解一些。

B: Good. Our leather bags have enjoyed a high reputation in the North American market because of their fashionable styles, fine workmanship and high-quality materials. We use advanced equipment imported from Spain. Besides, we keep a close eye on the style changes in the international market. Mr. Hayes, what in particular are you interested in?

很好。我们的皮包在北美市场有很好的口碑,因为它们款式时髦,做工讲究,用料上乘。我们用从西班牙引进的设备生产。另外,我们密切关注国际市场上款式的变化。海耶斯先生,你对哪个品种情有独钟?

A: Well, I find Article No. RH423 is rather attractive.

我觉得 RH423 号货很有吸引力。

B: It's our latest design. Its most distinguishing feature is its chic style. It sells very well. Feedbacks form different markets show that this model is appealing to even the pickiest buyers.

这是我们最新的设计。它最显著的特征是款式时髦。销售很火爆。从不同市场反馈的情况来看,即便对于最挑剔的买主来说,这个款式也极具吸引力。

A: Mr. Fang, compared with the various well-known brands from Italy, France and Spain, what gives your bags a competitive edge, in your opinion?

方先生,与意大利、法国和西班牙的各种名牌相比,你认为你们皮包的竞争优势在哪儿?

B: I would say prices. Our bags have the same high quality, but they are much more price-competitive, thanks to the low labor and raw material costs.

应该是价格。我们的质量同样好,但由于我们的劳动力成本和原料成本低,所以我们的皮包更具价格竞争力。

A: That's true. But in terms of highly personal items such as leather bags, brand names still matter a lot, and Italian, French and Spain products are still enjoying high customer loyalty. How can you make them buy yours?

这倒是真的。但就皮包这些极具个人色彩的物品而言,品牌还是很重要的,而且意大利、法国和西班牙品牌仍然享有很高的顾客忠诚度。你们将如何让这些顾客购买你们的产品?

B: I think customers can make their own judgment, despite their inclination to Italian, French and Spain brands. I believe once we have managed our way into these markets, these customers will be convinced.

我认为顾客是有自己的判断力的,尽管他们倾向于意大利、法国和西班牙品牌。我相信,一旦我们能够进入到这些市场,这些贵客一定会信服的。

Sample Dialogue 3   Inquiries and Offers

A: Can you show us your catalogue?

可以看一下你们的产品目录吗?

B: Certainly. Here's a catalogue for some of our popular items.

当然可以。这是我们一些畅销货的目录。

A: Thank you. We're very interested in some of your products. Here's an inquiry sheet we've drawn up.

谢谢。我们对你们的一些产品很感兴趣,这是我们拟订的询价单。

B: Thanks. We'll look into it carefully.

谢谢。我们会仔细研究一下的。

A：How about the supply position of your products?

你方产品供货情况怎么样？

B：We have a steady supply for most of them.

多数产品货源稳定。

A：Do you quote FOB or CIF?

你们报 FOB 价还是 CIF 价？

B：We usually quote on CIF basis.

我们通常报 CIF 价。

A：The market at our end has become pretty competitive. In order to sell successfully there, your goods will have to be competitive in price too.

我地市场竞争很激烈。为了成功的销售,你们的报价必须具有竞争力。

B：You'll find our prices are very attractive.

你们会发现我们的价格很有吸引力。

A：Would you give us an offer for Art. No. LM5217 CIFC3％ Hamburg now?

现在请给我们报 LM5217 号货 CIF 汉堡含 3％佣金价。

B：What's the quantity?

你们的订货量是多少？

A：We'd like to start with 20000 pieces. It's an attractive quantity, isn't it?

先订 2 万件。这个数量很可观,是吗？

B：When do you want the goods to be delivered?

你们要求什么时候交货？

A：Could you make it in October?

10 月份可以吗？

B：I think we could manage.

我想我们可以办到。

A：We pay by letter of credit.

我们用信用证支付。

A：OK. So now we can offer you 20000 pieces of Art. No. LM5217 at USD46 per piece CIF3％ Hamburg for shipment in October.

好的。现在我们向你们报价 LM5217 号货 2 万件,每件 CIF 汉堡 46 美元,含佣 3％,10 月份装运。

A：Thank you. How long will this offer be open?

谢谢。这个报价有效期多长？

B：It's valid for five days.

5 天。

A：I will study your offer with my colleagues and give you a definite reply in five days.

我将和同事们研究一下,5天内给你确切答复。

B: I'll be waiting for your good news.

我等候你的好消息。

Sample Dialogue 4　Prices

A: We are surprised to find that your price is 20% higher compared with other companies.

发现你们的价格比其他公司的高20%,我们很吃惊。

B: 20%? You can't be serious!

20%？你不是开玩笑吧！

A: That has been confirmed by our survey. I'm afraid I'll have to cancel the deal unless you reduce your price.

我们调查证实过了。恐怕我将不得不取消这笔交易,除非你降价。

B: But you fully know that our product is of superior quality. Other products can't be compared with it.

但你很了解我们的产品质量上乘,其他产品无法与之相比。

A: True. But it's also a fact that your price is too high.

是的。但你们的价格太高了,这也是一个事实。

B: Then what's your idea of a good price?

那你觉得什么价格合适？

A: I would say 15% off the listed price.

标价降15%。

B: Impossible. We won't make any profit at that price. 10% off is the best we can do.

那不可能。这样我们就无钱可赚了,最多降10%。

A: It's still too high.

还是太高。

B: Our quality is far beyond comparison. Besides, the market is advancing. Our goods can always find a good sale.

我们的质量是无与伦比的。而且行市上涨,我们的货物总会找到好销路的。

A: Other companies are also saying that their products are the best.

别的公司也都说他们的产品是最好的。

B: Let's meet each other half way. I'll drop another 3%. That's definitely my rock bottom price.

我们来折中一下吧。我再降3%,这绝对是最低价格了。

A: All right. That's settled.

好吧,就这么定了。

Sample Dialogue 5　Packing

A: Can we discuss the packing today?

我们今天谈一谈包装好吗?

B: Sure. We usually pack our shirts individually in polyethylene bags, eight dozens to one carton.

好的。我们的衬衣通常每件单独装一塑料袋,8 打装一纸箱。

A: Acceptable. But please pay attention to the design of the inner packing. All the packages must be ready for window display.

好。但请注意内包装的设计,所有的包装都必须适于橱窗展示。

B: Please don't worry. All the bags are beautifully designed to come in line with local market preference at your end.

没问题。所有的袋子都设计得很精美,符合你们当地市场的口味。

A: Have you got any samples here? I'd like to have a look.

这儿有没有样品? 我想看一看。

B: Here you are.

请看。

A: It does look good, especially the little swan.

确实漂亮,尤其是这个小天鹅。

B: Thank you. We understand that your people regard swan as a symbol of good luck.

多谢。我们听说你们那儿的人把天鹅当成幸运物。

A: Most of them do. But the background color should be a little lighter.

大多数人是的。但底色好像应该再淡一些。

B: No problem. What do you think of our logo?

好。你觉得我们的商品标识怎么样?

A: Very good. Maybe you should move it a little closer to the middle.

很好。再往中间靠一靠更好一些。

B: All right. Do you have anything to say about the outer packaging?

好。你对外包装有什么意见?

A: You mentioned cartons, didn't you? I'm afraid cartons are not strong enough.

你说的是纸箱吧? 恐怕纸箱不够牢固。

B: But we're only talking about shirts. They're not fragile goods. Besides, cartons are light and easy to handle.

但我们讲的是衬衣。衬衣不是易碎物品,而且纸箱轻便、容易搬运。

A: Well, I just mean they're easily breakable.

我是说纸箱容易破裂。

B: There's no need to worry. We can reinforce the cartons with straps.

这个不用担心,我们可以用条带加固。

A:Look, these goods will have to go a long way before they arrive at our port. What if dampness gets into the packages?

但这些货物必须经过长途运输才能抵达我港,包装受潮怎么办?

B:All the cartons are lined with plastic sheets, so they're absolutely waterproof, I can assure you.

所有纸箱都内衬塑料纸,我可以保证绝对防水。

A:As I just said, it's a long-distance transportation. I really don't want to take any chance.

正如我刚才所说,货物要经过长途运输,我实在不想冒任何风险。

B:You need have no fears about that. Our way of packing has been widely accepted by other clients, and we have received no complaints whatsoever so far.

你不用担心,我们的包装方式已经被其他客户广泛接受,目前为止还没有任何投诉。

A:Really? Then I suppose there is no other choice.

真的吗? 看来只能这样了。

Sample Dialogue 6　Shipment

A:Now that we've settled the terms of payment, is it possible to effect shipment during September?

我们已经谈妥了付款条件。是否能在9月份装运?

B:I don't think we can.

我看不行。

A:Then when is the earliest shipment we can expect?

那么最早什么时候可以装运呢?

B:By the middle of October, I think.

我想要到10月中旬。

A:It's too late. You see, November is the season for this commodity in our market, and our customs formalities are rather complicated.

那太迟了。你知道,在我们那儿11月是这个商品的上市季节,另外我们的海关手续相当复杂。

B:I understand.

我明白。

A:Well, the flow through the marketing channels and the red tape involved take at least a couple of weeks. So, after shipment it will probably be another four to five weeks before the goods can reach our retailers. So the goods really ought to be shipped before October, or we won't be ready for the season.

喔,通过销售渠道及繁琐的公文程序起码要花上两个星期。这样,装运以后还要四至五个星期我们的零售商才能收到货。所以10月份以前货物必须装上船,否则我们赶不上销售季节。

A: But our factories are fully committed for the third quarter. In fact, many of our clients are placing orders for delivery in the fourth quarter.

但是我们工厂第三季度的货已全部订满了。事实上,我们很多客户在订第四季度交的货。

A: Mr. Liu, you certainly realize that the time of delivery is a matter of great importance to us. If we place our goods on the market at a time when all other importers have already sold their goods at profitable prices, we shall lose out.

刘先生,你当然知道交货时间对我们来说是很重要的。如果当我们把商品投放到市场的时候,别的进口商早已脱手赚了钱,那我们就亏了。

B: I see your point. However, we have done more business this year than any of the previous years. I'm very sorry to say that we cannot advance the time of delivery.

这点我明白。但是今年我们做的买卖比以往任何一年都要多。非常抱歉我们不能提前交货。

A: I'm sorry to hear that. I sincerely hope you will give our request your special consideration.

太遗憾了。我衷心希望你对我们的请求给予特别考虑。

B: You may take it from me that the last thing we want to do is to disappoint a customer, particularly an old customer like you. But the fact remains that our manufacturers have a heavy backlog in hand.

你可以相信,我们最不愿意做那些使顾客失望的事情,特别是像你们这样的老客户。但是我们的厂家眼前生产任务压得很重,这是事实。

A: But can't you find some way to get round your producers for an earlier delivery? Make a special effort, would you? A timely delivery means a lot to us.

你不能想些办法说服厂家提前一些时候交货吗?请加一把劲,及时交货对我们很重要。

B: All right, Mr. Lewis. We'll get in touch with our producers and see what they have to say.

好吧,刘易斯先生。我们同厂家联系一下,听听他们的意见。

Sample Dialogue 7　Payment

A: Let's move on to the terms of payment. What would you say to payment by D/P?
接下来我们谈谈付款条件。你认为付款交单怎么样?

B: I'm afraid that won't do. It has been our customary practice to require irrevocable and documentary L/C payable by draft at sight.
恐怕不行。我们的惯例一直是要求不可撤销的、跟单的、凭即期汇票付款的信用证。

A: But I know sometimes you do accept D/P, don't you? Opening an L/C causes us many expenses because it requires a certain sum of deposit in the bank.

但我知道你们有时确实接受付款交单,对吧？开立信用证会造成很多开支,因为它要求付给银行一定数额的押金。

B: Yes, we do accept D/P, but only for some regular customers and a small amount involved in the deals. This is not the case with you.

是的,我们确实接受付款交单,但只是对某些老客户和小金额的交易而言。你们可不是这个情况。

A: I understand payment by L/C provides guarantee to both the sellers and the buyers. Considering the large amount, will a time L/C, say 60 days after sight, be acceptable? You see, we are making a concession. You should leave us some time to raise money.

我知道信用证支付对买卖双方都提供了保障。考虑到这次交易额巨大,使用远期信用证,比如说见票后60天付款行不行？你看,我们正在做让步。你应该给我们一些时间筹集资金。

B: It should have been all right. But as you said just now, it is not a small order, which means we have to bear great cost in producing the goods and preparing them for shipment. So I really have to stick to our usual practice.

远期信用证本来是没有问题的。但正如你刚才说的,这不是一笔小订单,这意味着我们得负担生产和备货装运过程中的巨大成本。所以我必须坚持我们的惯例。

A: OK, I understand your position. But I do hope that we can use easier terms of payment after we get more acquainted.

那好,我明白你的处境。但我希望我们相互更加了解之后,可以用更宽松的支付方式。

B: No problem.

当然。

Sample Dialogue 8 Insurance

A: Your quotation is on CIF basis. How do you cover insurance?

你们报的是 CIF 价,那么你们如何投保呢？

B: We always insure our goods with the People's Insurance Company of China as per their Ocean Marine Cargo Clause, Jan. 1, 1981 revision.

我们总是按照中国人民保险公司1981年1月1日的《海洋运输货物保险条款》向他们投保。

A: I have to say that I know very little about this clause. Can you explain it a little?

我得说我对这个条款了解得很少,你能不能解释一下？

B: OK. OMCC provides coverage of three basic risks, some additional risks and some special additional risks. The three basic risks are Free from Particular Average (F. P. A.), With Particular Average (W. P. A.) and All Risks (A. R.).

好的。《海洋运输货物保险条款》承保三种基本险,一些附加险和一些特殊附加险。这三种基本险是平安险(F. P. A.)、水渍险(W. P. A.)和一切险(A. R.)。

A: What do they mean respectively?

它们分别是什么意思?

B: Well, roughly speaking, F. P. A. covers total losses resulting from both natural calamities and accidents, and partial losses caused by accidents.

大体上说,平安险包括自然灾害和意外事故造成的全部损失和意外事故造成的部分损失。

A: What about W. P. A. ?

水渍险呢?

B: W. P. A. has a broader coverage. It covers everything in F. P. A. plus partial losses caused by natural calamities.

水渍险的范围广一些,除了平安险的范围外,还包括自然灾害引起的部分损失。

A: And all risks?

那么一切险呢?

B: All risks means W. P. A. plus additional risks, or extraneous risks, risks not incidental to transport by sea.

一切险就是水渍险加上附加险,或叫外来风险,即不是由于海上运输本身的特性所带来的风险。

A: I see. Now, for this particular article, what risks do you usually cover?

我明白了。那么我们这批货,你们通常投保什么险呢?

B: We usually insure against All Risks for 110% of the invoice value.

我们通常按发票金额的110%投保一切险。

A: Does All Risks include War Risk?

一切险也包括战争险吗?

B: No. War Risk is a special additional risk, and it has to be arranged separately.

不,战争险是一种特殊附加险,必须单独投保。

A: But judging from the recent situation in the Middle East, I think War Risk should be covered.

但是从中东目前的形势看,我认为应该投保战争险。

B: We can certainly do this, but it is subject to an additional premium, because our CIF quotation doesn't include this risk.

我们当然可以照办,但战争险要交额外的保险费,因为我们的CIF报价没有包括这种险别。

A: Additional premium? That's not a problem. There's no harm in doing things on the safe side.

额外保险费? 这没问题。做事安全一些总没坏处。

B：Then we will cover War Risk for you.
这样我们就替你们投保战争险。

A：Good. One more thing, what if I want 130% coverage?
好的。还有一件事,如果我想按 130%投保呢?

B：You mean 130% of the invoice value? This can be done, but you will have to pay an extra premium too.
你是说发票金额的 130%吗? 可以,但也要交额外保险费。

A：In this case I'd rather have 110%.
这样的话,我还是投保 110%吧。

Sample Dialogue 9　Conclusion of Business

A：So, now we have covered all the important points.
我们现在所有的主要问题都已经讨论过了。

B：Yes. I think so.
我想是的。

A：Before we draft the contract, let's examine the details.
在起草合同之前,我们先检查一下所有的细节。

B：OK. Under this contract, we will supply you with 3000 dozens T-shirts, S, M and L equally assorted, at USD87 per dozen CFR Rotterdam. Shipment in March. Payment by irrevocable sight L/C.
好的。根据这项合同,我们将向你们出售 3000 打 T 恤衫,大、中、小号平均搭配,每打 87 美元,CFR 鹿特丹价。3 月份装运,以不可撤销的即期信用证付款。

A：Perfect. But what I'm concerned about most is the time of delivery.
完全正确。但我最关心的是交货时间。

B：You may rest assured that shipment will be effected within the time limit stipulated in the contract. But there is also one point I'd like to stress.
你们尽可放心,我们会按照合同期限及时交货。但我也有一点想强调一下。

A：Yes?
是什么?

B：Your L/C must be opened at least one month before the time of shipment, otherwise we won't be able to catch the ship.
你方信用证必须在装运前 1 个月开出,否则我们将赶不上船。

A：No problem. I'll have the covering L/C opened as soon as I get back.
没问题。我一回去,就马上安排开立有关信用证。

B：Fine. I'm very glad our negotiations have arrived at a successful conclusion.
好,我很高兴我们的谈判取得了成功。

A：Me too. I hope this initial deal will result in further transactions between us.

我也是。我希望这首笔生意会带来我们之间更多的交易。

B: Of course. We will have the Sales Contract made out in two days.

当然了。两天之后合同就能备好。

A: Please remember to use both English and Chinese versions and both versions should be equally valid.

请记住用中英两种文字缮制合同,两种文本同样有效。

B: Naturally. Each of us keeps one original and two copies.

那当然。我们每人保留一份正本和两份副本。

A: Then I'll come along two days later to put my signature on it.

那么两天后我再来签字。

B: Good.

好的。

A: Well, Mr. Lin, it's been very pleasant talking to you.

林先生,跟您谈话真是非常愉快。

B: Thanks. By the way, do you have any plans for tonight?

谢谢。顺便问一下,今晚有什么安排吗?

A: None whatsoever.

还没有。

B: Why don't we have dinner together to celebrate the success of our first deal? There is a very nice restaurant round the corner.

为什么不一起吃个晚饭,庆祝我们的首次交易成功?附近有一家很不错的饭店。

A: I'd love to!

太好了!

Sample Dialogue 10 Complaints and Settlement

A: Good afternoon, Mr. Durant. I rushed here to look into the matter as soon as we received your claim.

早上好,杜兰先生。一收到你的索赔,我就赶到这里调查此事。

B: Glad to see you here, Mr. Zhao. We know complaint is an unpleasant thing, and we don't like complaining. But this time we feel we have to do it.

在这里看到你真高兴,赵先生。我们知道投诉是件不愉快的事情,我们不喜欢投诉。但这次我们是迫不得已。

A: What's happened exactly?

具体发生了什么事儿?

B: After your goods arrived, we immediately had them unpacked and examined. But to our surprise, we found that nearly 10% of them were not up to the contracted standard.

到货后,我们立即开箱检查,吃惊地发现将近10%的货没有达到合同规定的标准。

A: I'm sorry but I don't quite follow you. What do you mean by "not up to the contracted standard"?

对不起,但我没明白你的意思。什么是"没有达到合同规定的标准"?

B: The contract stipulates that you supply us with first grade oats. But I'm afraid 10% of the consignment are obviously second grade. Even an ordinary person can see the difference between these bags and the rest.

合同规定你向我方供应一级燕麦,但恐怕这批货的10%明显是二级。即使一个普通人也能看出这几袋子跟其他袋子的差别。

A: That really comes as a surprise. This has never happened before. Have you got any proof?

这可真让人吃惊。这种事情以前从未发生过。你有什么证据吗?

B: Here's the survey report issued by a reliable public surveyor. It shows clearly the oats in these bags are not first grade. They are only second grade at most.

这是一家非常可靠的公证行所出具的检验报告。上面清楚地显示这几袋子的燕麦不是一级的。它们充其量是二级货。

A: You may rest assured that if it's our fault, we'll certainly put the matter right.

你们放心,如果是我们的过失,我们一定会改正。

B: I hope so.

希望如此。

A: May I have a look at the goods?

我可以看看那批货吗?

B: Of course. We've left them in the warehouse at the port for your inspection.

当然。我们把它存放在码头的仓库里,以备你方检验。

A: (An hour later) It is true! These are second grade oats instead of first grade you ordered. Now I can only attribute it to our negligence at the time of dispatch. Please accept my deepest apology for any inconvenience caused to you.

(一小时之后)果然如此!这些都是二级燕麦,而不是你们所订购的一级品。我现在只能把它归因于我们发货时的疏忽大意。给你们带来了不便,请接受我最深的歉意。

B: Now the rights and wrongs are put clearly. And I appreciate your honesty and sincerity in this case. What are you going to do about this?

看来真相已经大白了。我们欣赏你对此事的诚信态度。你们准备怎么处理?

A: I promise to send the replacement immediately after I get back so that you may still catch the selling season.

我保证一回去就立即将替换品发来,以便你方仍能赶上销售季节。

B: All right. Then how should we deal with these few bags?

好的。那么这些袋子的货物怎么处理?

A: Actually, they are just lower grade products. The quality is not inferior at all. I propose you sell them off at a discount to cover the losses or extra expenses incurred in this case. I put it at your disposal. Is that OK?

事实上,他们只是等级稍低的产品,绝非劣质货。我提议由你们廉价卖出去来抵偿你方这次的损失和额外的费用。你看着办,这样行吗?

B: It seems we cannot but do so. Anyhow, we're so glad to have settled this case smoothly.

看来只能如此了。不管怎样,我们还是很高兴能顺利解决这一事件。

A: And we hope this incident won't affect future cooperation between us.

我们希望这件小小的意外不会影响我们今后的合作。

Sample Dialogue 11　Agency

A: I've come to talk about an agency agreement.

我是来谈代理协议的。

B: What do you have in mind?

你们有什么想法?

A. Ever since your product entered our market two years ago, it has shown a great market potential. But you can do even better if you develop some kind of sales network there.

你们产品自从两年前进入我们市场以来,显示出了很大的潜力。但如果你们能在那儿开发出某种销售网络,将会卖得更好。

B: To tell you the truth, I was just thinking about that.

说实话,我也正在考虑这事。

A: We are a well-established firm in the line of textiles, and we enjoy good relations with all the wholesalers, chain stores and distributors in Australia. You'll find it most worthwhile if you appoint us as your sole agent.

你知道,我公司在纺织业有良好的信誉,跟澳大利亚所有的批发商、连锁店和分销商都保持着很好的关系。如果指定我们为你们的独家代理,你们会觉得特别值。

B: Thank you for your intention to help promote the sales of our products, and we are quite satisfied with your performance in the last two years. But honestly, an annual sales volume of USD 1000000 does not justify a sole agency agreement.

感谢你们推销我方产品的意愿,对你们过去两年的表现我们也非常满意。但说实在的,100万美元的年销售量并不证明你们能胜任独家代理的工作。

A: If we are granted the sole agency, we can assure you that we'll double the turnover.

如果我们得到独家代理权,我们保证销售量可翻一番。

B: Do you mean to say that if we entrust you with the agency, you will sell USD 2000000 each year?

你的意思是说如果我们指定你们为代理,你将每年销售200万美元?

A: I couldn't have said it any better. But we expect a 10% commission, of course.

就是这个意思。当然我们要求10%的佣金。

B: Our agents in other areas usually get a 3%～8% commission.

我们给其他地区代理的佣金通常是3%～8%。

A: But your product is still new to our market, and we need to do a lot of work and spend a lot of money on the sales promotion. A 10% commission won't leave us much.

但我们市场对你们产品仍然不太了解,我们在推销过程中需要做很多工作,花很多钱。10%的佣金剩不下多少。

B: What duration are we talking about?

那么代理期限是多长?

A: Let's say two years to start with. After that the agreement can be renewed if we both agree.

先定两年吧。到时如果双方同意,可以续约。

B: Let's put it this way, we'll allow you a 10% commission if you guarantee an annual increase of USD 200000, starting from USD 2000000 for the first year.

我们这么说吧,如果你们保证第一年销售200万美元,然后每年增加20万美元,我们就给10%的佣金。

A: You certainly drive a hard bargain, Mr. Zhang. But I agree.

你真善于讨价还价,张先生。不过,我答应了。

B: The territory will be confined to the Australian market only.

代理地区将只限于澳大利亚。

A: Of course. Within the validity of the agency agreement, you should not supply your product to any other buyer in Australia, and we, on our part, shall not handle competitive products offered by other suppliers either.

当然,在协议有效期内,你们不能向澳大利亚其他买主供货,当然我们也不能经营其他供货商提供的竞争性产品。

B: Sure. Let's call it a deal.

当然。就这么定了。

A: When do we sign the agreement?

我们什么时候签协议?

B: We'll have the agreement made out within two days. Please come along at 3 P.M. the day after tomorrow.

我们两天之内就可以备好协议,请于后天下午3点过来签字。

A: I'll be here at 3 o'clock sharp.

3点钟我准时到。

参 考 文 献

[1] 祝卫,程洁,谈英. 出口贸易模拟操作教程[M]. 3版. 上海：上海人民出版社,2008.
[2] 祝卫,程洁,谈英. 国际贸易操作能力实用教程[M]. 上海：上海人民出版社,2006.
[3] 张晓明,刘文广. 国际贸易实训[M]. 北京：高等教育出版社,2009.
[4] 全国国际商务专业人员职业资格考试用书编委会. 国际商务英语口语[M]. 北京：中国商务出版社,2007.
[5] 安徽. 国际贸易实务教程[M]. 北京：北京大学出版社,2005.
[6] 陈胜权. 国际贸易实务经典教材习题详解[M]. 北京：对外经济贸易大学出版社,2005.

教学课件索取单

敬爱的老师：

感谢您使用我们出版社的教材。为了方便教学，教材配有相关教学课件。如果您需要，请您填写下面表格中的相关信息，并以**电子邮件**的形式发到我社，我们在核对您的信息后，即免费向您提供教学课件。

我们的联系方式：

地址：上海市中山西路 2230 号 1 号楼 907 室　　邮编：200235
电话：(021)64391590　　传真：(021)64391590
联系人：王老师　　电子邮件：gzjw@lixin.edu.cn

教材名称				作者姓名	
教师姓名		性别		身份证号	
学　校		院系		教研室	
学校地址				邮　编	
职　务		职称		办公电话	
E-mail		手机		宅　电	
通信地址				邮　编	
教材用量	册	委托订购单位			

您对本教材的意见和建议是：